# BEING AND BECOMING VISIBLE

A *Feminist Formations* Reader

# Being and Becoming Visible

## Women, Performance, and Visual Culture

EDITED BY **Olga M. Mesropova and Stacey Weber-Fève**

The Johns Hopkins University Press
*Baltimore*

Printed in the United States of America on acid-free paper
9 8 7 6 5 4 3 2 1

The Johns Hopkins University Press
2715 North Charles Street
Baltimore, Maryland 21218-4363
www.press.jhu.edu

ISBN 13: 978-0-8018-9494-7 (hardcover: alk. paper)
ISBN 10: 0-8018-9494-8 (hardcover: alk. paper)
ISBN 13: 978-0-8018-9495-4 (paperback: alk. paper)
ISBN 10: 0-8018-9495-6 (paperback: alk. paper)

*Library of Congress Control Number:* 2009940297

A catalog record for this book is available from the British Library.

*Special discounts are available for bulk purchases of this book. For more information, please contact Special Sales at 410-516-6936 or specialsales@press.jhu.edu.*

The Johns Hopkins University Press uses environmentally friendly book materials, including recycled text paper that is composed of at least 30 percent post-consumer waste, whenever possible. All of our book papers are acid-free, and our jackets and covers are printed on paper with recycled content.

# Contents

# Introduction

OLGA M. MESROPOVA AND STACEY WEBER-FÈVE

*The Visible Woman* was conceived as a celebration of feminist scholarship on performance and visual culture previously published in the *National Women's Studies Association Journal* (*NWSA Journal*). As editors of this collection we have aimed to bring together essays that cross geographical and disciplinary borders while examining female representation in a variety of performative and visual media. In this vein, the present volume includes case studies related to such diverse genres and media as theater, cinema, painting, television, performance activism, and photography from South Africa, Australia, New Zealand, Germany, the United Kingdom, and the United States. We have also sought to offer a wide range of feminist theoretical approaches to the study of performance and visual culture and thereby examine women both as the producers of images as well as a commodified or politicized spectacle of the media's gaze. Most significantly, the present collection of essays situates the disciplines of visual culture and performance studies within two conceptual frameworks—multicultural and feminist—through the overarching thematic trope of visibility.

"Becoming visible," understood in the broader sense as a means to legitimize underrepresented groups (gendered, sexual, racial, and so forth), is perhaps one of the most essential concepts of feminist theory and practice. Scholars regard visibility as a central component of identity that allows certain individuals, groups, and communities to celebrate the very same "visible signifiers of difference" that have traditionally targeted them for discrimination (Walker 1993, 868). The essays in the present anthology employ the notion of female visibility in both a literal and figurative sense, while examining the sociopolitical and cultural influences surrounding the production of female identity. Viewed collectively, our contributors discuss a complex web of female visibilities that range from women's use of activist art to empower themselves and their communities to representations of female subjects as they are constructed (that is, made visible) in a variety of visual and performative works.

While highlighting multiple systems of visual representation in distinct cultural settings, this book echoes ongoing theoretical debates on global intervisuality. Introduced by Nicholas Mirzoeff, the theory of intervisuality (or visual intertextuality) refers to the visual cross-referencing between various media while attempting to explain how viewers interpret images in light of other visual texts (Mirzoeff 2000). The essays in this collection all point to the underlying intervisual themes, tropes, and patterns that form various modes of female visibility in performance and visual culture. While focusing on the role of visual and performative media within specific cultural contexts of production and reception, *The Visible Woman* exemplifies the relationality of female representations as they transgress geographical, cultural, and sociopolitical boundaries. By presenting the visible woman from the critical perspectives of diverse academic disciplines, we also strive to multiply lines of inquiry from which scholars may study gender, performance, and visual culture. It is our hope that, by directly and indirectly presenting several levels of critical interpretation, this project will provide feminist scholars and teachers with inspiration for their own research and teaching of female (self-)representation in performance and visual culture.

The space for critical reflection created by this volume is, in some ways, reminiscent of a museum exhibition in terms of scope and objective. Museums of all types purport to define relationships among communities, nations, and peoples through objective and subjective (as well as personal and collective) interpretations of artifacts, experiences, and environments. To situate the anthology's essays within the unified framework of a museum exhibition (whose goal is to assemble, preserve, showcase, and inspire), we begin with Margaret D. Stetz's essay, "Feminist Exhibitionism: When the Women's Studies Professor Is a Curator." The comparison of this anthology to a museum display logically gives rise to the issues of curatorship. Stetz addresses the role of the curator and explores the potential of museums and other institutional exhibitions as sites for conducting critical feminist work. Stetz bases this important claim on her extensive experience teaching Alice Walker's *In Search of Our Mothers' Gardens* in her introductory courses in women's studies. Stetz explains that she supplements her instruction of Walker's essay with a 1992 British-made documentary film about Walker in which the novelist expresses her dislike of museums, describing them as an elitist example of Western society's treatment of art. For Stetz, Walker's attitude poses a dilemma because she wants her students to take Walker's words seriously but not automatically dismiss museums and curatorship as elitist. In the remainder of her essay Stetz takes the reader through an autobiographical journey of professional experiences that illustrate the ways in which exhibition work may advance and even embody feminist pedagogical principles. Through a discussion of interdisciplinarity, political activism, and community outreach, Stetz calls on women's studies faculty to assume the role of guest curator—a position that crosses boundaries and allows one to teach about race, class, sexual orientation, and gender to a wider audience.

Stetz's discussion of the guest curator also extends to the other essays included in this anthology. Each part of this collection approaches the issue of the visible woman from a different perspective. In part I, entitled "Spectators, Spectacles, and Cultural Icons," we group four essays that treat photography, painting, television, and film. This part situates the visible woman within two specific unifying tropes of image and persona, while also considering the spectator's engagement with the visual text. The essayists in this part examine image and persona across constructions and interpretations of five Anglo-American cultural icons: Princess Diana, the Madonna, Mary Poppins, Maria from *The Sound of Music* (1965), and Lucille Ball.

As its title suggests, Jill R. Chancey's essay, "Diana Doubled: The Fairytale Princess and the Photographer," investigates representations of Princess Diana in photography, specifically in the tabloid press. Chancey's work explores the image (or simulacrum) of Princess Diana that both British and American media have created since her death. By focusing on the photographs that surfaced in the media after Diana's passing, Chancey discusses how the princess's image suddenly changed in a very specific way. Diana was no longer portrayed in a negative manner, as she had been shortly before her death. Instead, the media focus turned to images of Princess Diana as mother, humanitarian, and fairytale princess. In this essay Chancey employs several critical theories of Jean Baudrillard, Pierre Bourdieu, and Linda Dégh to examine the context of the tabloid, the myth of the fairytale heroine, and the use of photography in the construction of Diana's images. As Chancey analyzes these frozen images, she asserts that the posthumous version of Princess Diana—especially in her role as mother—is invariably coded in a positive light ("beautiful") as opposed to the frequently negative ("inappropriate" or "unfeminine") portrayals of the princess during her lifetime.

The construction of motherhood takes a very different form in the second essay in part I, Denise Bauer's "Alice Neel's Portraits of Mother Work." Moving from the quasi-ethereal "feminine" constructions of Princess Diana, we come upon a hyperrealistic image of motherhood and femininity represented in Alice Neel's paintings. Bauer maintains that Neel consistently made the experiences of mothers the subject of her work by transgressing, parodying, and critiquing the Madonna and child painting genre, while simultaneously reflecting on the social construct of "mother" as it shifted throughout the twentieth century. Drawing attention to class and race analyses of motherhood and family in Neel's art, Bauer discusses many of Neel's portraits of mother work that chronicle the shifts in definitions and understandings of maternal subjectivity. Bauer concludes that not only did Neel privilege the tasks of motherhood but also her images brought and still bring to light the inner struggles women face in caring for their children within a largely unsupportive cultural and political context.

A different approach to parenthood emerges in Anne McLeer's "Practical Perfection? The Nanny Negotiates Gender, Class, and Family Contradictions in 1960s Popular Culture." McLeer's essay examines two popular mid-1960s films, *Mary Poppins* (dir. Robert Stevenson, 1964) and *The Sound of Music* (dir. Robert Wise, 1965). The author contends that, despite their foreign settings, British stars, and historical time frames, these two films reveal social and political concerns regarding the constitution of the family that were common in 1960s America. McLeer ascertains that both films address anxieties surrounding masculinity, motherhood, and domestic gender roles. By investigating the construction of the nanny's persona in these two films, McLeer sees a link between this liminal figure and the reinstallation of the father's role as head of the household, a familial structure that was believed to be in jeopardy in mid-sixties America.

The construction of persona and domestic gender roles also figures largely in the fourth essay of part I, Lori Landay's "Millions 'Love Lucy': Commodification and the Lucy Phenomenon." Landay opens her essay with a discussion of how mass consumer culture is central to understanding and interpreting all levels of the Lucy phenomenon. Landay traces this notion across individual episodes that revolve around the advertisement and consumption of commodities. More specifically, her essay deals with the "good life" portrayed in the series, Ball's public persona as "just a housewife," and the myriad of consumer goods tied to the show in the fifties (that are also popular today). Landay provides a close reading of the episode "Lucy Does a TV Commercial" in relation to this construction of the Lucy phenomenon as well as to gender and middle-class life in the postwar era. She concludes that Lucy was framed by and broke the framework of commodification. Landay asserts that, while the Lucy show participated in the mass consumer economy of its time, its comedy played on conflicts and anxieties about consumption and domesticity.

Moving from the issues of female image and persona presented in the first part of this anthology, the volume's second part, "Explicit Selves, Explicit Bodies," brings together four essays that explore the image of the female body both as a locus of powerful personal stories and as a presentation of sociocultural and political perspectives. The term "explicit body" originated with Rebecca Schneider's *The Explicit Body in Performance* (1997), a study of feminist performance artists who use their own bodies as a site for cultural criticism. In her book Schneider compares female bodies to symbolic stages across which the performers reenact social dramas and traumas (Schneider 1997, 6–7). In this anthology we apply the notion of explicit bodies to a diverse range of subjects as well as performative and visual media, including feminist cancer theater, a cinematic biography of Tina Turner, photography in Weimar Germany, and a photographic exhibit developed by low-income, single-parent students in the United States. Through an explication of bodies in visual art, performance, and activism, this part's contributors discuss the power of female explicit bodies (and explicit selves) to facilitate a critical dialogue with mainstream representations of women.

One example of a direct exploration of "explicit body" performance theory is Mary K. DeShazer's essay "Fractured Borders: Women's Cancer and Feminist Theater." This essay examines theatrical representations of breast, ovarian, and uterine cancer in four feminist plays from the 1990s: Margaret Edson's Pulitzer Prize–winning *Wit*, Maxine Bailey and Sharon M. Lewis's *Sistahs*, Susan Miller's *My Left Breast*, and Lisa Loomer's *The Waiting Room*. Combining close interpretative readings of these plays with postmodern theories of the body, writings of French feminists, and performance theory, DeShazer frames her discussion within two principal trajectories. First, she foregrounds personal narratives that highlight female cancer victims' sense of agency, despite their grim individual experiences with the disease. Second, DeShazer reveals how the feminist playwrights question, and at times condemn, both the impersonality and inefficiencies of the U.S. health care system. While juxtaposing cancer's private and public domains, as well as disturbing and graphic depictions of individual suffering performed on stage, DeShazer's essay considers how feminist cancer theater can elicit empathy and activism from its audience.

The investigation of the public/private dichotomy also shapes Diane Shoos's essay "Representing Domestic Violence: Ambivalence and Difference in *What's Love Got to Do with It*." Here Shoos examines Brian Gibson's 1993 film based on the autobiography of American pop diva Tina Turner. While reading the film's narrative in the context of recent feminist and clinical debates on domestic violence and female victimization, Shoos analyzes the film's counterpunctual presentations of Tina Turner's private relationship with her abusive husband and public images of the two as a happy professional couple. Interpreting the film through the disturbing lens of an explicitly violated female body, Shoos critiques Gibson's filmic portrayal of domestic violence. Applying Stuart Hall's discussion of "visibility" and "invisibility" in black popular culture, Shoos argues that, despite the film's powerful and clearly "visible" depiction of domestic violence, Gibson's cinematic battered woman ultimately remains tacitly invisible. Moreover, instead of calling attention to domestic violence as a serious social problem (and to battered women as an oppressed group), the film offers comfortable positions that affirm social stereotypes of race, class, and gender.

Societal stereotypes resurface in Vivyan C. Adair's essay "The Missing Story of Ourselves: Poor Women, Power, and the Politics of Feminist Representation." In this essay Adair discusses a nationally touring photographic and narrative exhibit produced and organized by low-income, single-parent students. The concept of "explicit bodies" discussed earlier in reference to feminist theater is also applicable to the visual and verbal codes of this installation. While the images that Adair discusses do not have the overtly corporeal nature of feminist theater (although poverty has undoubtedly left its mark on the women's faces and bodies), the photographic and textual presentations of impoverished parents serve as sites of broader social significance. In this capacity the exhibit not only conveys individual (hi)stories of women from diverse ethnic and religious backgrounds but also provides an insider's perspective on perceptions of poverty and government welfare reforms as well as broader problems of political economy. As Adair argues, through their powerful and disturbing messages, these pictorial self-narratives have given a voice to each individual woman while simultaneously permitting them to express their collective identity. As in feminist theater, these "stories from the margins" give prominence to an underrepresented group while advocating activism and compassion among the exhibit's viewers.

The role of photographic images in the empowerment of the female subject is also central to the final essay in this part, Mila Ganeva's "Fashion Photography and Women's Modernity in Weimar Germany: The Case of Yva." While focusing on the fetishization of the explicit female body in the context of conspicuous consumption, Ganeva's essay deals with the work of Yva, a prolific professional photographer in Germany during the 1920s and early 1930s. A creator of a unique visual language that combined the aesthetics of fashion photography, advertising, and conventional portraiture, Yva was also highly innovative in her presentation of female models. Ganeva contends that, at a time when photographic images of women (intended for the voyeuristic gaze of the male consumer) began to proliferate in various forms of commercial culture, Yva attempted to undermine the standard appearance of female models as stereotypical sexual symbols. The author demonstrates how this female photographer created overtly sexual images of women's bodies as consumerist objects ("explicit bodies" in the literal sense) while simultaneously representing her subjects as active agents of modern life.

The third part of the anthology, entitled "Iconographies of Communal Identity," examines visual and performative (self-)representations of women within the wider sociocultural contexts of place-based rituals, traditions, and communities. While analyzing the discourses of culturally liminal, underrepresented, or traumatized groups, this part's contributors all point toward the transformative and empowering potential of visual culture and performance. Through close readings of diverse ethnic and cultural female representations, these three essays address visual and performative modes of expression as sites of female self-realization, agency, and activism.

The convergence of art and activism is central to Kim Miller's essay, "Iconographies of Gender, Poverty, and Power in Contemporary South African Visual Culture." This essay introduces the reader to the Philani Project, a women's textile art cooperative in the impoverished township of Crossroads, South Africa. Originally conceived as an antipoverty initiative aimed at training unemployed mothers for careers as commercial textile designers, the cooperative has afforded women the opportunity to employ visually powerful designs in both creative production and community-based activism. Contrary to traditional scholarly discourses of poverty that either victimize or romanticize the poor, Miller stresses that the women of the Philani Project have aestheticized their disadvantaged socioeconomic situation as images of dignity and empowerment. Using bell hooks's concept of "liberatory imagination," Miller notes that, through the creation of their visual autobiographical narratives, these textile artists have developed a strategy of resistance by combining disturbing narratives with bold colors and brilliant designs. In this capacity, in addition to gaining relative economic independence through the sale of their work, these women artists have also used their art to speak as active agents on behalf of impoverished women in postapartheid South Africa.

Emmanuel David's essay, "Cultural Trauma, Memory, and Gendered Collective Action: The Case of Women of the Storm following Hurricane Katrina," provides further exploration of the role of feminist art in activist movements. Focusing on what he terms the "gendered performance activism" of the New Orleans–based organization, Women of the Storm, David demonstrates the pivotal role that this group's performances have played in the region's recovery after Hurricane Katrina. The group originally conceived their activities as a means of lobbying the U.S. Congress to pass federal legislation regarding the restoration and protection of the Gulf Coast. David argues that—in addition to their original requests for material resources—Women of the Storm have also engaged in a larger symbolic attempt "to repair a sense of home and community." While appropriating sociohistorical practices, traditional symbols, and rituals unique to New Orleans culture (such as traditional jazz funerals and second line parades), the group became a public face for those affected by the Katrina catastrophe. Through a detailed description of one of the group's dramatizations in New Orleans' City Park, the author exemplifies how these women's collective "performative actions" evoked the rhetoric of trauma and remembrance while promoting the preservation of their city's cultural memory.

The theme of place-based communities and their respective rituals and symbols is further investigated in Caroline Brown's essay "The Representation of the Indigenous Other in *Daughters of the Dust* and *The Piano*." This essay focuses on the cinematic representations of two indigenous communities as they interact with nonnative women. The two films analyzed in this essay were released in 1992 and 1993 respectively; the former is an independent film written and directed by American filmmaker Julie Dash, the latter is the work of New Zealand director Jane Campion. While employing Gayatri Spivak's discussion of the marginalization of the subaltern and Laura Mulvey's theory of the gaze, Brown discusses these two films' constructions of native groups (Gullah and Maori) as "cultural others." Brown argues that, although both directors acknowledge and represent the complexity of aboriginal cultures, the films' indigenous characters never play a fully formed role. Instead, the Gullah and Maori communities serve as a silenced backdrop that facilitates the nonnative (that is, European) heroines' self-empowerment and affirmation. Although both directors seemingly marginalize the native communities, Brown poses the question whether a character's centrality to the narrative is essential to the creation of powerful representations of "otherness." Through a close reading of the two films' narratives, the author demonstrates that a discourse that ostensibly bears traits of cinematic Orientalism can ultimately be read as a challenge to established representations of indigenous groups.

Viewed collectively, the three parts of this volume treat the visual and performative (self-)representations of women within a broad range of sociocultural, political, and geographical contexts through a thematic lens of visibility. As editors of this project we have attempted to bring together essays that address the trope of visibility from two overarching perspectives. One group of essays examines the potential of performative and visual art to provide empowering visibility to culturally liminal or invisible groups. Essays dealing with South African textiles, feminist cancer theater, feminist performance activism in New Orleans, and a photographic exhibit by single-parent students are all salient examples of the visibility that these underrepresented groups acquire through their artwork. The other group of essays in this collection addresses the commodification and manipulation of female visibility. Ranging from images of Princess Diana, photographic models in Weimar Germany, a cinematic portrayal of Tina Turner, and the televised persona of Lucille Ball, these case studies examine the construction of female hypervisibility as it is negotiated in high and low cultural contexts. Unified by the organizing theme of a museum exhibit, the essays in this book point to the multilayered nature of visibility as both a site of inclusion and agency and a form of spectacle and exhibition. This collection does not claim to be exhaustive in its scope of methodologies, geographical contexts, or visual forms. However, it is our hope that the essays in this anthology will inspire further cross-disciplinary, multicultural, and intervisual approaches to the study of gender as well as its diverse modes of being and becoming visible through performance and visual culture.

## References

Mirzoeff, Nicholas, ed. 2000. *Diaspora and Visual Culture: Representing Africans and Jews.* London: Routledge.
Schneider, Rebecca. 1997. *The Explicit Body in Performance.* London: Routledge.
Walker, Lisa M. 1993. "How to Recognize a Lesbian: The Cultural Politics of Looking Like What You Are." *Signs: Journal of Women in Culture and Society* 18(4):866–90.

# BEING AND BECOMING VISIBLE

CHAPTER ONE

# Feminist Exhibitionism: When the Women's Studies Professor Is a Curator

MARGARET D. STETZ

While teaching Alice Walker's classic 1974 essay "In Search of Our Mothers' Gardens" in my introduction to women's studies courses, I have for the past nine years supplemented it by showing an excerpt from a filmed documentary. This 1992 British-made documentary about Walker features readings from her work, dramatizations of scenes from the novel *Possessing the Secret of Joy*, historical footage from the civil rights era in the United States, and commentary by various "talking heads," such as Gloria Steinem and the late Barbara Christian. But most important, it relies on interviews with Walker herself, portions of which are intercut throughout.

In the section of the documentary that I show in class—the segment devoted to the creation and impact of the central argument of "In Search of Our Mothers' Gardens"—Walker's on-camera presence is particularly arresting and inspiring, as she talks about the unacknowledged artistry of poor African American women in the rural South. Yet every year, I present this powerful feminist statement to my classes with some hesitation and misgivings. Why? Because the students both see and hear Walker accompanying her celebration of the arts of women of color with the following slam: "I don't like museums, which is a very white Western notion of what you do with art, because it takes it out of context of life, and I think for many indigenous people, earth people, you create beautiful things because beauty is all around you. I mean, what else would you do?" (Shaw 1992).

For me, Walker's words pose a dilemma. I want my students to take Walker's perspective seriously, yet I don't want them to dismiss out-of-hand either the achievements or the potential of museums and other institutional exhibition spaces, such as those in university galleries and libraries, as sites for doing feminist and antiracist work. On the contrary, I would like them to consider such established spaces as opportunities for feminist pedagogy and outreach, not merely as irredeemable symbols of elitism. Indeed, I would like my students to feel equally inspired and challenged by the alternative point-of-view of African American women artists such as the sculptor and printmaker Elizabeth Catlett, who has exhibited in libraries such as the Main Public Library in Las Vegas, Nevada, using community-based galleries as though they were museums,

Originally published in the Summer 2005 issue of the *NWSA Journal*.

on the principle that "making my work available . . . where it is accessible to Black working people is very important to me" (LaDuke 1992, 138).

Like bell hooks, I choose to believe that "art constitutes one of the rare locations where acts of transcendence can take place and have a wide-ranging transformative impact" (1995, 3). As she says in her 1995 essay, "Art on My Mind," art "can enhance our understanding of what it means to live as free subjects in an unfree world" (8–9). I take this faith to the next step and remain unable and unwilling to give up on organized exhibitions, either as occasions for presenting the visual arts in various guises and media or for educating viewers about them and about their relationship to gender, race, and class issues. If women's studies is truly to be interdisciplinary in practice, rather than in name only, then its faculty should be ready to enter into and engage with the spaces and locations that other disciplines value and that they use regularly. Sometimes, that must involve moving out of the classroom and into the kinds of places where women who are either professional creators of or commentators upon the fine and the decorative arts usually bring their efforts before the public.

Rosemary Betterton, a leading British feminist art historian, has admitted that "women have an ambiguous relationship to the visual image. This is because they are represented so frequently within images and yet their role as makers and viewers of images is scarcely acknowledged" (1987, 3). At the same time, women rarely have been "in a position to direct the production, circulation and consumption of visual imagery . . . in the major institutions . . . of the art world" (5). Yet to deny that women (including women of color and women of the global South) have managed, particularly over the past 30 years, to exercise some degree of agency and authority in the exhibition world would be wrong. Many museums and galleries, though especially those dependent upon public funding, have undergone revolutionary change in terms of their dedication to increasing access and appealing to populations that previously were neglected or shut out. They have done so at the level of the individual exhibition or program, but also at the administrative level; women are now found often in the role of director, not merely as support staff. (At my home institution, for instance, a woman occupies the position of director of university museums, serving as the overseer of all university exhibition spaces.)

From a political perspective, it would be counter-productive for feminists to cede to anyone a space that still exercises so much cultural influence. But from the perspective of women's studies faculty, it also seems unwise to dismiss the museum or gallery as a sphere that has nothing to do with feminist education, either actually or potentially. To do that, moreover, is to disregard an important piece of feminist history and achievement, losing ground won through enormous effort by the women's art movement of the 1970s. It is worth remembering that in 1973, at the very moment when early women's studies programs were being established at universities around the country, feminist artists and scholars came together in Los Angeles to create the Woman's Building. The original project laid out studios and workshops and a theater, but also a Center for Feminist Art Historical Studies alongside artists' exhibition galleries. As Judith Brodsky, a former president in the 1970s of the Women's Caucus for Art, has reported, the goal then was to integrate and unify: "Central to the vision of the founders [of the Woman's Building] was the notion that art and feminist education should not be separated from the other activities of the burgeoning women's community" (1994, 109). Also in the decade of the 1970s, Chicana feminists in Texas, as Shifra Goldman has noted, demonstrated their own importance in the cultural life of their state, when they founded "the art group Mujeres Artistas del Suroeste . . . and organized exhibits for Chicana and Latina women" in the gallery-studio they opened in Austin (1988, 191). For these earlier feminists of color, control of art spaces was a necessary and hard-won step toward political visibility, influence, and power.

The opportunities that exhibition sites open, as places situated within community life and integrated into the experience of individuals at all stages of their lives, must appeal to women's studies educators who feel the constraints of the classroom and of the traditional four-year college education. Ordinarily, students take a course, then graduate, and afterwards often are lost to us. The positive lessons, moreover, that we offer them in classroom settings are tainted with a touch of the compulsory. We invite students to transform their lives, but insist that, while doing so, they turn in papers and take exams, that they be measured and graded—requirements that may mar the experience. The knowledge we can share through the medium of an exhibition, however, comes unspoiled by such considerations and is thus more likely to be associated with unalloyed pleasure on both sides.

As I make this special pleading, I admit that my stake in the question is also a personal one. I like to call myself a *feminist exhibitionist*. My use of that term is only half-facetious. Committed though I am to campus spaces such as women's studies classrooms and women's centers, I confess that on numerous occasions I have felt great exhilaration in moving outside of them to curate exhibitions. My formal academic training was in literature, not in art history or museum studies. Yet I delight in all aspects of curating: selecting books, watercolors, prints, paintings, manuscripts, letters, posters, photographs, textiles, and decorative objects for display; researching the works chosen; arranging objects in cases or on walls; and, most of all, producing essays for catalogues, writing interpretive labels for individual items, and creating fact-based narratives for the wall panels that introduce a show. To perform such work is not merely to immerse myself in the forms of another discipline, but inevitably to leave my own stamp upon them—to arrive at a new synthesis that reflects a literary and gender-conscious perspective on the visual arts.

Surely one of the goals of an academic women's studies program or department is to go beyond multidisciplinarity and to model *interdisciplinarity* instead, both to students and to colleagues. I can think of few ways for professors to do this more explicitly than by stepping outside of their own disciplinary comfort zone. When we attempt to work in unfamiliar modes and genres—when, for example, we write interpretative labels for objects, instead of articles for feminist journals—we still bring to that project the methods of gender analysis that we have developed in another sphere; yet the methods themselves are reshaped by being adapted to a new context. We have the pleasure then of telling about and through the item at hand a different story. It will differ from the narrative that a museum professional might provide, for it will always put gender at the center. But it will also differ from the sort of abstract writing that we might do elsewhere, as well as from the generalized discussions we ordinarily have in classrooms. As curators, we can explore the challenges and joys of dealing with individual *things* in their material particularity, and we can then bring back to our women's studies teaching an enhanced respect for the role of material culture in women's histories and experiences.

Equally satisfying, though, is another aspect of exhibitions, one that certainly must appeal to other faculty engaged in women's studies: the opportunity for collaboration. Much of my exhibition work has been done with a co-curator, and such partnering is common in the world of museums and galleries. Yet the kinds of collaborations available through these alternative spaces go beyond those we might find in ordinary academic situations, such as the co-authoring of books or team-teaching. If the mounting of a visual arts show resembles anything, it is the staging of a play. Exhibitions demand that you work alongside a host of nonacademics (many of whom are women), from library or gallery or community center directors to administrative staff members, including those engaged in everything from conservation to book delivery to public relations to printing. For a professor, it can be a humbling, yet salutary, experience to test the limits of her own expertise and to discover how much she needs to rely on the expertise of others who have training very different from that of faculty with Ph.D.s.

But for women's studies faculty, the main question must be: In what ways can exhibition work advance and even embody feminist pedagogical principles? The answers are sometimes obvious and sometimes not. To begin with the less obvious, I would suggest that the physical act of encountering a theme-based or idea-based exhibition as a spectator is an experience that is consonant with feminist ideals. From the other side, curating such a show is also an activity that supports feminist methods of teaching.

An exhibition, for a start, can be one of the least coercive and most individualized forms of education. Unless viewers are there with a school group, their presence is wholly voluntary. Viewers pace themselves according to their own interests, their learning styles, and their ability or willingness to absorb either visual or written information. Ordinarily, they do not have to follow a linear, consecutive progression; they can move from case to case, room to room, in any order they wish. They can read labels or ignore them. They can come alone and be silent, but if they prefer, they can be there with friends or family and talk about what they see, either during or afterward, to make the experience collective. Many major museums in the world give access only to those who can afford steep admission charges, while college or university galleries, library exhibition spaces, student centers, and off-campus community centers are almost always free and open to the entire community, both academic and nonacademic. Although women's studies courses have always had great appeal to nontraditional students, college courses require a commitment of time and tuition that shuts out many working people. Populations, however, that might never enroll in women's studies classes are far more likely to walk through a gallery space for an hour, now and then. (Right now, for instance, to enter the Smithsonian's new Museum of the American Indian on the Mall in Washington, D.C., and to see the diverse crowds represented there is to feel cheered by the prospects for exhibitions to attract viewers across the lines of class, as well as gender and ethnicity.) If the public cannot come to the feminist classroom, then the valuable ideas generated within the feminist classroom can go out to the public by other means. Certainly, the opportunities for advancing projects that unite gender-based and antiracist approaches are myriad. As Elizabeth Catlett has said of her own works on paper and sculpture, "When I exhibit, Black people come. . . . White people always come. . . . If we exhibit together, it brings us all together" (LaDuke 1992, 140).

For faculty whose classroom pedagogy must always operate within restrictions, curating an exhibition can be liberating. There is no need to think in terms of time, of what presentations will fit within 50 minutes or 75 minutes. This teaching comes without the pressures of finding ways to measure and rank student performance, for there are no exams to administer, no grades to give. The sense of abstraction and distance that can pervade classroom learning falls away here, for both the objects themselves and the commentaries or narratives provided by the curator about those materials exist side by side. And unlike course evaluations, which appear only after the end of a semester (and unlike the reviews that appear months or years later in conventional scholarly publishing), the feedback from an exhibition is immediate. Just try standing anonymously in any room of your show and listen, or look at the blank book for written comments at the exit that some galleries provide.

This does not mean, of course, that a curator operates with total autonomy, any more than a professor does, no matter what lip service we might like to pay to the concept of "academic freedom." Given the collaborative nature of exhibition work, the curator's judgments—whether about the ideological content of a show, the selection of materials, or the language and even length of wall texts or of labels—are always subject to review and to editorial alteration at a variety of levels, whether for political or for pragmatic reasons. This is no more or less of a problem than it would be in team-teaching or in any other cooperative endeavor more familiar to women's studies faculty. In women's studies departments or programs, moreover, our course schedules usually reflect what we are asked or required to teach, rather than what we choose to teach. But exhibitions, especially in smaller venues such as on-campus spaces, are often initiated by a guest curator, who approaches the museum or library director with an idea and a proposal for carrying it out. Exhibitions, too, can be accompanied by educational programming for public outreach—from formal lectures to informal gallery talks; from scholarly symposia to public conversations with living artists or designers in an interview-format; from film and video screenings to hands-on workshops—as creative and wide-ranging as the curator can imagine and as budget constraints will allow.

If women's studies faculty reading my essay are unmoved by these marvelously selfish reasons for taking on the role of guest curator as a supplement to teaching in the classroom, then let me offer a selfless one. The museum world needs you right now—it needs your perspectives and your experience as feminist educators. Recently, both Julia M. Klein, in the 6 September 2002 issue of the *Chronicle of Higher Education*, and Bernice Yeung, in the Fall 2002 issue of *Bitch* magazine, have commented upon the growing numbers of museums devoted to women's history that have been opening or will open shortly. As Klein notes, however, so far the exhibitions at some institutions have favored the "antiquated 'great woman' approach to history"; the "next phase—and the challenge for the new generation of women's museums," as she says, will be "to present exhibits that go beyond celebration to historical complexity, that don't shrink from tackling contentious issues in a provocative way" (B15). Reviewing one show at the new Women's Museum in Dallas, Julia Klein, who is not an academic but rather a reporter and critic, seems to call out for curatorial participation by feminist scholars and theorists: "Because it shows rather than tells, the display resembles installation art, and visitors can provide their own take on what they see. But a more in-depth presentation of the issues covered, including the concepts of femininity, body image, and aging, would have been even better, particularly since they aren't given their due elsewhere in the museum" (B16). Or, to put it another way, this looks like a job for a women's studies professor!

The involvement of faculty with women's studies experience could also prove helpful in another regard. Bernice Yeung's article, "Making History Hers," suggests that debates over the desirability of separate institutions dedicated to women are still ongoing, even at this late date, with many museum professionals arguing instead for the "mainstreaming" of material about women (2002, 26). This is an area in which women's studies faculty have informed perspectives, since most of us have been through discussions, either on campus committees or at conferences, about whether and why women's studies should offer a freestanding major, should be administered through a program or an independent department, and should turn itself into gender studies or not. We are familiar with and can speak to the arguments on both sides about inclusion versus separatism and can advise those who are wrestling with such matters in the nonacademic sphere.

We can also be useful in other current controversies. Mark Fisher's article in the British *Times Literary Supplement* of March 2002, "Objections to the Object: Are We Losing Confidence in the Idea of the Museum?" and Janet Tassel's essay in the September–October 2002 issue of *Harvard Magazine,* "Reverence for the Object: Art Museums in a Changed World," are recent, high-profile expressions of the backlash that has set in against the so-called politicization of museums. Both articulate a nostalgia for museums as "sacred precincts" that will play a "civilizing role," as Tassel quotes James Cuno, director of the Harvard Art Museums, as saying (99). After having supposedly "politicized" college classrooms and curricula for three decades, without seeing either the institutions of higher education or the world at large come tumbling down, women's studies faculty certainly can be a resource to embattled museum staff under attack for nontraditional approaches to exhibitions or to public education. We can support those who, in the words of Ron Chew, attempt to "awaken conscience, deepen understanding, and enrich the public dialogue" through politically engaged shows and sometimes receive "hate calls at the museum and at home" for their efforts (2004, 40). Those of us who are professors can use the clout of our scholarly reputations and of the institutions we represent in defending innovations and also speak out from the security of tenured positions, a luxury that most museum professionals, whose jobs are on the line every day, do not have.

Feminist academics can weigh in, too, on a different sort of backlash—the reaction against exhibition labels. Blake Gopnik, a staff writer for the *Washington Post,* articulated this response in December 2001, with his article, "Read All About It: With Explanatory Labels Papering Museum Walls, Are We Still Looking at the Pictures They Explain?" After calling many such labels "mistaken," "plain dumb," "obviously absurd," and "unintelligible," Gopnik writes, "But even the very best of wall texts . . . risks leading people astray in a more fundamental sense. The very existence of such enhancements implies that works of art can be reduced to single, pat, 100-word paraphrases that 'explain' them, or explain them away" (G6). Listening to this, women's studies professors may hear echoes of those students who insist that any classroom interpretation of a literary work, a film, or a magazine ad constitutes "reading too much into it." I would hope that our experience in dealing with texts of many kinds—including visual ones—might enable us to argue against seeing them as somehow above and beyond commentary, even as it encourages us to treat them respectfully, without drowning out their voices with our own.

Those of us in women's studies are already boundary-crossers. But as I wish to emphasize, more of us should be crossing the thresholds of exhibition spaces, involving ourselves as curators, and bringing our years of work as interdisciplinary educators, teaching about race, class, sexual orientation, and gender, to a different sphere. We have a lot to contribute there. And, based on my own experience, I can also say that we have a lot to gain. As faculty, we sometimes grow complacent about our success in initiating positive change through the classroom alone. Are we setting our sights too low? If we believe in the feminist ideas we teach, then we should also be carrying them elsewhere, planting them in new venues, and, like Alice Walker's mother in her garden, watching those flowers blossom into beauty.

## References

Betterton, Rosemary. 1987. "Introduction: Feminism, Femininity, and Representation." In *Looking On: Images of Femininity in the Visual Arts and Media*, 1–17. London and New York: Pandora.

Brodsky, Judith K. 1994. "Exhibitions, Galleries, and Alternative Spaces." In *The Power of Feminist Art: The American Movement of the 1970s, History and Impact*, ed. Norma Broude and Mary D. Garrard, 104–19. New York: Harry N. Abrams.

Chew, Ron. 2004. "Taking Action! Advocates? Or Curators of Advocacy?" *Museum News* 83(2):38–43.

Fisher, Mark. 2002. "Objections to the Object: Are We Losing Confidence in the Idea of the Museum?" *Times Literary Supplement*, March 22, 13–4.

Goldman, Shifra. 1988. "Portraying Ourselves: Contemporary Chicana Artists." In *Feminist Art Criticism: An Anthology*, ed. Arlene Raven, Cassandra Langer, and Joanne Frueh, 187–205. New York: Icon Editions.

Gopnik, Blake. 2001. "Read All about It: With Explanatory Labels Papering Museum Walls, Are We Still Looking at the Pictures They Explain?" *Washington Post*, December 9, Arts, G1.

hooks, bell. 1995. "Art on My Mind." In *Art on My Mind: Visual Politics*, ed. Gloria Watkins, 1–9. New York: New Press.

Klein, Julia M. 2002. "Women's History through Different Doors." *Chronicle of Higher Education*, September 6, B15–16.

LaDuke, Betty. 1992. *Women Artists: Multi-Cultural Visions*. Trenton, N.J.: Red Sea Press.

Shaw, Susan. 1992. "Alice Walker." The *South Bank Show.*

Tassel, Janet. 2002. "Reverence for the Object: Art Museums in a Changed World." *Harvard Magazine* 105(1):48–58, 98–9.

Walker, Alice. 1983. "In Search of Our Mothers' Gardens." In *In Search of Our Mothers' Gardens: Womanist Prose by Alice Walker*, 231–43. San Diego and New York: Harcourt Brace Jovanovich.

Yeung, Bernice. 2002. "Making History Hers: New Museums Aim to Put Women on a Pedestal—in a Good Way." *Bitch* 18:25–8, 88.

# PART I Spectators, Spectacles, and Cultural Icons

CHAPTER TWO

# Diana Doubled: The Fairytale Princess and the Photographer

JILL R. CHANCEY

> Photography is the inventory of mortality.
>
> —Susan Sontag, 1977

Diana, Princess of Wales (1961–1997), has been an object of global fascination and obsessional documentation in the mass media since she started dating Prince Charles in 1980. Photographs, especially those found in the weekly tabloids in both the United Kingdom and the United States, have fed (perhaps created?) the documentation frenzy. Despite the best efforts of postmodern academics to bring into question the transparency and veracity of photography, photographs still carry the weight of evidence, and are understood to provide a view through a window onto someone else's real life. In the case of Diana, her photograph has come to stand in for the woman herself; the body of photographs of Diana in the tabloids is the equivalent or simulacrum of seeing her in the flesh.

In the following pages I discuss the subject matter and nature of presentation of photographs of Diana. These photographs are drawn from a survey of tabloids, news magazines, and memorial publications that were available in the month prior to and several months following her death. A close examination of this material leads to the conclusion that the image of Diana has been edited in the wake of her death. Diana serves as an interesting case study here because the response to her death was so overwhelming and so global. Press coverage of her death received more column inches per week (in the two months following her death) in the British papers than did World War II; billions of people watched her funeral, yet only a tiny percentage of those viewers ever met the woman, and even fewer knew her intimately (Bowman 1997). It is photographs, I would argue, that have allowed the public to feel as if they (we) know her intimately, and that same body of photographs contributed to the enormous outpouring of grief across the globe upon her death.

This phenomenon is, I believe, an excellent case study in the manifestation of Baudrillard's concept of a simulacrum (1981). Baudrillard argues that "reality" is irrelevant in the face of the ever-proliferating, mass-produced images of the information age: "It is the image-creating postmodern communication technologies—especially television—which proliferate self-generating, self-mirroring, depthless images. Experience

---

Originally published in the Summer 1999 issue of the *NWSA Journal.*

everywhere [is] now superficial" (quoted in Selden and Widdowson 1993, 180). In reference to the Gulf War, Baudrillard has argued the extreme position (since moderated) that the war was not real, but a fabrication of television, entirely staged (Baudrillard 1995). Nonetheless, it is clear that it is impossible for us to know the "real" Gulf War, or the "real" Princess Diana, from the multiple representations of her in film, video, newspapers, magazines, and on the Internet.

What has been constructed by this mass of representation is a simulacrum, one that is ever-shifting and never entirely knowable because of its enormous size and scope. Yet the hunger for new information about this simulacrum continues to grow even after the death of a flesh-and-blood woman, who has now become a multibillion-dollar image industry.[1] It is relevant here that photography was one of Baudrillard's referents in his discussion of the "hyperreal," the condition of postmodern culture in which all is simulacrum without depth: "Reality itself founders in hyperrealism, the meticulous reduplication of the real, preferably through another, reproductive medium, such as photography" (Harrison and Wood 1992, 1049). Photographs, which are infinitely reproducible and continue to function as evidence for the mass media and its audience, not to mention the judicial system, are the very means that produced the simulacrum-Diana.[2]

The simulacrum-Diana, Baudrillard would argue, would be just as real as the flesh-and-blood Diana, because "the real is not only that which can be reproduced, but [also] that which is always already reproduced: the hyperreal" (Baudrillard 1993, 73). Yet the simulacrum, I believe, never yields an entirely satisfactory experience. Without the depth beyond the image, a meeting with Diana in the mass media is incomplete, which leads to a desire for yet another encounter, hopefully more satisfactory than the last. The depthless simulacrum yields only temporary pleasure; hence the billion-dollar industry of the celebrity-oriented tabloid press, which provides more and more Diana-commodity, even more than a year after her death.

I invoke the Baudrillardian simulacrum as a way of understanding this body of images; I do not want to be misunderstood as speaking of the "real" Diana. Like nearly all mass media consumers, I can only know Princess Diana through the media's representation of her life in pictures that is under consideration here. I intend to demonstrate how the simulacrum-Diana was first manifest in the tabloid press as bad-girl/whore and later altered after her death to represent the fairytale princess. The Diana memorabilia industry is still in high gear long after her death. Commodities such as porcelain Diana dolls, commemorative stamps and plates, picture books from a number of publishers, and memorial cassette tapes and CDs trade on the image of Diana, drawn from or relying entirely upon the extensive photographic record of her life. The business is so brisk and varied that the Diana, Princess of Wales Memorial Fund has copyrighted a Diana logo for use on officially approved merchandise, a percentage of whose profits go to a philanthropic trust set up in her name.[3] This legal maneuver, however, has not stopped the flow of merchandise not endorsed by her estate.

While photographs of Diana have appeared across the entire spectrum of the mass media, the tabloid industry has been a significant purveyor (and purchaser) of all sorts of celebrity photographs and, in particular, photographs of Diana. Since the advent of the carte-de-visite in the middle of the nineteenth century, celebrity has been created by, mediated by, photography. The first images of celebrities were posed official images, made with the consent and cooperation of the celebrity involved (royalty, literati, actors) whose desire for recognition encouraged their participation in the process. However, with the advent of faster, portable cameras by the turn of the century, it became possible to take unofficial, unapproved photos of celebrities (and others) and to publish them in the illustrated newspapers that sprang up in the 1890s (Szarkowski 1989, 83, 144). Since then, celebrity photographs have proliferated.

Photojournalistic exploitation has remained remarkably consistent for more than a century: there have been complaints about the sleaziness and intrusiveness of tabloids and paparazzi photographs since the nineteenth century. A published drawing of Queen Victoria holding the infant Prince of Wales provoked an outcry against the picture as an invasion of privacy. In the 1930s and 1940s, both *Look* and *Life* published gory photos of violence victims (Guimond 1991, 156). From the 1950s to the early 1970s, the heyday of exploitation tabloids in Canada and the United States, several dozen tabloids with names like *The Confidential Flash* and *The National Exploiter* published sensational stories about sex, violence, and celebrity gossip (Betrock n.d., 6). By the 1970s, most of the smaller tabloids in the United States had folded, and the field was reduced to the six major tabloids available today (owned by only two companies, MacFadden Holdings Inc. and Globe Communications), which still provide weekly doses of sex, violence, gossip, and fantasy to a mostly female, mostly working-class, mostly white, and mostly middle-aged or older audience (Bird 1992, 8).

The celebrity photograph has been a staple of tabloids since the turn of the century and continues to attract readers by the millions. Today the tabloids will pay top dollar for the most invasive photos imaginable, whether they be of the corpses of Elvis Presley or Bing Crosby in their coffins, the Duchess of York having her toes sucked, or crime scene photos of the corpses of Nicole Brown Simpson and Ronald Goldman. James Guimond believes that the celebrity photograph appeals to its audience because the reader of the illustrated journal "is no longer one of the mass who had always been excluded" (1991, 156). Critic Elizabeth Bird has shown how the celebrity component of the tabloid formula dates to the earliest incarnations of the tabloid in the 1880s (1992, 16–17).[4]

The death of Diana has invoked an almost global argument about the limits and responsibilities of the paparazzo or celebrity photographer. The tabloids are a multibillion-dollar industry; in the wake of her death, each participant in the economy of the tabloid has laid blame elsewhere. Neither photographers, publishers, or customers will take responsibility for the escalation of Diana-chasing. There has been a rush to separate tabloid photographers from journalistic photographers, mostly by those wishing to distinguish themselves from the paparazzi.[5] Distinctions between photographic journalism and paparazzi photographs tend to rely on unquantifiable "high standards" regarding the important news value of celebrity photos. One such distinction was outlined by the editor of *People* magazine following the fatal car accident:

> From its first issue, *People* has applied rigorous standards to its journalism. We employ a staff of researchers to check all facts before publication. Unlike much of the tabloid press, we do not pay story subjects or sources. We are also very careful about the photographs we use . . . we work hard to avoid buying pictures by the so-called stalkerazzi. . . . we use paparazzi pictures . . . weighing the *news value* of a picture against a story subject's right to peace and privacy. In the wake of this tragedy we will redouble our efforts to maintain the standards that you have come to expect of us. (Wallace 1997, 8, emphasis mine)[6]

These are high-minded words from a magazine whose cover that week was originally going to be "THE BEST AND WORST DRESSED 97," a magazine whose cover Princess Diana graced more than any other public personality, some 43 times in the last sixteen years. The point here is that *People* rushed to define itself as "unlike much of the tabloid press" at a time when tabloids were under fire (Wallace 1997, 8).

The photographer plays a role in the creation of the simulacrum-Diana beyond the simple production of photographs. The public's awareness that there were photographers constantly following the princess also contributed to the process. Seventeen years of constant press about the princess have made it public knowledge that there were photographers with telephoto lenses wherever she went. That knowledge contributes to the belief that any blurred, distant photo of a leggy blonde wading in the surf or running toward a plane might represent Diana. Although we might be astonished to find our own vacation photos on the cover of the *National Enquirer*, it is entirely within the realm of reason to believe that a paparazzo could aim his telephoto lens at a distant princess as she climbed into a sailboat or went for a swim, thus capturing her image. The paparazzo functions as the audience's virtual voyeur; instead of actually lurking about in the hedgerows, the viewer can live vicariously through the lens of a "royal-chaser," as they are often called.

Susan Sontag has noted that taking a photograph of someone is a kind of violation that "turns people into objects that can be symbolically possessed" (Sontag 1977, 14). This formulation allows the tabloid reader to not only see Diana, but to partake in the hunt, and eventually to own her or, rather, a simulacrum of her. The fact that there is no male counterpart to the "most photographed woman in the world" is surely symptomatic of the way the female body and identity are commodified in contemporary consumer culture.

The precise nature of Princess Diana's often adversarial, sometimes collaborative, relationship with the mass media may be difficult to pin down, as the major sources are the media themselves. However, what is clear is that the press began to follow her on a daily basis in mid-1980, at about the time she began to date Prince Charles. Its attention was intense enough to induce both tears and fear in her, even before the wedding of June 1981, and it only increased in the years afterward. By December 1981, the Queen of England had called a meeting with press members to ask them to give the then-pregnant princess some privacy (Davies 1992, 135–7). Even the queen could not stop the paparazzi, and by the following year the press had begun its intense scrutiny again. By 1989, "photographers would follow her on motorbikes with linking walkie-talkie radios and mobile phones" (Davies 1992, 204).

In December 1993, Diana announced that she would retire from public life and asked the press to grant her more privacy than it had in the past. This move only intensified the media invasion into her private life. In a now-chilling book called *Dicing with Di: The Amazing Adventures of Britain's Royal Chasers*, two freelance photographers detail three years of what was essentially the stalking of Princess Diana (Harvey and Saunders 1996). In the foreword, they explicitly date the beginning of the "hunt" to the date of Diana's withdrawal from public life.

In a tone alternating between smug, catty, and defensive, the two photographers have published what amounts to a stalker's diary, replete with tales of secret hiding spots and confrontations with Diana. It is a virtual paparazzo bragbook of intimidation and harassment, detailing the photographers' car chases, day-long hunts, and constant references to the money to be made from Diana photographs. Given the events leading to her death, the text is fairly disturbing. The authors provide the following disclaimer: "As press photographers, our job is to take pictures. We do not see ourselves as part of Diana's problems. We do not accept an accusation of harassment, intrusion, or invasion of privacy" (Harvey and Saunders 1996, 2). In other words, they invoke the notion that everything a celebrity does is "news," to which the public has a right. Sontag has noted that "the information that photographs can give starts to seem very important at that moment in cultural history when everyone is thought to have a right to something called news" (1977, 22). Apparently, by 1993, the audience's desire for more news of Diana was insatiable, and Saunders and Harvey felt they were providing a public service (while at the same time being highly paid).

As late as 1996, Diana was granted an injunction against a paparazzo, who had to stay more than 300 meters from her.[7] This photographer, Martin Stenning, made comments curiously similar to those of Saunders and Harvey. He insisted that Diana used the press for her own ends, was friendly to him on occasion, and that he never invaded her personal space. While Saunders and Harvey also make these claims, the fact is that the paparazzi, in an effort to satisfy an ever-increasing lust for more and more photos of Diana, became more invasive and offensive to her as the years passed.

These paparazzi are among the collective authors who have fabricated the simulacrum-Diana. The audience, too, participates in the creation of what Baudrillard calls the *hyperreal.* A mass media phenomenon such as this is authored by no one and everyone: mass media outlets, consumers and, in some ways, Diana herself. Diana was certainly aware of the importance of her image, but rarely had the kind of control she would have liked over it. And as the photographs proliferated exponentially, there came to be a certain look associated with Diana. She was what we call *photogenic,* which, as Sontag notes, has become a term equivalent to beautiful: "We learn to see ourselves photographically: to regard oneself as attractive is, precisely, to judge that one would look good in a photograph. Photographs create the beautiful" (Sontag 1977, 55).

The fact is, one can find photos of Diana that distinctly *don't* look like Diana; that is, they don't conform to the characteristic "shy Di look." A Christie's catalog published shortly before her death contains a candid photograph of Diana that is nearly unrecognizable. She looks directly at the camera, doesn't smile, and holds her head up straight.[8] She looks as if she has been interrupted in the midst of conversation, and simply does not wish to put on that famous Diana smile. Most of the photographs of Diana published in the tabloids in the weeks prior to her death could have been photographs of just about any long-legged blonde with a similar haircut. We simply must trust that the photographer—and the publication—aren't lying to us about who is in the fuzzy distance. What is often missing from such photos is the standard Diana look: head slightly turned down, tilted to right or left, eyes looking up from that tilted face, and a frequently closed-lipped, but always quite practiced, smile. That the "shy Di look" is so easily defined is a result of the thousands of photographs of Diana published in the last several decades. When the formula is strayed from, she suddenly does not look quite right; whether it's a smile that appears to be genuine and not practiced, a fully raised head, or a head-on glance, the deviation stops us from recognizing the Diana we think we know. This sense of familiarity with a celebrity is surely a function of photography; we think we can know a total stranger through her image, but when the image contradicts our expectations, we have difficulty recognizing her. The expectations do not come from a familiarity with Diana, but rather from a familiarity with hundreds or perhaps thousands of photos of her. A quick perusal of the website of a Diana impersonator shows only photos with the patented head-tilt and up-and-sideways glance.[9] One of these pictures is almost entirely convincing, as it is a restaging of a widely published official photo of Diana by Lord Snowdon.

In the months since her death the content and definition of the photographic image of Diana changed. The character of the simulacrum-Diana changed to parallel almost exactly the "folklore heroine" narrative delineated by the folklorist Linda Dégh (1994). This biography of the fairytale heroine, according to Dégh, defines the heroine in terms of a series of relationships to men: father, husbands, sons, and lovers. The narrative reinscribes the conventional roles for women in story after story, and this is the narrative that the memorial industry tells of Diana. This story is told via a careful selection of photographs, images which may have been culled from the tabloid/paparazzi archives, but which do not transgress the conventional roles of the folklore heroine. Many memorial publications have appeared, mostly filled with photographs and only a smattering of text. These publications are remarkably consistent in character and have created a canon of appropriate images of Diana, excising many scandalous and unflattering photos that appeared in the years since her separation from Prince Charles. Sontag has noted that "as the fascination that photographs exercise is a reminder of death, it is also an invitation to sentimentality"; such a view holds true for these memorial publications (1977, 71).

In many tabloids, even the condition of death does not prevent an invasion of privacy. However, when it is a celebrity's death instead of a stranger's, the terms of what is appropriate shift from scandalous to sentimental. The sociologist Pierre Bourdieu has argued that the convention of amateur photography is this: one photographs what "must" be photographed, and one only photographs what "may" be photographed (1990, 34). Yet, my examination of tabloid photography demonstrates that those involved in celebrity journalism are willing to publish what "may *not*" be photographed as long as the celebrity is alive. For example, there are several tabloids which predate Diana's death in which the headlines blare, "Di in Vicious Street Brawl," "Di in NEW Sex Scandal," "Fat Di: Princess Binges on Junk Food and Packs on 15 Lbs," and "Psychic Warns Di: Dump Dodi." The accompanying photographs show the princess sunbathing, swimming, and accosting a photographer. They are unflattering; some are blurry, most would be barely identifiable out of context or without a caption, and none were taken with her permission.

A comparison of the material that was published after her death in these same tabloids yields an entirely different crop of photos: the princess, for the most part, at official functions, dressed to go out to a social function (many pictures of her in a tiara), engaged in humanitarian activities (which were nearly always accompanied by invited press photographers), images of her wedding and her funeral, and a great quantity of pictures of Diana as mother. Suddenly her image must be appropriate—the photos are those which "may" and "must" be taken—formal events, holidays, social occasions, family events. These are the photos that tell the story of the fairytale heroine, that emphasize the important events in her life in relation to men: her wedding, her motherhood, her divorce, and her new love interest. Not only does this postmortem visual biography almost exactly parallel that of the folklore heroine delineated by Dégh (1994), but Diana began her career in the public eye with what was widely referred to as a "fairytale wedding."

Those photos that made her so unhappy—and the pursuit of which some say may have led to her death—are eliminated entirely from the memorials' photographic record of her life. In the numerous tributes to Diana published in the months following her death (the publication of which quickly became a multimillion-dollar industry), I have been unable to find a single photograph that goes beyond that which "may" and "must" be photographed.[10] The pictures generally fall under a few basic headings: childhood photos, wedding photos, Diana as mother, Diana as humanitarian, Diana as victim of bulimia and of the royal family, Diana as fashion plate, funeral photos. Yet even the pictures that emphasize her troubled times were taken at official functions, where she was seen as pensive, distant, or looking generally miserable.

Judging by these photographs, it appears that the last taboo in photojournalism (or tabloid photography) is this: one should not speak ill of the dead. At least, not right away. The tenor of the coverage could change, but considering a November 1997 headline in the *Star*, "Di's Secret Miracles," one doubts that the coverage will grow any less worshipful and sentimental in the near future. Clearly the field of imagery is being edited in the wake of her death, which yields yet a new and more socially conventional simulacrum of Diana, one in which she performs all of the roles of traditional femininity (mother, wife, princess) and has no transgressive qualities (sexually active, aggressive, aging). Now that the flow of images must stop, the press has stopped to sift through the extensive photographic evidence of her life and republish those photos that are respectful and sentimental. Even many disrespectful or satiric websites have self-censored themselves since her death, such as one that consists merely of an official portrait of Diana, and the following statement: "If you came to this page from Altavista, you were expecting to find a joke here. The original picture is now in extremely poor taste, and I have removed it. The world is a poorer place for our loss of a truly good person, Diana, Princess of Wales. Godspeed."[11]

In the midst of all of this reconstruction of a royal identity there remains one problem: what to do about those pictures of her in the wrecked Mercedes. There are photographs, somewhere, taken of Diana and her companions shortly after the car crashed, but before the ambulance arrived. Since the crash, the German magazine *Bild Zeitung* has published photos of the bloodied passengers, still in the car, whereas the tabloid *National Enquirer* chose to take the "high road" and announce on television (within hours of Diana's death) their boycott of the photos, which they claimed to have been offered within hours of the crash. Perhaps to forestall competition, they challenged their colleagues in the tabloid industry to do the same. Thus far, the photographs have not been published in the United States.

However, photos of bloody car crashes and other tragedies are no anomaly in the world of photojournalism. The American photographer Weegee, for example, made his reputation in New York City in the 1930s as the spot-news photographer with an instinct for where the next tragedy would be, filling the New York papers with photos of bloodied gangsters, car-crash victims, and scenes of tenement fires and their victims.[12] Warhol's *Black and White Disaster* (1962) and *Green Disaster* (1963) were both created using silkscreens of news photos of car crashes. Some of the most famous photographs of our day involve death and violence: Kent State, 1971; a Viet Cong execution, 1968; the Zapruder film of Kennedy's assassination, later used to such horrifying effect in Oliver Stone's movie, *JFK*; Lee Harvey Oswald's televised death at the hands of Jack Ruby; and scenes of police and their dogs attacking civil rights protesters in the early 1960s, also appropriated by Warhol in his *Red Race Riot* (1963).

Yet pictures of Diana in a car crash have been deemed almost universally to be in bad taste. I would argue that this is due to the image reconstruction process I have described, which eliminates the ugly, inappropriate, or transgressive in favor of emphasizing the traditionally feminine aspects. There is clearly nothing "feminine" or fairytale-like about being bloody and broken in the back of one's lover's Mercedes. The photograph published by *Bild Zeitung* is actually quite difficult to read; mostly what one sees is a crashed car with some amorphous blobs of color inside the car.

Ironically, the *Philadelphia Inquirer* (a news daily, not to be confused with the *National Enquirer*), has published on its website a very tiny reproduction of the cover of *Bild Zeitung* in order to condemn the German magazine for publishing the car crash photo.[13] Another website included a photo of a bloodied blonde victim being pulled out of the backseat of a black car with accompanying text that stated that the photo may or may not be a fake.[14] The unresolved identity of the victim in the backseat highlights the differences in news value that pictures of a celebrity like Diana or a noncelebrity victim carries. Additionally, a photo of an unknown victim would not cause the sort of public outrage that a photo of a dying Diana would cause. Why? Because such a photo would contradict everything the mass audience thinks, or wants to think, about the dead princess. These photos would serve as concrete, incontrovertible evidence that the fairytale princess did not live happily ever after.

As her death becomes more and more distant, the simulacrum that photography has created becomes more contained, more altered, and more appropriately feminine. Those sex scandals, street brawls, and bad cellulite days are being edited out of the record. Instead of the living and complicated Diana defined by scandals, eating disorders, and friction within the royal family, a newer, streamlined, prettified postmortem version is being created. The Diana memorial industry has edited the massive visual record of Diana's life so that we see only the fairytale side of her life; even her tribulations are part of a folklore heroine's life, according to Dégh. Those pensive photos of a too-thin or depressed-looking princess at official functions, which are generally placed about midway through the series of photos, serve to show that she suffered trials and tribulations before nearly achieving the final goal of every folklore heroine: marrying the "prince." Dodi Fayed's (the prince of Harrod's?) courtship of Diana did not end in marriage, but it is clear from the memorial books and articles (see References) that her happiness in the last months of her life were considered the "happy ending" of her fairytale, and her eventual marriage to Dodi almost a given (despite the considerable obstacle of his Muslim faith).

The final photos in these books, however, are always of Prince Charles and her sons at her funeral. Thus, the pictorial story of Diana's life ends just as it began,with Prince Charles, for the memorial books usually begin their visual narrative with the months preceding her marriage. Furthermore, the final photos are staid, formal, and official. Diana's life is wrapped up in a tidy package by these books. She is codified in these publications as mother, princess, wife, humanitarian, beautiful, and never, ever, "inappropriate" or "unfeminine." It is only in death that her visual biography has begun to fit the fictional narrative of ideal womanhood. The simulacrum is no longer evolving, but rather has been pinned in place, slowed if not stilled, by the Diana memorial industry.

## Acknowledgments

I would like to thank Professor John Pultz and my colleagues in his seminar on Vernacular Photography, High Art, and Popular Culture, held in the Fall of 1997. The patience and hard work of the editorial staff of the *NWSA Journal* has been invaluable.

## Notes

1. For example, a simple search on "Princess Diana" on an Internet search engine yielded several hundred thousand hits; many of these websites originated after her death.

2. One wonders if the relationship between Diana and her simulacrum-self might prove to have been the source of much of her misery regarding the press; unfortunately the details of such a relationship can only be speculative.

3. http://britain-info.org/bis/monarchy/diana/links.htm

4. Bird points out that tabloids are the descendants of broadsheet ballads and the penny press, and are an extension of ancient oral traditions going back long before the invention of photography.

5. All of the major network news shows, the national newspapers, and news magazines quickly editorialized about the incident. Each carefully distinguished its own journalism from "stalkerazzi" celebrity-chasers.

6. As I write this, *People*'s latest issue contains a gossipy cover story on Chelsea Clinton's personal life, despite the protests of her parents.

7. Rachel Donnelly, "Injunction granted to princess is a load of rubbish, says photographer." www.irish-times.com/irish-times/paper/1996/0817/for11 .html. Originally published in *The Irish Times*, 17 August 1996.

8. My thanks to Professor John Pultz for bringing this particular photo to my attention.

9. Julie Woolley/Diana, Princess of Wales. http://members.aol.com/fboyprods/ jwdi01.htm (5 December 1997).

10. It is impossible to note all of these tributes, but a few examples are listed after the references.

11. "In Memoriam: Diana, Princess of Wales." www.hypertype.com/smile .html (5 December 1997). Given self-censorship on the Internet and the

lack of archived back issues of tabloids, one wonders if the entire photographic record of the transgressive, scandalous Diana will one day be impossible to retrieve.

12. Weegee, born Arthur Fellig, was nicknamed after the Ouija board because of his apparent ability to sense disaster and be the first on the scene (Szarkowski 1989, 197).

13. Susan Caba, "Photos of Diana in wrecked car fueling ethics debate," www.phillynews.com/inquirer/97/Sep/03/national/PHOTO3.htm (5 December 1997).

14. www.glr.com/crash.htm (5 December 1997).

## References

Baudrillard, Jean. 1981. *Simulacre et simulation.* Paris: Éditions Galilée.

———. 1993. *Symbolic Exchange and Death.* Trans. Iain Hamilton Grant. London: Sage Publications.

———. 1994. *Simulacra and Simulation.* Trans. Sheila Faria Glaser. Ann Arbor: University of Michigan Press.

———. 1995. *The Gulf War Did Not Take Place.* Trans. Paul Patton. Bloomington: Indiana University Press.

Betrock, Alan. n.d. *Sleazy Business: A Pictorial History of Exploitation Tabloids, 1959–1974.* Brooklyn, N.Y.: Shake Books.

Bird, S. Elizabeth. 1992. *For Enquiring Minds: A Cultural Study of Supermarket Tabloids.* Knoxville: University of Tennessee Press.

Bourdieu, Pierre. 1990. *Photography: A Middle-Brow Art.* Trans. Shaun Whiteside. Stanford, Calif.: Stanford University Press.

Bowman, Daniel. 1997. "Pictures of an Execution: How to Look at Diana's Final Photos." Online. Available at www.salonmagazine.com/sept97/diphotos970908.html.

Davies, Nicholas. 1992. *Diana: A Princess and Her Troubled Marriage.* New York: Birch Lane Press.

Dégh, Linda. 1994. *American Folklore and the Mass Media.* Bloomington: Indiana University Press.

Guimond, James. 1991. *American Photography and the American Dream.* Chapel Hill: University of North Carolina Press.

Harrison, Charles, and Paul Wood. 1992. *Art in Theory, 1900–1990: An Anthology of Changing Ideas.* Cambridge, Mass.: Blackwell.

Harvey, Glenn, and Mark Saunders. 1996. *Dicing with Di: The Amazing Adventures of Britain's Royal Chasers.* London: Blake.

Junor, Penny. 1983. *Diana, Princess of Wales.* New York: Doubleday.

Lester, Paul. 1991. *Photojournalism: An Ethical Approach.* Hillsdale, N.J.: Lawrence Erlbaum Associates.

Selden, Raman, and Peter Widdowson. 1993. *A Reader's Guide to Contemporary Literary Theory.* Lexington: University Press of Kentucky.
Sontag, Susan. 1977. *On Photography.* New York: Anchor Books, Doubleday.
Szarkowski, John. 1989. *Photography until Now.* New York: Museum of Modern Art.
Wallace, Carol. 1997. "Letter From the Editor." *People Magazine,* 15 September, 8.

## Magazine issues either devoted to Princess Diana or featuring a cover article about Princess Diana

*The Globe*: 5 August 1997; 16 September 1997; 7 October 1997.
*Majesty*: July 1997.
*National Enquirer*: 16 September 1997; 23 September 1997.
*National Examiner*: 2 September 1997.
*Newsweek Commemorative Issue: Diana, A Celebration of Her Life*: October 1997.
*The New Yorker*: 15 September 1997.
*People*: 16 September 1997; 22 September 1997; 13 October 1997.
*Star*: 16 September 1997; 23 September 1997; 30 September 1997.
*Time Magazine Special Report*: 8 September 1997.
*Vanity Fair*: July 1997.

## Specially produced commemorative publications

*Diana: Life of a Legend.* 1997. Montreal: Globe International.
*Diana, The People's Princess: Her Royal Life in Pictures.* 1997. Red Bank, N.J.: Fanzine International.
*A Final Farewell: Diana, the World Says Goodbye.* 1997. Red Bank, N.J.: Fanzine International.
*Princess Diana: Her Life in Words and Pictures.* 1997. Radnor, Pa.: NewsAmerica Publications.

CHAPTER THREE

# Alice Neel's Portraits of Mother Work

DENISE BAUER

> I always had this awful dichotomy. I loved Isabetta, of course I did. But I wanted to paint.
>
> —Alice Neel

It is inviting to look at romantic, artfully staged portraits of mothers and children—cherubic, irresistible children and serene, smiling mothers—because they offer us the fantasy of a privileged ideal. But what the ubiquity of these images also implies is that only the most beautiful, loving moments with our children count. These Madonna and child-inspired images belie the messy realities of mothering and raising children; they are relics of an androcentric historical tradition in which maternal subjectivity was invisible and women artists were (are) largely silent and silenced.

The American portraitist Alice Neel (1900–1984) was never silenced, however. She was unafraid to reveal, alongside the tenderness and joy mothers experience, the ambivalences, conflicts, and fears women face as mothers, too. Neel's approach to the representation of mothers was characteristic of her overall style of both penetrating social artifice and dignifying the realities of all people. She had a courageous, brutally honest approach to rendering an individual's character. Neel's portraits of mothers and children brazenly defied the social norms and transgressed the Western art tradition of the Madonna and child. In a major retrospective of her work that was organized by the Philadelphia Museum of Art and toured several major U.S. museums in 2000–2001, Alice Neel's courageous vision has been fully on display.

Unfortunately, however, while the accompanying catalogue, *Alice Neel* (2000), edited by Ann Temkin, does address some feminist aspects of this artist's work, it does not delve very deeply into the radical feminist implications of such works. The exhibition itself leaves out many of Neel's most feminist images as well. Despite the great interest her art typically generates among feminists, there is limited feminist scholarship available on Neel's work other than a few brief essays dating from the 1970s.

As has historically been the case with Neel, reviews of the retrospective tended to focus on the most sensational and outrageous images in her oeuvre, such as the male nude with three penises, *Joe Gould* (1933),

Originally published in the Summer 2002 issue of the *NWSA Journal*.

or Neel's portrait of a bare-chested and wounded *Andy Warhol* (1970). The less glamorous, but more ordinary human experiences of mothering and raising children, a major motif of Neel's, attracted much less critical attention. In this essay, I will explore a select number of Neel's mother and child portraits, most of which were not included in the retrospective, to examine how evocatively she casts light on mother work and the interrelationships of mothers and their children, which I believe are among her most important contributions to feminist art and cultural history.

The example of Neel's still life, *Thanksgiving* (1965), depicting a raw turkey indecorously splayed in a kitchen sink beside a jar of Ajax, is representative of her deliberately irreverent style. Just as in this exposé of an undressed Thanksgiving turkey before its formal presentation at the dinner table, Neel's portraits of mothers and children expose their inner experiences and unguarded private moments, often as they are lived within the domestic sphere and outside the frame of those more familiar and idealizing portraits.

While Neel was a traditional easel painter working in conventional genres, she also transgressed those same conventions with her own subjective vision and understanding of the complexities of the human and, in particular, the female condition. Neel's portraits were a radical departure from the flattering commissioned works of Old World Masters. Never resorting to cliché, her portraits of women include a crouching self-conscious young woman, a bold nude girl, a *degenerate Madonna*, and a series of pregnant nudes, all of which flew in the face of conventional notions of how the feminine was to be understood and represented. Painting for decades prior to the shift in mass consciousness resulting from the second wave feminist movement, Neel's portraits of women anticipated and contributed to the emergence of feminist art in the 1970s. Today, many of these portraits of women have entered the canon of feminist art history.

Alice Neel has long been a favorite among feminists and leftists. Although she had been an art world presence in New York starting in the 1930s, it wasn't until the 1970s that her work began to gain wider mainstream recognition. Combined with her colorful life story, ebullient personality, and passion about showing her work, Neel and her riveting portraits of public figures like pop artist Andy Warhol (1970), politician Bella Abzug (1975), and New York City's mayor Ed Koch (1981) began to attract the media's attention. In 1970, she was commissioned to paint a portrait of Kate Millet for a *Time* magazine cover. During the 1970s, she was featured in the pages of *Newsweek*, *People*, and appeared twice on the *Johnny Carson Show*. Since her death in 1984, her work has gained greater critical attention, culminating most recently in her major touring retrospective, 2000–2001.

Much of Neel's work is unmistakably autobiographical. As feminist art critic Ann Sutherland Harris has described, Neel's oeuvre stands as a "kind of diary" to the people, events, and experiences of her life (1978, n.p.). Not only did she paint her own experiences as a mother, starting with the birth of her first child in the late 1920s, she also painted her daughters-in-law and grandchildren from the 1960s until her death in 1984. She also painted the mothers and children around her—her friends, neighbors, other artists, critics, and people from the art world. Together, these portraits stand as a kind of Neel family album of the people and personalities who came in and out of her life.

Alice Neel was born in Merion Square, a suburb of Philadelphia, in 1900 to a middle-class family. Her father, whom Neel described as a "very refined . . . wonderful, kind man" (quoted in Hills 1983, 12) was the head of the Per Diem Department of the Pennsylvania Railroad. He came from a family of opera singers. Neel's mother, Alice Concross Hartley, a descendent of a signer of the Declaration of Independence, was a homemaker and an intelligent, well-read, and strong-minded woman who took Neel regularly to concerts and the theater. Neel was a highly sensitive and nervous child, the fourth of five children (one of whom died), who remembers feeling completely bored with small-town life. She credits her mother with being the only one who "stimulated [her] mind" (quoted in Hills 1983, 12).

From an early age, Neel had a heightened awareness of class distinctions and a disdain for bourgeois conventions. As a young adult she enrolled herself at the Philadelphia School of Design for Women, but rejected the impressionist style that was in favor there, stating in her characteristically witty way, "I never saw life as a picnic on the grass" (quoted in Hills 1983, 13). Instead, she was influenced by the Ashcan School of Realism through one of its main proponents, Robert Henri, who had taught at the Philadelphia School of Design. The Ashcan School made urban ghetto life its subject and asserted the importance of using feeling in art. This subject and sensibility appealed to the young Neel who remembered how "on the way to school I would pass old gray haired women who had been scrubbing office floors all night and would feel guilty to be drawing classic statues" (1971, M-7). Her social conscience was later developed in the leftist climate of Greenwich Village, where she moved in 1927, and later, like many artists and writers of the time, she briefly joined the Communist Party. Although she said she was "never a good Communist" because she "hate[d] bureaucracy" (quoted in Hills 1983, 60), she remained committed to its ideals and, in particular, remained loyal to its members, many of whom she painted through the McCarthy era and up until her death in 1984.

Despite Neel's blond, angelic appearance and charming manners, she had a mercurial nature, a ribald sense of humor, and a sardonic wit. Neel was a true bohemian who deliberately chose a lifestyle free of many conventional, middle-class notions of propriety. For most of her life, she was a struggling artist and single mother, a white woman who lived from 1938 to 1962 alone with her children in the New York neighborhood, Spanish Harlem, which today is known as *El Barrio*. As a young woman, she married a Cuban art student, Carlos Enriquez, who came from an aristocratic and wealthy family. They had two children—one died in infancy and the other was raised by Neel's in-laws. Throughout her life, Neel had several stormy relationships with often-troubled men, including one who slashed scores of her paintings. She had two more children, Richard and Hartley, and later in life became a devoted, although somewhat eccentric mother and grandmother. She enthusiastically included her grandchildren in her art openings but was less likely to babysit them or participate in their daily care.

Neel's own unconventional lifestyle, precarious class status, and political sensibilities were shaped in part by living and socializing within Latino communities periodically through her life. This put her in a unique position to see through the markings and pretenses of social class, the ethnocentrism of the controlling white culture, and the dominant ideologies around mothering, family, and femininity as they shifted and changed over her lifetime. It was her displacement from mainstream social and political norms that permitted Neel to capture the rich complexities of women's lives, as they existed outside of, and often in tension with, such ideological confines.

Mothers and children were a major motif throughout Neel's career, no doubt stemming from her own often tormented experiences as a young mother, her early ambivalence about having children, her difficult experiences as a single mother, and in later years, her view of the changing roles of mothers in society, mainly as observed through her daughters-in-law and grandchildren. Neel consistently made the experiences of mothers, the interrelationship of mother and child, and familial relationships the subjects of her work.

But also, and as is a pattern in Neel's work, these issues were emblematic of larger cultural changes. Following on the heels of the first wave feminist movement, the early part of the twentieth century was marked by challenges to the nuclear family as women won the right to vote, began to enter the workforce in larger numbers, and began to seek higher education. With more life options and the drive for "voluntary motherhood" being espoused by early proponents of birth control, motherhood began to be seen as an option rather than a requirement. Women's friendships with each other were highly valued and there was an increase in the visibility of lesbian relationships (Kaplan 1992). (Interestingly, Neel's double female nude portrait, *Nadya and Nona* [1933], might have been influenced by this changing cultural context.)

Neel's earliest mature works date from the end of this period in the late 1920s, by which time the first wave's ethos of social reform had been significantly eroded. In its place, the more individualistic image of the New Woman who combined career, family, and marriage took precedence. However, with little social or political supports to enable the New Woman to exist among the masses of women, this remained a largely unrealized ideal. Growing up during the first wave feminist movement, but coming of age during a period of political retreat, left Neel and many others of her generation in an awkward place. They were sufficiently inspired to create new lifestyles as women; however, they had little direction or support in actualizing new life patterns (Ware 1997). Neel's struggles with motherhood were reflective of these conflicts.

During the late 1920s, Neel created both traditional, posed, as well as parodied images of motherhood. Neel poignantly chronicled the death of her first child, Santillana, from diphtheria, in a number of early expressionist works. *Requiem* (1927) is an eerie work in which an amorphous figure, suggestive of a mother holding an infant, lies at the bottom of a dark, undulating sea. *Futility of Effort* (1930) is a very spare painting of a small child with her body half-severed, hanging from the bedpost. Neither idealizes nor sentimentalizes motherhood; in fact, both cast the experience of mothering and having babies in a tragic manner.

The birth of her second child, Isabetta, followed shortly after the death of her first. As Neel explained: "In the beginning I didn't want children, I just got them" (quoted in Hills 1983, 21). Within a few weeks of Isabetta's birth, Neel painted *Well Baby Clinic* (1928), a highly expressionist, surrealistic work that depicts scores of writhing red-brown naked babies and their intent mothers in a starkly white hospital-like setting (Hills 1983). In the foreground, a mother with an exaggeratedly large mouth, whom Neel describes as "talking like mad" sits beside a silent doctor who is holding out pills to her. As Neel herself explained, "*Well Baby Clinic* makes my attitude toward childbirth very dubious" (quoted in Hills 1983, 23). The title parodies this nightmarish scene of naked babies and earnest mothers.

One of Neel's most wry commentaries on mothering is a small watercolor titled *The Intellectual* (fig. 3.1). In this amusing work, Neel illustrates her childless actress friend Fanya Foss, in the foreground, disproportionately larger than the other women pictured, languishing in a chair with her breasts hanging out over her dress. According to Neel, she is speaking with an attentive but smaller, equally elegant, high-heeled woman beside her, "of intellectual things" (quoted in Hills 1983, 26). In a very witty way, Neel depicts herself looking on, with three arms and three legs, as she tries to manage her small child while also attempting to participate in their conversation. The contrasting life choices of these women are made very apparent. Foss's highbrow attitude—suggested in

3.1 *The Intellectual,* 1929. Watercolor on paper, 10½ × 15 inches, 26.7 × 38.1 cm. 

her larger size, her appearance in the foreground of the work, and her exaggeratedly relaxed pose—appears arid and pompous beside the mundane physical struggle Neel is having with her small child. While Neel is clearly mocking Foss's pretentiousness, she is also expressing, in a whimsical way, her own frustration at an inability to pursue intellectual matters as the mother of a small child.

Such frustrations and whimsical images were relatively short-lived, because by 1930, Neel's already deteriorating marriage to Carlos was over and their child, Isabetta, was left in the care of his wealthy Cuban family. Owing to a variety of circumstances, including financial problems, Neel's nervous breakdown, and a rivalry that emerged between Neel and her husband, Carlos's family then raised Isabetta. *Isabetta* (1934) was painted when she had returned from Cuba for a visit with her mother. When explaining this turn of events, Neel said, "I always had this awful dichotomy. I loved Isabetta, of course I did. But I wanted to paint" (quoted in Hills 1983, 29). Neel's dichotomy was the classic conflict between motherhood and creative work. This clash of identity and the resulting tensions it generates is articulated quite distinctly in her early portraits of mothers and children, when these issues were most raw for her personally and when cultural supports were less for working mothers. This dichotomy appears again, as a sympathetic awareness in her later works after 1960, when new social and political issues began to recast the mother's role.

Following the end of her marriage and the loss of her two children—one in death, the other to her in-laws—Neel was institutionalized in a mental hospital for a year. Unable or unwilling to conform to the dictates of "womanhood" or "motherhood," Neel instead painted. Like many of her female peers, she was determined to combine career, motherhood,

3.2 *Degenerate Madonna,* 1930. Oil on canvas, 31×24 inches, 78.7×61 cm. © The Estate of Alice Neel/Courtesy David Zwirner, New York.

and marriage despite the obstacles. The only apparent answer for her was sacrifice; Neel felt forced to give up marriage and motherhood. "At first," she explained after Carlos and Isabetta left, "all I did was paint, day and night" (quoted in Hills 1983, 29).

In a macabre inversion of the Madonna and child tradition, Neel painted the wildly expressionistic *Degenerate Madonna* in 1930 (fig 3.2). The subject is Neel's childless friend Nadya, whose sexuality Neel later explored in two nude portraits, *Nadya Nude* (1933) and *Nadya and Nona* (1933). However, in this moralizing work, Neel casts Nadya as the "bad mother" (Hills 1983, 188). Nadya never had children, perhaps because she had had multiple abortions from which she suffered permanent physical damage (Neel Arts Inc. 1997–2001). Here Neel plays with the virgin/whore dichotomy that persists in Western culture in which a bad mother would also be a sexual one, just as she undoubtedly gives expression to her own feelings about her failed mothering efforts.

*Degenerate Madonna* is a startlingly crude, mostly black and white painting of a disfigured bare-breasted woman and her deformed child. One half of the background is painted a deep red; the other half bears a sinister reflection of the child's distorted head. When it was shown at the Washington Square Park annual outdoor art exhibit in 1932, the local Catholic church demanded that it be removed, viewing its monstrous image of the Madonna as sacrilege. Since circumstances and her own life choices had denied Neel the conventional role of middle-class mother and wife, Neel no doubt saw herself at this time as a "degenerate Madonna."

While Neel's portraits of mothers and children still resonate in contemporary culture, they can also be read as representative of shifting ideologies around mothering throughout twentieth-century American culture. In her book, *Motherhood and Representation*, feminist critic E. Ann Kaplan outlines how a major cultural shift relating to motherhood began after World War II (1992). Developing most rapidly during the 1960s political movements, and specifically the women's movement, this shift was marked by the mother "com(ing) into subjectivity" (26). While the father's subjectivity has been constant in culture, until recently, the representation of the mother was an "absent presence" (3). That is, while the representation of the mother was ubiquitous, it was usually seen through an androcentric perspective and/or the male gaze.

Neel's images of mothers and children both predate and exemplify this particular cultural shift in a number of ways. Starting in the 1940s, when her two sons were born, she begins to privilege the mother's roles and experiences more extensively from outside the male gaze. In fact, she only sometimes includes fathers in her portraits of families. Instead, she represents mutuality between mothers and children, as they embrace, nurse, and communicate with each other. Neel's exploration of maternal subjectivity is best exemplified in her pregnant nude series, done in the

1960s and 1970s, where the *mother-in-becoming* (with no children in sight) is the literal subject of the work. In a *New York Times* special issue magazine, *The Shadow Story of the Millennium: Women,* one of Neel's pregnant nudes was reproduced as an example of this cultural shift toward an understanding of mother as subject in her own right (Cotter 1999, 96).

By the early 1940s, Neel begins to develop a more sympathetic and intimate view of mothers and children in which she expresses a much more tender feeling of mother for child. This coincides with the birth of her sons, Richard in 1939 and Hartley in 1941. In the drawing *Mother and Son* (1942), a standing mother bends toward her standing son, her arms around his abdomen in a simple gesture of maternal caretaking. In *Hartley on the Rocking Horse* (1943) (fig 3.3) Neel makes her son's simple pleasure the subject of a painting; she pictures herself reflected in a small mirror in the background. Although minimal, the inclusion of her

3.3 *Hartley on the Rocking Horse,* 1943. Oil on canvas, 30×34 inches, 76.2×86.4 cm. © The Estate of Alice Neel / Courtesy David Zwirner, New York.

own image points to the emergence of a maternal subjectivity and is a rare self-portrait done well before her singular and now legendary self-portrait in which she is nude at the age of eighty. Significantly, she portrays herself as the engaged artist, paintbrush in hand, in much the same way she does in her much later *Self-Portrait* (1983). In *Hartley on the Rocking Horse,* she is both the artist and the mother, finally integrating both identities and captured in a simple moment of joy. And, in a dramatic departure from her earlier views of motherhood, in this work she is simply enjoying her child's pleasure.

In a more grief-stricken and clearly autobiographical portrait, *Alice and Richard* (1943) (fig 3.4), Neel depicts herself as hollow-eyed and shocked as she embraces the small head of her son, who is resting on her chest with his eyes shut. In this work, her maternal expression is no longer a featureless face as in the earlier Madonna-like images; instead, its expression is clear and bold. The unusually vivid colors—deep blues and purples—intensify this expression. The focus on the mother's and son's faces make their emotional anguish, and specifically a mother's horror at her child's pain, the obvious subject of the painting. Richard was suffering from an eye infection that resulted in near blindness, and this painting was done during a period when Neel had been caring for him alone (Neel Arts Inc. 1997–2001). Neel credited another of her unusually vivid works, *Still Life with Fruit* (1940), with having been inspired by her own hyper-awareness of color as a result of Richard's near loss of sight (quoted in Hills 1983, 70). The autobiographical nature of these tormented works makes them all the more poignant.

Neel single-handedly raised Richard and Hartley under conditions that weren't always ideal. Her sons had different fathers, neither of whom was consistently supportive, financially or emotionally. Despite much insecurity, Neel was a loving and caring mother who prepared regular meals, took them for walks in the park, and arranged for their private educations (Neel Arts Inc. 1997–2001). Much to her credit, they both graduated from Columbia University and went on to become respectable professionals; Richard became an attorney and Hartley became a medical doctor.

The traditional, nuclear-family arrangement was highly visible and idealized in mass culture during the post–World War II baby boom, from the late 1940s into the 1960s. Interestingly, art historian Pamela Allara points out the irony of the typical, middle-class family portrait of this period, in which the father/breadwinner was always "front and center" despite being "absent for the better part of each day" (1998, 139). However, this was not the norm for the Neel family or for many of their neighbors in Spanish Harlem. The Latino and African American mothers and children of their neighborhood, who were the subjects of many of Neel's portraits from the 1940s and 1950s, were often depicted as

3.4 *Alice and Richard,* 1943. Gouache on paper, 22½ × 15½ inches, 57.2 × 39.4 cm. © The Estate of Alice Neel / Courtesy David Zwirner, New York.

"families" without fathers, or if a father was included, he was usually only minimally mentioned in the work. Although rendered invisible within mass culture of the time, this "fatherless" family was more the norm for this particular segment of the American population (Ware 1997, 242–3).

Sometimes the father's absence was due to illness, a harsh reality in this poor community, especially during this period in history. For example, one of Neel's most famous portraits, *T.B. Harlem* (1940) is a sad depiction of one of Neel's friends, a young Puerto Rican man who was sick with tuberculosis. It is a companion piece to the less-well-known portrait, *The Spanish Family* (fig 3. 5, 1943), which pictures the wife and children of the sick man (Neel Arts Inc. 1997–2001). *T.B. Harlem*, one of Neel's most famous works, is owned by the National Museum of Women in the Arts and was included in the 2000–2001 retrospective. But *The Spanish*

3.5 *The Spanish Family*, 1943. Oil on canvas, 34 × 28 inches, 86.4 × 71.1 cm. © The Estate of Alice Neel / Courtesy David Zwirner, New York.

*Family* was not included, and is rarely reproduced, another example of the erasure of mothering experience from our cultural landscape.

In *The Spanish Family*, a young, strong-faced woman sits with her two small children on either side of her, and with a baby on her lap. The small family sits closely together against a backdrop of ornate grillwork. The central placement of the mother in the composition, the squared shape of her seated body, and the resolute look on her face give her a strength and solidity as the head of the family. The children are diminutive and vulnerable beside her, their rounded eyes and sorrowful expressions register pain and fear, one clutches her mother's skirt. But the mother's presence seems to hold their vulnerability in a kind of protective sheath that connects them together as a family.

Neel often painted mothers and children as a single, joined form in a style sometimes reminiscent of German expressionist Käthe Kollwitz's huddled mothers protecting their children. For example, in Neel's drawing *Mother and Children* (1942), a mother encircles her arms around two children who lean into her lap. A third child leans against her, his body contouring to hers. The children are represented as overlapping additions to the mother's body; the mother's embrace invites their connection. Neel described how children remained virtually connected to their mothers for the first two years of their lives (Neel Arts Inc. 1997–2001). This sense of the mother-child relationship is visually expressed through the pattern of a single, joined form. This is again apparent in a drawing of her own daughter-in-law and grandchildren, *Family* (1978), which will be discussed in detail later in this essay. Furthering the connection between mother and child, Neel also painted portraits of nursing mothers, like the drawing *Mother and Child* (1956) and the painting *Carmen and Judy* (1972). These literally picture the physiological connection between mother and child and the deep intimacy of breastfeeding. As she did with pregnancy, Neel records this ordinary feminine experience as a "fact of life" (quoted in Hills 1983, 162). Like the earthy images of nursing mothers done by nineteenth-century painter Paula Modersohn-Becker, these portraits are striking for their depiction of a human experience that is virtually invisible in Western art history.

As in *Alice and Richard, The Spanish Family*, and this drawing, *Mother and Children*, the mother appears to be consoling children who are sad or grieving. This too is a similar theme in Kollwitz's images of mothers and children, who were often depicted as the victims of poverty and war. Neel's twentieth-century images of mothers and children express a psychological victimization. However, unlike the emotional idealism that impressionists like Mary Cassatt brought to bear in the mother and child genre, Neel privileges a wider range of emotions within the mother-child relationship than is customarily revealed in traditionally posed family portraits.

For example, she captured the difficulties and struggles of becoming a new mother in a magnificent portrait of her daughter-in-law and first grandchild, *Nancy and Olivia* (1967) (fig 3.6). This work vividly captured Nancy's first bewildered experience with mothering. As Neel described this portrait: "Olivia was three months old and Nancy looks afraid because this was her first child. Olivia was very active" (quoted in Hills 1983, 123). Young and wide-eyed, Nancy's face speaks of the fear, fatigue, and perplexity that come with the often-shocking transformation into "mother." Neel accentuates this sense with an unsteady, teetering composition in which Nancy is awkwardly seated and the background is skewed. Nonetheless,

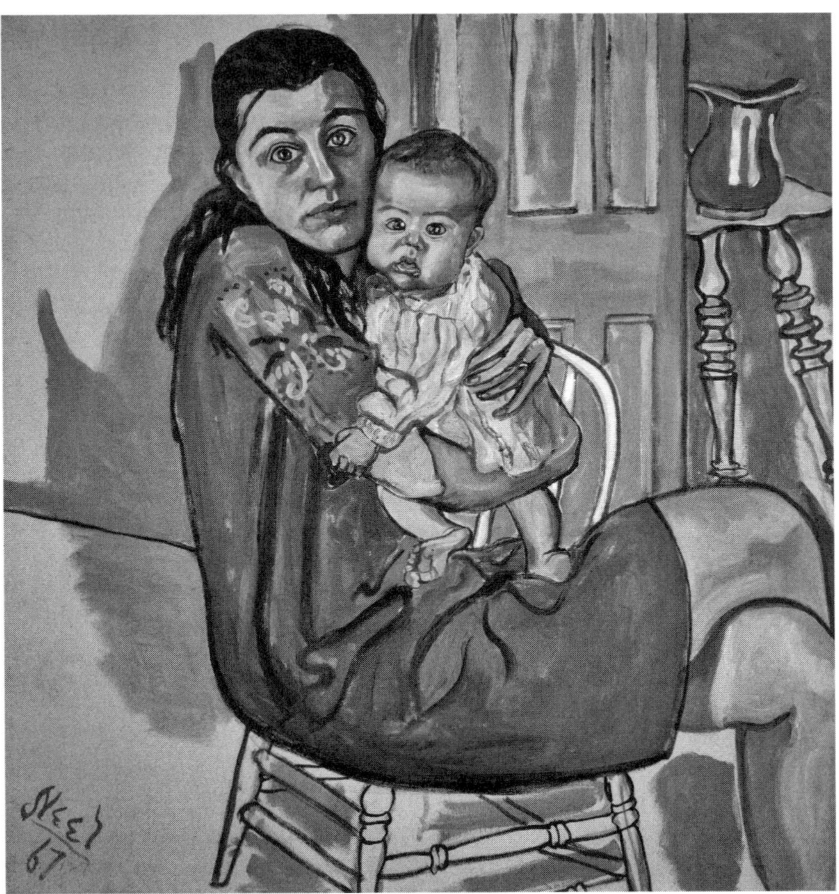


3.6 *Mother and Child* (*Nancy and Olivia*), 1967. Oil on canvas, 39¼×36 inches, 99.7×91.4 cm. © The Estate of Alice Neel/Courtesy David Zwirner, New York.

Nancy holds her squirming baby, whose movements are captured with an upturned foot and darting glance, tightly and securely. Their face-to-face embrace is the focal point of the composition, emblematic of the demand placed on them by their forced mutual interdependence.

The subject of this work—the difficulties and struggles of becoming a new mother—is a highly unusual theme within the mother and child genre, which more typically presents an idealized, trouble-free relationship between mother and child. Neel's treatment of the subject is extraordinary because without devaluing the primacy of the mother-child bond, she still includes the real struggles that make that bond possible. Such representations recognize the fact that such caretaking is not so much innate as it is learned through the process of parenting.

Another revealing portrait of mother work is the drawing, *The Family* (1978) (fig 3.7), which takes as its subject the birth of a new baby in a family—another topic that is generally absent in the mother and child genre. *Family* depicts Neel's daughter-in-law, Ginny (wife of Hartley), and their first child, Elizabeth, just after the birth of their second child, Andrew. Neel had a studio at Hartley and Ginny's home in Vermont where she would visit and paint the New England countryside and her son's growing family. As she did with the many family portraits of Nancy Neel (wife of Richard) and their children, Alice Neel was particularly adept at capturing the most intimate and often subtle aspects of child rearing and family life through her observations and experiences with her sons and their families.

The often complex and emotionally charged reaction of the first child to the arrival of a second, and the concern and awkward emotional and physical juggling of the newly created mother of two is wonderfully rendered in this simple drawing. With barely a line serving as a seat, the drawing consists solely of the three figures, mother and children, seated so closely together that they seem to constitute a single entity. Ginny has the new baby on her lap, but her head—a darkly outlined and shaded oval that serves as the drawing's focal point—leans toward Elizabeth who is seated beside her.

In this work, Neel's trademark skewed perspective is more exaggerated than usual and there is a dynamic interaction between the nearly overlapping figures, an appropriate aesthetic treatment for such a tumultuous time in a young family's life. Ginny's leaning toward Elizabeth, while still clutching the new baby, appears to almost steady this skewed perspective. At the same time, however, Elizabeth's facial expression is fixed, her right leg and arm are stiffened and her fist is clenched so that she seems to be almost pushing her mother and brother downward and out of the tilted composition altogether. Ginny explained that at the point that this drawing was done, "Elizabeth [was] just getting used to another 'being' in the family and [was] clearly still needing reassurance

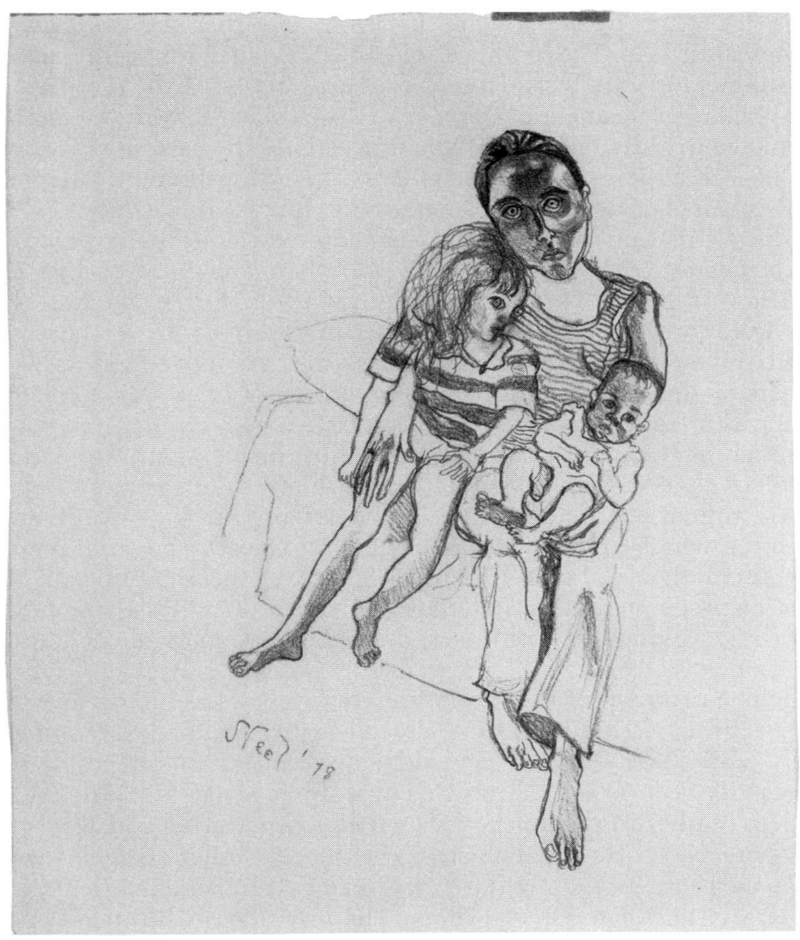


3.7 *The Family,* 1978. Pencil on paper, 16 × 12 inches, 40.6 × 30.5 cm.


that she [was] not losing me" (Neel Arts Inc. 1997–2001). Baby Andrew teeters on the far end of Ginny's lap. This work has been in private ownership and has never before been reproduced, another example of how the common details of mother work too often remain unrecognizable and invisible in contemporary art.

In another intimate portrait that reveals yet another view of mother work, Neel painted her Haitian housekeeper with her disabled baby in *Carmen and Judy* (1972). This work pictures the mother with one breast exposed and the nude child's mouth open, as if about to nurse. With the baby's disconcerting blank stare, it is not clear that she can even suck without some help. The mother's face, lined but smiling, seems somehow accepting of her child's sad fate. Neel's exaggeration of the mother's oversized hands was meant as a reference to the hard work she had done all her life (quoted in Hills 1983, 161), including perhaps the hard work of mothering this sick child, who was one of five. This sympathetic treatment of a poor woman of color's struggles with mothering is vintage Neel.

During this same period, Neel also painted traditionally posed, full-length portraits of white professional mothers and children like *Linda Nochlin and Daisy* (1973) and *Ann Sutherland Harris and Neil* (1978). Both were (are) respected feminist art historians who at the time of the sitting were key figures in the feminist art movement as well as mothers of small children. This combination of roles was increasingly the norm for educated white middle-class women, owing in part to the changes brought about by the women's movement. Again capturing the feminist *zeitgeist*, Neel first includes children in her portraits of well-known women during this time. The emerging ideology of the mother as subject, which Kaplan identifies being strongest in cultural representations of motherhood from 1978 to 1988, is perfectly exemplified in Neel's series of pregnant nudes and these portraits of professional mothers with their children. In both cases, mothers are seen as subjects in their own right.

The construction of the mothering experience has changed dramatically over the twentieth century, which roughly spanned Neel's lifetime. Rarely have these shifting definitions and understandings of maternal subjectivity been so well chronicled by a single artist. Not only did Neel privilege mother work, but she did so with a penetrating and deeply compassionate vision that brought to light the real inner struggles women face as they care for their children within a cultural and political context that largely does not support them. The fact that such images and the radical critique they make were omitted and/or diluted in the Neel retrospective suggests that Neel's vision of maternal subjectivity has still not been fully realized by the larger culture. Neel, it seems, even on her one-hundredth birthday, is still ahead of her time.

## References

Allara, Pamela. 1998. *Pictures of People: Alice Neel's American Portrait Gallery.* Hanover, N.H.: University Press of New England.

Cotter, Holland. 1999. "Through Women's Eyes, Finally." In *The Shadow Story of the Millennium: Women. New York Times Magazine Special Issue,* 16 May:92–6.

Harris, Ann Sutherland. 1978. "Alice Neel Drawings and Watercolors 1926–1978." *Alice Neel: A Retrospective Exhibition of Watercolors and Drawings.* New York: The Graham Gallery, 1978.
Hills, Patricia. 1983. *Alice Neel.* New York: Harry N. Abrams.
Kaplan, E. Ann. 1992. *Motherhood and Representation: The Mother in Popular Culture and Melodrama.* New York: Routledge.
Neel, Alice. 1971. "By Alice Neel." *Daily World,* 17 April:M-7.
Neel Arts Inc. 1997–2001. Series of interviews, phone calls, and e-mail discussions with Nancy Neel, Ginny Neel, Hartley Neel, and Richard Neel.
Temkin, Ann, ed. 2000. *Alice Neel.* Philadelphia: Philadelphia Museum of Art.
Ware, Susan. 1997. *Modern American Women: A Documentary History.* New York: McGraw-Hill.

CHAPTER FOUR

# Practical Perfection? The Nanny Negotiates Gender, Class, and Family Contradictions in 1960s Popular Culture

ANNE McLEER

In the mid-1960s, two family films starring British actress Julie Andrews garnered much popular and critical acclaim in the United States. Although *Mary Poppins* (Stevenson 1964) and *The Sound of Music* (Wise 1965) are both set in overseas locales, and feature many well-known English actors, they can nevertheless be seen as belonging to the canon of American popular culture. Both films were produced by American companies—Walt Disney in the case of *Mary Poppins* and Twentieth Century Fox in the case of *The Sound of Music*—and were popular among audiences in the United States. *Mary Poppins* was nominated for best picture in the 1965 Academy Awards, and Julie Andrews won the Oscar for Best Actress for her performance in the film. The following year, *The Sound of Music* won Oscars in the categories of best picture and best director for Robert Wise, among other awards. Julie Andrews was nominated but did not win.

In this essay, I argue that despite (or indeed because of) their foreign settings and non-American stars, these films speak to the "Hollywood imaginary," addressing in their oblique, allegorical manner concerns and anxieties that surrounded the notion of the family and changing gender roles in the United States of the 1960s. Such concerns were probably pertinent throughout middle-class families across Western Europe, and these films, no doubt, also had much social resonance in Britain and Canada.

Much like science fiction or speculative texts, films set in a different era or geographical location to their time and place of production often have as much, if not more, to say about that place and time than about their imaginary historical locales. Bruce McConachie contends that the popular, 1950s, *Oriental* musicals of Rodgers and Hammerstein resonated with Cold War ideology and American foreign policy in Vietnam in the 1960s. He suggests that *The King and I*, for example, although set in Siam in the 1860s, nevertheless used metaphors, images, and narrative structures that were prevalent in American postwar culture and thus "prepared its spectators to accept U.S. intervention into Southeast Asia as responsible, benevolent, and necessary" (McConachie 1994, 396).[1]

I will argue that in *Mary Poppins* and *The Sound of Music*, foreign historical situations that would have been meaningful to a 1960s American

Originally published in the Summer 2002 issue of the *NWSA Journal*.

audience—the loosening of Victorian family relations in pre–World War I Britain and the Austrian position vis-á-vis Nazism just before World War II—are used as allegories for the United States.[2] In both films, the historical setting can be read as a metaphoric response to contemporary social upheavals. I read these responses at the level of the "political unconscious," assuming the ability of texts to imaginatively address, resolve, or complicate social contradictions and tensions that are irreconcilable in the social realm from which texts emerge (Jameson 1981). By making this assertion I am implying that all films, whatever their historical setting, always speak to the moment of their production in some way. This idea (that films always speak to the moment of production) coincides with Fredric Jameson's notion that all cultural products are ultimately political (20).

In the United States of the mid-1960s, a counter ideology was beginning to emerge that challenged women's so-called traditional domestic role in society. This ideology was bolstered by the increasing employment of wives and mothers in the marketplace. The challenge appeared from a number of different quarters; African American women in the Civil Rights Movement; young female students discontent with their treatment in the youth/student movement; middle-class, professional white women addressing employment discrimination; and housewives responding to Betty Friedan's exposure of the "problem that had no name" (1963, 15).

Political initiatives, such as the establishment in 1961 of the President's Commission on the Status of Women and the addition of the category *sex* to the prohibitions against discrimination in employment in the 1964 Civil Rights Act, also helped to circulate questions surrounding the problematic situation of women in American society (Freeman 1983, 19). Sara Evans points out that the commission and its report, published in 1968 under the title *American Women,* were important "less in the specific changes they generated directly than in the renewed interest in 'women's place in society' which they reflected" (1980, 17).

In this essay, I suggest that these films—despite their displacement to foreign, historical settings—address social contradictions brought about by concerns surrounding "women's place in society" in the United States. Women's activism and the emergence of 1960s feminism can be seen as a response to the previous twenty-five years of domestic containment ideology and its contradictions. The films *Mary Poppins* and *The Sound of Music* can be understood as an oppositional response to this feminism. Both films establish family or private stability, defined by the secure positioning of the patriarch, as the basis of national and public stability. In the case of *Mary Poppins,* family stability is analogous to the foundation of security as well as modernization in the capitalist marketplace, whereas in *The Sound of Music* it represents the foundation of nationalist struggle against military and ideological aggression. Through the use of recognizable situations in unfamiliar settings, these films could evoke contested issues of their time by cloaking them in allegory, while at the same time making the films seem to be about something else. According to George Banks, the faltering patriarch of Mary Poppins's adoptive family, 1910 England was "the age of men." These films attempt to redress the fact that the "age of men" was swiftly coming to a close for many Americans.

## Nostalgia for 1950s Domestic Containment

In order to understand the conflicts and upheavals surrounding the family, and men's and women's roles in the domestic and public spheres in the 1960s, the prescriptions of the 1950s nuclear family ideal must be understood. In middle-class America of the 1950s, a new postwar conception of the nuclear family was established and a popularized narrative of the domestic ideal was widely circulated in cultural texts. The "qualitatively new phenomenon" of the domestic ideal was the suburban nuclear-family unit (Coontz 1992, 25). Isolated from the extended family, this ideal domestic configuration was composed of a breadwinning father and an appliance-dependent, housekeeping mother of four.[3]

This new domestic ideal was bolstered by the ideology of educators, sociologists, psychologists, and other popularized *experts*. For example, sociologists such as Talcott Parsons and psychologists such as David Goodman insisted that correct sex-role identification in children came only through mimetic relations with the appropriately feminine, submissive, and continually present mother and the appropriately masculine, breadwinning, often absent, and dominant father. The 1950s domestic ideal built up the *traditional* family as a mainstay of patriotism. If the correct parental power structure was observed, the family should produce girls and boys whose correct displays of femininity and masculinity indicated their status as ideal American children. In the ideology of domestic containment, "A 'normal' family and vigilant mother became the 'front line' of defense against treason" (Coontz 1992, 33). The notion that the family was the basic unit of a secure society and strong nation was more than propaganda or political rhetoric. Many Americans believed in such a notion as a social truth. The public, politicians, the media, and experts extolled the virtues of nuclear-family life and believed that "suburbia would serve as a bulwark against communism and class conflict, for according to the widely shared belief articulated by Nixon, it offered a piece of the American dream for everyone" (May 1988, 19–20).

Scholarship and experience has indeed shown that contradictions between the ideal and the reality of 1950s suburban life abounded (Coontz

1992; Meyerowitz 1994). Spurred by financial necessity, more married women than ever joined the workforce into low-paying, "female" occupations. Commentators have shown that, ironically, in order to achieve the middle-class suburban ideal represented by the nuclear family, many families depended on the income earned by wives as well as husbands (Evans 1980; May 1988; Coontz 1992). The idea that women found true personal fulfillment in the home was bolstered by mass media. To show that women did not seek or find a sense of achievement in the public sphere, mass media used the fact that women were segregated into low-paying, noncareer jobs as evidence. Even if women were no longer confined to the home, their home and family were still of chief concern (Spigel 1992). In cultural, as well as political realms, the contradictions surrounding womanhood in the 1950s may have been concealed under the ideology of domestic containment, but they were not reconciled (Spigel 1992; Evans 1980).

Race, youth, and gender revolt, fomenting under the surface of the American dream in the 1950s exploded in the 1960s. Many commentators responded to burgeoning youth rebellion and juvenile delinquency by calling for more male domination in the home. The problems of racial inequity and the socially underprivileged position of African Americans were blamed on the high numbers of female-headed households in the black community (Griswold 1993). The American dream-that-never-was of the 1950s came to signify a lost ideal for many conservatives in the 1960s. A coded desire for this *lost* family structure and a certain ideological understanding of the relationship of the domestic and the public are evident in the popular texts of the 1960s. Joel Foreman writes that a text is "a field within which the competing forces of tradition and cultural innovation may be exposed" (1997, 4). In *Mary Poppins* and *The Sound of Music*, the forces of tradition act by restructuring the family to the 1950s traditional domestic ideal at a point in American history when great social and ideological upheavals were brewing. Both films, however, modernize this ideal by reconceptualizing the relationship of the patriarch to the domestic household, in response to mid-1960s cultural anxieties over American masculinity and the role of fathers.

Ironically, conservative anxieties over the structure and role of the nuclear family in 1960s America, a family ideal predicated on the lack of outside interference, are resolved in *Mary Poppins* and *The Sound of Music* by the intervention of the nanny, a domestic *threshold figure* (McClintock 1995, 94–5). As a cultural figure, the nanny not only intervenes in nuclear-family isolation, but she represents the breakdown of the distinction between public and private spheres by existing simultaneously in both spheres, being at the same time family and not-family. Both these films posit a nuclear-family structure under the control of a caring patriarch as a crucial element in national security and stability. Both films suggest that the father's removed and disciplinary relationship with his children is at the root of nuclear-family dysfunction, and metonymically, at the root of social and public problems. The role of the nanny is to restore family order by modernizing the father-child relationship according to the rubrics of the childcare experts of the time, thus restoring him to his position as head of household. Although positioning the father at the head of the household is as old a notion as patriarchy itself, the emphasis in these films on nondisciplinary, friendly, father-child relations is something new.

Although Betty Friedan was urging women in 1963 to break out of the "feminine mystique" and seize part of the public sphere for themselves, these films made a coded appeal to women to return to the private sphere and reorganize their families' lives there (1963). A few years before feminism burst into mainstream public awareness by gaining media attention, however negatively, these films attempted to piece together previously held ideals about the family and gender roles.[4] These ideals, having proven unsatisfactory in practice, were beginning to be seriously undermined. Although contemporaneous with straightforward representations of ideal nuclear families, such as television shows like *The Donna Reed Show* (1958–1966) and *The Adventures of Ozzie and Harriet* (1952–1966), these films carried out a more covert or symbolic reinforcement of conservative ideology through the figure of the nanny. Representations of nonnuclear, indeed non-American, families in these films (with the presence of the nanny as family interloper) nevertheless work to bolster the ideal American family structure of breadwinning father, stay-at-home mother, and children.

## The Contradictions of 1960s Motherhood

In *Mary Poppins,* the "practically perfect" eponymous nanny arrives at the chaotic Banks household as Jane and Michael Banks's fifth nanny of the year is packing her bags to leave. Mary Poppins's childcare abilities are contrasted not only with her short-lived predecessors, but with the mother of the children, first wave feminist Winifred Banks, who spends most of the film out of the home engaged in suffragist activism. In *The Sound of Music,* a young novice nun, Maria, comes to the estate of Captain von Trapp to take up a temporary position as governess to his seven children. She had been forced to leave the convent because of her disruptive high spirits. Maria eventually wins the affection of the children and the love of their father, ousting his fiancée, the wealthy aristocratic Baroness Schraeder, to become his wife. In both of these films, the nanny functions to represent one side of a dyadic split in a contemporary notion of womanhood, her counterpart being, in the first case, absent mother Winifred Banks, and in the second, the husband-hunting but nonmaternal Baroness Schraeder.

This split emerges from the presence of certain irresolvable contradictions in the prescriptive concept of femininity in 1960s America. According to Lauri Umansky, "Although the role of the mother had been riddled with post-Freudian angst, so that it was nearly impossible to be considered a *good* mother, the dictate to 'go forth and mother' remained in place" (1996, 20). The film, *Mary Poppins,* sets about trying to reconcile the social contradiction that makes it "nearly impossible to be considered a *good* mother" (or to represent one), while at the same time promoting motherhood to women. The text contrasts the errant mother, who cares more for feminism than for her mother role, and "practically perfect" Mary Poppins who brings the ideal balance of nurturance and discipline into the children's lives. Mothers in the 1950s were becoming defined by their inability to carry out their mother role and by the dangers that such ineptitude posed to future generations of American children. The role of mother was so intersected by the advice and censure of experts that no mother came up to the mark. In the 1940s, books such as Philip Wylie's *Generation of Vipers* (1942) and David Levy's *Maternal Overprotection* (1943) produced widespread beliefs that American mothers had rendered their sons effeminate through overprotective mothering, a sentiment that became known as *momism,* and which persisted as a widespread notion into the 1960s. Umansky also cites books such as Joseph C. Rheingold's *The Fear of Being a Woman: A Theory of Maternal Destructiveness* and Dan Greenburg's *Be a Jewish Mother: A Very Lovely Training Manual* as examples of the many "markedly misogynist," "mainstream mother-blaming tracts" circulating in the 1960s (1996, 18). Marynia Farnham, an influential psychiatrist, and Ferdinand Lundberg, a sociologist, wrote *Modern Woman: The Lost Sex* (1947), a general disparagement of all women, which castigated American mothers for many of the perceived ills of society. Women's magazines of the 1950s and 1960s emphasized the importance of mothers' dependence on experts in articles and advice columns. Although the appearance of experts in the discourse of motherhood greatly reinforced the mother role as imperative for women, paradoxically this rhetoric of experts inscribed all mothers as inadequate.[5]

The contradiction created by the impulse of male experts and educators, as well as men and women psychologists and journalists, to characterize motherhood by its own failure and yet encourage motherhood as proper and fulfilled womanhood, is resolved in the fictitious world of the nanny in *Mary Poppins.*[6] The film shows the dangers of absent mothers unconcerned with their mother role exclusively, while showcasing ideal motherhood through the nanny as stand-in, ersatz mother. Mary Poppins follows the prescription of 1960s child-rearing experts, such as Benjamin Spock, in encouraging self-expression and imaginative play in her charges. She gets them to take medicine through song and games rather than by exerting her authority. She sits by the fire in the nursery and lulls them to sleep by singing. She fills their days with enjoyable activities, yet is the first nanny to have been able to make them behave. Although *Mary Poppins* shows American audiences how to bring harmony to the family through correct mothering, the message to American mothers is not that they should go out and hire a nanny. Rather they are being told that a woman's chief and most satisfying role in life is in the home, and that their dissatisfactions therein can be solved by rearranging family configurations. Both films restore the authority of the patriarch and his control over domestic affairs, but they also reestablish a mother figure in the home. At the end of *Mary Poppins*, Winifred Banks is seen alongside her husband and children flying kites in the park near their home. In *The Sound of Music*, Maria becomes the children's new mother by marrying their father.

Significantly, Mary Poppins proves to be a civilizing influence not only on the two children of the Banks household, but on the household as a whole, much in the same manner that the white, middle-class, American suburban mother of the postwar era was supposed to be on the nation as a whole. In *Mary Poppins*, the ideology of the call to motherhood for American women is upheld without violating the cultural edict to represent motherhood by its own failure. The text can show ideal mothering and castigate women as "bad" mothers at the same time.

In *Mary Poppins*, the nanny displays ideal mothering while the children's real mother engages in political activism and disregards much of her domestic role.[7] In *The Sound of Music* the children's real mother is dead, and two contrasting figures of womanhood are presented in Maria and Captain von Trapp's fiancée, the Baroness Schraeder. In this film, as in *Mary Poppins*, ideal mothering behavior is showcased through the figure of the nanny, Maria. In Maria's case, she is not compared with a "real" mother, but competes with the wealthy Baroness Schraeder to attain motherhood status as Captain von Trapp's future wife. The character of Maria differs from Mary Poppins in that she becomes the romantic interest in *The Sound of Music*, ultimately completing the family unit by marrying Captain von Trapp, while Mary Poppins is excluded from the family unity she brought about at the end of *Mary Poppins*.

In the terms of popular, postwar-era Freudianism, Maria can be seen as representing the *libidinal mother*. The libidinal mother was a popularized construct of postwar psychologists who supposedly would be "the ideal mother to go with the permissively raised child—one who would find passionate fulfillment in the details of child care" (Ehrenreich and English 1978, 221). The libidinal mother acted on her instincts and fulfilled all her desires by giving her child unconditional, spontaneous love. This mother-child bond was based on maternal regression to a childlike state (223). Maria's character in *The Sound of Music* exemplifies the infantilization of mothers. She runs, sings, dances, climbs trees, cycles, and falls into a lake, in company with the children in her care.

Maria wins the contest to attain position of wife to her employer and mother to his children by displaying the correct signifiers of the woman/wife/mother conflation of conservative 1960s America. She is attractive but not glamorous, nurturing but not afraid to get her hands dirty, fun but not frivolous, and resourceful but not independent. The baroness, in contrast, despises the children, is overly sexualized, and has her own source of income. The baroness's financial self-sufficiency is an implicit threat to the notion of male breadwinning, one of the elements of the masculine gender role in jeopardy at the time (Ehrenreich 1983). Maria's purity is also an important measure of distinction between her and the widowed baroness. When she marries the captain, Maria becomes the virgin-mother of the Trapp children, reflecting the impossible Christian ideal of womanhood encapsulated by her namesake the Virgin Mary.[8] The association of sexually mature womanhood with religion is forged in the film in the wedding scene where Maria walks down the aisle of a magnificent church in an extravagant white dress and veil accompanied by the singing of the convent nuns' choir.

In both *Mary Poppins* and *The Sound of Music,* notions of motherhood can be seen to intersect with ideas of feminine dependence (male power), class relations, and sexuality. These highly popular texts set out to articulate motherhood with purity, simplicity, subordination, naiveté, and domesticity in womanhood. This articulation may have been an attempt, albeit at the level of the "political unconscious," to restore an ideal of femininity for the American women in the audience, although such connections (and implied disconnections) may not have been a possibility for all women.

## Masculinity in Crisis and the Reconfiguration of Domestic Patriarchy

In *Mary Poppins* and *The Sound of Music,* before the arrival of the nanny, the father has a disciplinarian, behaviorist technique for dealing with his children and household, which in both stories is shown to be a failure. In both films, the children misbehave and feel distanced from their father until the nanny remedies the situation. These changes resonate with changing understandings of child rearing and family structure that had been emerging in postwar America. Childcare experts and psychologists rejected the previous generation's strict disciplinarian methods of child rearing, as advocated by behaviorists such as John Watson (1928), for the more *laissez-faire* methods of "Dr. Spock" (1954). This change is seen to be consistent with a general cultural trend away from the self-denial of the prewar period and toward the self-fulfillment that was an important element of the emerging new postwar consumerist economy. Inculcating indulgence and self-regulation, as did the permissive school of child rearing, resonated with ideas of individuality and gratification that were the necessary ethics for a consumer-based economy (Margolis 1984, 63). The fathers' belief in strict discipline at the outset of both films is shown to be out of kilter with up-to-date notions of individual self-expression, which are more readily embodied by Mary Poppins and Maria.

By the 1960s, however, doubts had arisen in some quarters about the prudence of the permissive school of child rearing. The demoralization of American troops in Korea, the low standards of literacy among American as compared to Soviet children, and escalating youth unrest began to be seen as the result of a lack of parental discipline in the postwar, postbehaviorist era (Ehrenreich and English 1978; May 1988). Even Dr. Spock himself began to advise against overpermissiveness in his book, *Problems of Parents* (1962). Maternal authority, or lack thereof, in the home was also held to blame for juvenile delinquency. At the same time, dominating, authoritarian fathers were considered to produce profascist sons (Griswold 1993). The films *Mary Poppins* and *The Sound of Music* negotiate the terrain between permissiveness, advocated by childcare experts and concurrent with a consumer society, and conservative fears of declining male-dominance in the home, by demonstrating a reconfiguration of the father's role in domestic patriarchy. The father's authority is restored while his authoritarian tendencies are removed.

As *Mary Poppins* opens, George Banks is deluded that he has everything under control in both his personal and professional life, despite the fact that both are on treacherous ground. He believes that he is "Lord of my castle, the sovereign, the liege." However his position as traditional patriarch in the home is being eroded by his wife's (and servants') feminism and his children's rejection of his beliefs in "tradition, discipline, and rules." The Banks household is in turmoil when Mary Poppins magically arrives (she floats down aided by her umbrella from the clouds over London). The children are out of control, persistently running away from their frequently resigning nannies. They have an alienated relationship with their father, whom they want as a caring playmate while he insists on playing the role of the distant disciplinarian. Their mother, Winifred Banks, is absent from the household most of the time due to her suffragist activism. The other servants are discontented and always fighting with each other (though not discontented with their employment situation, it seems, as they return to passivity when the family order is restored). The winds of change blow in with Mary Poppins and she makes the necessary modernizing alterations to Mr. Banks and his household that allow a new patriarchal order to begin. At the end of the film, George Banks is reinstalled in a modernized position as patriarch, an improved relationship with his children, and a reharmonized home and family.

A similar situation exists in the Trapp household when Maria is first employed as a nanny in *The Sound of Music*. She is the twelfth governess the seven Trapp children have had since their mother died, her employer informs her, the previous one lasting only two hours. When the children come downstairs to first meet Maria, their father, a former navy captain, summons them with his navy whistle. He orders them to stand in line military style and to step forward to announce their names when he blows their individual whistle signal. Maria is horrified, refuses to be assigned a whistle signal of her own, and rebukes the captain for treating people like dogs. The captain spends little time with his children, allows them no leisure or playtime, and forbids music or singing in the house. Before Maria's arrival, the children were constantly getting into mischief in order to gain their father's attention. Nevertheless, the captain is convinced that he runs an effective home and initially balks against Maria's suggestions that his child-rearing strategies need to be altered. The first two-thirds of the film traces how Maria succeeds in making Captain von Trapp rethink his military style of parenting, bringing father and children back into intimacy. The father can now assume a new kind of control, patriarchy is saved, and Maria completes the family circle by becoming Mrs. von Trapp.

Both films respond, through the use of historical metaphor, to fears that arose in the 1960s surrounding the position of men in the domestic sphere. Such fears developed out of the so-called crisis of masculinity "discovered" by postwar sociologists and psychologists (Ehrenreich and English 1978; Ehrenreich 1983). Experts feared that a national "flight from manhood" (Buhle 1998, 125) was underway, evinced not only by the many men who could not psychologically cope with the trauma of combat in World War II (also a concern during American interventions in Korea and Vietnam) but also by rising levels of male homosexuality and what was considered a lack of assertiveness and confidence in black men (Ehrenreich 1983; Griswold 1993). In the ideology of momism, mothers' influence on sons in the home was held to blame (Buhle 1998; Ehrenreich and English 1978; Griswold 1993).

By the 1960s, it was a widely circulated notion that a man's position as provider in the home was being eroded by women's employment and consumer power (Ehrenreich1983). To redress the "flight from manhood" in boys by removing them from the influence of overprotective mothers, and to reestablish a role for men in the home beyond that of provider, a new role for men in the domestic realm was suggested. The ideas of sex-role psychologists such as Talcott Parsons (1955), who claimed that the development of feminine and masculine traits in girls and boys comes directly from observing and interacting with their parents, were furthered and popularized in the late 1950s/early 1960s by authorities in child rearing (Ehrenreich 1978). In his 1954 edition of *Baby and Child Care,* Spock writes that "a boy needs a friendly, accepting father" who will enable his son to pattern his maleness after his father and other men through fun activities and approval (242–3). The friendly father can also give his daughter confidence in her femininity by "approving of her dress, or hair-do, or the cookies she's made" (243).

The popularization of changing notions of fatherhood is evident across popular culture. In accordance with changing theories of child psychology, 1960s popular culture began to represent the father role as expanding beyond that of breadwinner and husband. Popular culture representations showed fathers interacting with their children and offering them emotional as well as economic security. From the early 1960s, advertising in women's magazines began to show images of this newly involved father. They showed fathers cooing over babies and spending time with older children. The success as a novel, film, then television series of *The Courtship of Eddie's Father* (also published in digest form in *Good Housekeeping* of August 1961) indicated that the relationship of fathers to their children (particularly boys) was now a major social concern (Toby 1961).

Magazine articles also promoted the notion of fatherhood as healthy for men, the family, and society as a whole (Keller 1994). Although the father was not to displace the mother, fathers were now represented as nurturing and carrying out the emotional work of parenthood. Indeed, their presence was considered a form of damage control against the influence of mothers (Ehrenreich and English 1978). This new representation of fatherhood was not necessarily a call for gender equality, but rather "allowed a man a purpose in the home without his losing authority in it" (Keller 1994, 154). The emphasis in *Mary Poppins* and *The Sound of Music* on the father's relationship with his children, a relationship which must be transformed from removed disciplinarian to friendly interactive Dad, coincides with the increasing emphasis on the father-child relationship. Fathers' encroachment into the previously female domain of domestic parenting also set limits on women's power and decision making in the home. By assuming the role of concerned and loving father, men could reestablish masculinity in the home as a return to, rather than a flight from, manhood. Representations such as these work to ensure the father's enduring authority in the home in an era when definitions of male and female roles were changing.

## National Unity and the Erasure of Class Difference

Class difference, therefore class conflict in Marxist terms, is elided and erased in both these films, ironically through the nanny, a figure that represents bourgeois appropriation of the domestic labor of women. In both films, class conflict/difference is subsumed under family and, by extension, national stability. In *Mary Poppins,* the nanny figure is used to represent the erasure of class conflict as a prerequisite to family unity, which is in turn posited as the necessary basis for successful capitalism. In *The Sound of Music,* a similar family unity, with modernized and restored patriarch, is considered to be the vital mainstay of national unity, and erasure of class difference is represented as class assimilation through bourgeois idealization of the peasantry.

Mary Poppins can be seen as a figure who traverses the space between the British working class, represented in its various stereotypes by her friend the street painter, chimney sweep, one-man-band Bert, and the British bourgeoisie, represented by the Banks household. George Banks is a banker, his name signifying the correlation of capitalism and the family in the text. Mary Poppins, who has clearly had dealings with the working class before her arrival in the Banks household, comes (literally) from out of the sky, a nonclassed, ahistorical space. Yet she performs all the behavioral requirements of the bourgeoisie, and is capable of inculcating the appropriate signifiers of British *middle-classness* in the Banks children. She is thoroughly "respectable," or class-appropriate, despite the implication that she has been romantically involved with Bert the chimney sweep. As a threshold figure, a familiar position of the nanny, she frequently crosses from the working class to the bourgeoisie, seeming to belong in both. However, this is not to be read as a signifier of the possibility of class mobility, but rather as an indication of the lack of conflict between the classes posited by this text. Mary Poppins's daily movements in and out of the Banks household with the children, Jane and Michael, are movements from the bourgeoisie in and out of the working class. She and the children spend their days with Bert, other chimney sweeps, and members of the working class without class conflict ever arising. American audiences of the 1960s may have understood class to be a principal organizing factor in British society (particularly in pre–World War I eras), unlike popular conceptions of contemporary America. Nevertheless, the metaphoric patterns in the film, the way the film endorses lack of conflict between differently situated social groups, may be read as a caution against the incitement of the social divisions and strife that were beginning to rend the conservative fabric of 1960s America.

In *Mary Poppins*, the capitalist order, represented by the bank where George Banks works, is modernized alongside the family. This modernization of capitalism in the film is structurally connected to father-child relations. One of the first attempts that Mary Poppins makes to reconcile father and children is when she suggests (while making him believe that it was his idea) that George Banks take the children with him on an outing to the bank where he works. On the evening before they are to go with their father, Mary Poppins lulls the children asleep with a song and story about the "bird lady" of St. Paul's Cathedral, who sits on the steps of the church selling breadcrumbs at "tuppence a bag" with which to feed the birds. The following day, on their way to the bank with their father, the children see the bird lady, and Michael wants to buy a bag of breadcrumbs. His father, of course, refuses, and when they get to the bank, he insists that Michael use the tuppence to open an account. Michael refuses and causes a scene when the partners of the bank, led by the bank's elderly director Mr. Daws, try to take the tuppence from him.

Chaos ensues when bank customers start to panic about their money and cause a "run on the bank," and in the melee the children run away and get lost. After spending some frightening hours lost on the dingy streets of London, the children are found accidentally by Bert the sweep, who returns them to their home. The disorder caused by Michael's challenge to capitalism and the banking system is temporary, but it ultimately causes the demise of the old order of capitalism by being the catalyst for the change in his father. Later that evening, George Banks is summoned to the bank and humiliated, then dismissed by the partners and director. In this scene, Banks finally makes the transition from the patriarchal decorous banker to fun-loving informal Dad. He begins to dance around in front of his former employers, laughing at a joke told earlier to him by the children, and at the meaningless but transformative expression taught to him by Mary Poppins—"supercalifragilisticexpialidocious." Banks leaves the meeting and returns to his home, where the next morning he assumes his new role as interactive, caring Dad by fixing the children's broken kite, and bringing them and his wife to the park to fly it. In the park, they meet the bank partners, also flying kites. One of the partners, the younger Mr. Daws, son of the director, informs Banks that his father died laughing at Banks's joke, and that they would like him to fill the opened position as partner.

Ultimately, because of the chaos the children caused, the outmoded form of capitalism passes away, symbolized by the death of the elderly Mr. Daws. It is replaced by a new order, indicated by the transformation of the other partners from crumbling, humorless bureaucrats to joyful kite flyers. This new order is characterized by pleasure seeking, informality, and togetherness. These elements are posited as essential to the functioning of successful and happy families. The bank now constitutes a family, in the modernized sense, with pleasure and informality taking the place of rigid hierarchical roles, and the demise of the disciplinarian patriarch indicating the rise of family-based interactive masculinity (all the partners are men).

In *Mary Poppins*, family relations dislodge class relations as the organizing system of society. Nuclear-family stability and functionality is seen to be the structural basis for successful capitalism. The relationship of the bourgeois home to the bank, or the private sphere to the public sphere, is seen as structural and formative. The position of the patriarch in the home, in the case of George Banks, must be secured in order for capitalism to also successfully adapt itself to change. George Banks has to accept the consumerist ethos of pleasure and indulgence personally, and in his relationship with his children, as a prerequisite to the bank's transformation. These patterns in the film have symbolic bearing to the United States of the 1960s, an era when industrial production was waning; the service, entertainment, and consumer sectors of the economy growing; and interpersonal relations were becoming important in the economic world. The bank, a traditional bastion of capitalism, needed to shed its image as vengeful patriarch of the marketplace as much as the father in the home needed to shed it in his familial relations.

Positing such a connection between the stability of nuclear families and the stability of capitalism allows the film to raise the stakes concerning erosion of the nuclear-family structure and gender roles. Voices and changes that challenge patriarchal family hierarchy and therefore national security can now be represented as a danger to larger social and economic structures.

## Maria, Class, and Nationalism

The character of Maria, in *The Sound of Music*, also seems to seamlessly cross class barriers. She comes from a mountain (presumably peasant) family, yet can carry out all the behavioral prescriptions of the bourgeois dinner table. She woos her employer, Captain von Trapp, by displaying her affiliation to the Austrian peasantry, rather than to the middle classes. As Stacy Wolf points out, Maria slips easily from the role of nanny to the role of wife-mother. Wolf contrasts Maria with the representation of the Southern "Mammy" who never makes such a transition. Maria's whiteness and thinness allow her "unlimited class mobility" (1996, 57). Maria's move from servant to wife, however, indicates more than class mobility: a symbolic erasure of class difference (conflict) in the interest of constructing a concept of nationalism. Austrian nationalism, in the face of encroaching Nazi aggression in the Europe of 1939, shares metaphoric patterns and, I believe, would be capable of eliciting similar emotional responses to American patriotism in the face of perceived Soviet expansionism in the ideology of 1960s anticommunism, as well as to concerns of internal social unrest. I argue that throughout the film, the concept of nationalism in prewar Austria structurally mirrors that of American Cold War nationalism. In both cases, patriotism is constituted by lack of conflict between social groups, the correct positioning of traditional femininity and masculinity in the nuclear family, and the positing of the normative patriarchal family as the frontline against foreign aggression.

In the beginning of the film, Trapp has classist reservations about how Maria deals with his children. In a scene where Trapp is driving near his estate with the baroness, returning from a long trip to Vienna, they see Maria and his children climbing trees on the roadside. When asked by the baroness what is going on, he replies, "Oh, nothing, just some local urchins," embarrassed to admit to her that his children would behave in such a manner. Later, he berates Maria for the incident. Trapp's anxiety about Maria's influence at this stage in the film reflects a bourgeois fear that has existed historically in terms of real nannies and governesses since the nineteenth century. It was widely feared that nannies would be "the conduit through which working-class habits would infiltrate the middle-class home" (Poovey 1989, 233).[9] In *The Sound of Music*, however, the reverse occurs when the bourgeois family assimilates the peasantry into its own representations of nationalism. Despite her peasant origins, as Wolf points out, in marrying Trapp, Maria "wears the clothes and the demeanor of Mrs. Captain von Trapp with frightening ease" (1996, 57). Maria does not desert her peasant origins when she becomes Mrs. von Trapp, however, rather those origins are assimilated into the ideal of a national femininity upon which is built the ideal of a national family then employed in the fight against the Nazis.

Nationalism as a trope facilitates Maria's move into the middle class, while simultaneously setting her up as the personification of Austrian national femininity, which then allows the film to elide class difference. Maria and Trapp first become obviously attracted to each other during a party held at his villa when they dance an Austrian folk dance together. She is dressed in a simple, peasant-like costume of plain fabric, in contrast to the baroness's tight and slinky evening dress of glittering gold lamé. As they dance and look deeply into each other's eyes, Maria becomes emblematic of Austrian womanhood through the sexualizing male gaze. From this moment on it is clear that the captain is in love with Maria, and, as the baroness later jealously points out, she with him. This scene is significant not only because it represents the moment when Maria comes to embody the nation-as-woman, but also because the captain initiates this personification. The peasant/working class is defined through the gaze of the middle class, femininity defined by masculinity, and the call to national unity and class erasure comes from the ranks of the bourgeoisie. Class is not transcended here by Maria, rather the bourgeois male gaze constructs a femininity that erases class difference, not just prioritizing national difference/conflict over class conflict, but suggesting that class antagonism is a danger to national stability and security. National unity, according to this ideology, is premised on the disappearance of internal conflict—a metaphoric pattern that resonates with conservative antirevolutionary discourse of 1960s America that bemoaned the social unrest going on in the era. The film attempts to resolve dominant anxieties in the United States of 1965 surrounding the internal race, class, and generational conflicts going on in the middle of a Cold War, and at the time of America's deepening involvement in the Vietnam conflict. For many conservatives these movements were destroying national unity (symbolized by the consensus and containment metaphor), and weakening the "nation" (Ehrenreich and English 1978). *The Sound of Music* resonates with these conservative values by displaying national unity in the face of ideological threats, whether they are Nazism in Austria of 1939 or communism, both real and imagined, in the United States of 1965.

Maria cannot fight Nazism alone, however; national femininity must be placed in its proper social position, and the nuclear family must be united under a benevolent patriarch. The idea that Maria is not a full person before her integration into the patriarchal/nationalistic family is indicated by the fact that, before her marriage to the captain, she does not seem to have a last name but is known simply as Maria. From the beginning, Maria's purity, the perfection of the Austrian landscape, and the "sound of music" have been metonymically linked. The opening scenes of the film place Maria as a natural part of the Austrian landscape and the "sound of music" as the uninhibited expression of this landscape/womanhood conflation. Maria's femininity is conflated with nature and beauty, and situated within a discourse of nationalism.

Song in the film can be seen as an expression of the natural order, an order that includes the "innocent voices of our children"—a nationalist trope for everything "good in this country." During the party at Trapp's estate, there are tensions between the local Nazi supporters and the captain, who has prominently displayed the Austrian flag in his ballroom. When Herr Zeller, a local official and Nazi supporter, retorts, "Would you have us believe that Austria alone holds a monopoly on virtue?" the captain replies, "Some of us prefer Austrian voices raised in song to ugly German threats." The Trapp children here become a trope for all Austrian children and Maria's folksy femininity and instinctual mothering will organize Austrian children's voices in song against external threats, but only with the addition of the final ingredient, the father. All the structures are now in place for Maria to marry the captain. Family and national unity is achieved when the Trapp Family Singers perform at the Salzburg Folk Festival, and the crowd joins in singing the Austrian anthem *Edelweiss.* The film suggests that national unity is only possible if preceded and predicated on family unity, a unity based on a particular ideal of womanhood and gendered domestic power positions. The combination of the natural, "libidinal" mother-of-the-nation with brave, patriotic children headed by the expressive, loving father is a family configuration that as much expresses the Cold War family ideal in the ideology of consensus and containment in postwar America as it does prewar Austria. This type of family unity significantly implies rejection of generational, as well as gender, conflict, an important symbolic strategy in the generation-torn America of 1965.

The ideologies of patriotic containment and anticonsensus radicalism are in opposition in this text, the first represented by the modernized, unified, nationalist family, the second by the forces in the film that threaten to pull that family apart, in particular, Nazism. To a 1960s audience, the threats posed by Nazism in Austria of the late 1930s could be understood to resonate with the threats posed by communism to the "free world." In the 1938 *Anschluss,* Nazi forces overtook Austria without resistance. At this point in the film, the Trapp family decides to flee Austria, as the captain has been ordered to return to military duty with the navy of the Third Reich. The Nazi occupation of Austria can be seen to symbolize fears of both communist expansionism in the Cold War era as well as threats to the conservative nation from internal generational, racial, and gender movements and counter-culture ideologies. In *The Sound of Music,* the character of Rolf, the all-Austrian telegram boy who joins the Nazis, emphasizes the vulnerability of American youth to the persuasive forces of evil foreign ideas. Unlike the Trapp family, Rolf lacks the strength as an individual to stand up to foreign indoctrination.

The virtues earlier inculcated in the children by Maria coincide with mid-1960s notions of American individualism in the face of the totalitarian rigidity that was believed to characterize both Soviet communism and wartime Nazism (Griswold 1993). In both films, the importance of spontaneity, expressiveness, and a sense of adventure in children is emphasized and inculcated in them by their respective nannies. Mary Poppins brings the children dancing on rooftops and riding merry-go-round horses in a fantasy countryside, much to the chagrin of their father who prefers them to be clean, obedient, and silent. Maria is compelled by nature toward song and impulsiveness. Her inability to follow the rules and routines of the convent, because nature calls her from outside the convent gates, is the first example we are given of her resistance to uniformity and rules. Later on in the film, she insists that the children have play clothes to replace the uniforms their father wants them to wear. This individualism both attracts Trapp to Maria and allows her to symbolize nationalism.

In the United States of the 1950s and 1960s, many observers "agreed that the authoritarian personality was a threat to democratic society" and sociologists claimed that dominating fathering could produce intolerant, even fascist, offspring (Griswold 1993, 208).[10] American individualism was considered a component of the struggle against anti-American ideologies. "With Nazism as a backdrop and the Cold War well under way, how could obedience, conformity, and dependence measure up against self-direction, freedom, and independence as desirable values to foster in children" (1993, 212)?

As I discussed above, permissiveness in child rearing and family relations could go too far, and in *The Sound of Music*, the correct sort of individualism in the children is contained within the newly perfected family circle, with the father clearly back in control.

## Conclusion

Susan Douglas points out that since the 1950s, representations of women in the mass media have involved "a complex struggle between feminism and antifeminism that has reflected, reinforced, and exaggerated our culture's ambivalence about women's roles for over thirty years" (1994, 13). Elyce Rae Helford argues that fantasy television shows such as *I Dream of Jeannie* and *Bewitched* allowed popular culture of the 1960s to incorporate ambivalence about women's changing social position in the era. These shows maneuvered between allowing "symbolic articulations of women's (at least white, middle-class women's) aspirations for respect in roles other than wife and mother," while at the same time avoiding the risk of alienating conservative viewers by representing these women within the "traditional" suburban ideal (2000, 2). Lynn Spigel writes that postwar television (and I would add mainstream film) not only contributed to the ideological dominance of the white normative family ideal, but also, in contrast, "precipitated cultural dialogues about women's place, gender relations, sexuality, childhood, class, and racial relations" (2001, 11).

This ambivalence surrounding the representation of women in popular culture is also evident in *Mary Poppins* and *The Sound of Music*. Although the conservative position dominates in the films' resistance to changing domestic gender roles, nevertheless, both the characters of Mary Poppins and Maria (at least initially) embody many of the characteristics of the "liberated" woman according to the 1960s feminist rubric. Both women are opinionated, unconventional, and self-possessed; if necessary, they are willing to speak back to their (male) employer or stand up for their own beliefs. Yet the work they carry out in both films restores insecure patriarchal rule. An incorporationist strategy allows the film, *Mary Poppins*, to depict the eponymous nanny as embodying what Chris

Cuomo calls "certain liberal feminist egalitarian values and even some radical feminist critiques of femininity" (1995, 215), while using her powers and charms to bring the patriarchal home back into (modernized) order. A similar point may be made about Maria in *The Sound of Music*, whose initial tomboyishness and androgyny allows her to succeed in repairing the relationship between the captain and his children, yet she is rapidly heterosexualized by her marriage.

Both films certainly suggest a solution to certain "problems" that were being experienced by white, male-dominated bourgeois culture: the rise of subcultures among middle-class whites, youthful challenge of authority and the government, white youths' interest in racial integration and their participation in the Civil Rights Movement, and crucially, women's challenges to traditional notions of gender roles. *Mary Poppins* and *The Sound of Music* proffer that men needed to readjust and reassume their positions of power in the family, and that the family should position itself as the bedrock of politics and society. This strategy not only reified patriarchal power relations in the nuclear family, but also established this nuclear-family formation as the exclusively correct structure on which to model public policies and institutions.

## Notes

1. Rodgers and Hammerstein also wrote the music for *The Sound of Music*.

2. Another well-known historical text that allegorizes the Cold War era and McCarthyism is Arthur Miller's play *The Crucible* (1953).

3. This new suburban, nuclear-family structure was facilitated by an array of circumstances: government housing policy that enabled many urban families to relocate to the suburbs, the GI bill that gave higher educational opportunities to many men who otherwise would not have moved into the middle class, the government project to build 37,000 miles of highway that began in 1947 and enabled suburban culture to grow, among others (Coontz 1992).

4. Most scholars agree that the protests against the Miss America pageant in Atlantic City in September 1968 were "a watershed in American history," and the moment when feminism begins to be given widespread public attention, most of it negative (Douglas 1994, 140).

5. See Ladd-Taylor and Umansky for more examples of maternal failure in the United States in this and other periods (1998).

6. Obviously there were representations of the "perfect" mother that were popular at the same time, such as the mother in *The Donna Reed Show*, but

these shows ignored or erased the contradiction rather than address it. Culture also produced texts such as *Mary Poppins* and *The Sound of Music* that reinforced ideology through attempts to resolve rather than ignore social contradictions.

7. Winifred Banks is not shown as a neglectful wife, but one who panders to her husband throughout the film while at the same time not spending time with the children.

8. It is interesting to note that the unmarried, and presumably chaste, Mary Poppins also has this first name.

9. Gathorne-Hardy writes that the employers of wet nurses often feared that working-class attributes would be passed on to their children through breast milk (1973).

10. See Else Frenkel-Brunswik, "Parents and Childhood as Seen through the Interviews," in Theodor W. Adorno et al.'s *The Authoritarian Personality*. She shows that men whose fathers spent time "playing and 'doing things' with their sons" were found to be in general unprejudiced and those with stern and distant fathers were found to be intolerant (1950, 361).

## References

Adorno, Theodor W., Else Frenkel-Brunswik, Daniel J. Levinson, and R. Nevitt Sanford in collaboration with Betty Aron, Maria Hertz Levinson, and William Morrow. 1950. *The Authoritarian Personality*. New York: Wiley.

Buhle, Mari Jo. 1998. *Feminism and Its Discontents: A Century of Struggle with Psychoanalysis*. Cambridge, Mass.: Harvard University Press.

Coontz, Stephanie. 1992. *The Way We Never Were: American Families and the Nostalgia Trap*. New York: Basic Books.

Cuomo, Chris. 1995. "Spinsters in Sensible Shoes: Mary Poppins and Bedknobs and Broomsticks." In *From Mouse to Mermaid: The Politics of Film, Gender and Culture*, ed. Elizabeth Bell, Lynda Haas, and Laura Sells, 212–23. Bloomington: Indiana University Press.

Douglas, Susan. 1994. *Where the Girls Are: Growing up Female with the Mass Media*. New York: Times Books.

Ehrenreich, Barbara. 1983. *The Hearts of Men: American Dreams and the Flight from Commitment*. Garden City, N.Y.: Anchor Press.

———, and Deirdre English. 1978. *For Her Own Good: 150 Years of the Experts' Advice to Women*. New York: Anchor Press.

Evans, Sara. 1980. *Personal Politics: The Roots of Women's Liberation in the Civil Rights Movement and the New Left*. New York: Vintage Books.

Farnham, Marynia, and Ferdinand Lundberg. 1947. *Modern Woman: The Lost Sex*. New York: Harper.

Foreman, Joel, ed. 1997. *The Other Fifties: Interrogating Midcentury American Icons.* Urbana: University of Illinois Press.

Freeman, Jo, ed. 1983. *Social Movements of the Sixties and Seventies.* New York: Longman.

Friedan, Betty. 1963. *The Feminine Mystique.* New York: Norton.

Gathorne-Hardy, Jonathan. 1973. *The Unnatural History of the Nanny.* New York: Dial Press.

Goodman, David. 1959. *A Parent's Guide to the Emotional Needs of Children.* New York: Hawthorne Books.

Griswold, Robert L. 1993. *Fatherhood in America: A History.* New York: Basic Books.

Helford, Elyce Rae. 2000. *Fantasy Girls: Gender in the New Universe of Science Fiction and Fantasy Television.* Lanham, Md.: Rowman and Littlefield.

Jameson, Fredric. 1981. *The Political Unconscious: Narrative as a Socially Symbolic Act.* London: Methuen.

Keller, Kathryn. 1994. *Mothers and Work in Popular American Magazines.* Westport, Conn.: Greenwood Press.

Ladd-Taylor, Molly, and Lauri Umansky, eds. 1998. *"Bad" Mothers: The Politics of Blame in Twentieth-Century America.* New York: New York University Press.

Levy, David. 1943. *Maternal Overprotection.* New York: Columbia University Press.

Margolis, Maxine. 1984. *Mothers and Such: Views of American Women and Why They Changed.* Berkeley: University of California Press.

May, Elaine Tyler. 1988. *Homeward Bound: American Families in the Cold War Era.* New York: Basic Books.

McClintock, Anne. 1995. *Imperial Leather: Race, Gender and Sexuality in the Colonial Contest.* New York: Routledge.

McConachie, Bruce. 1994. "The 'Oriental' Musicals of Rodgers and Hammerstein and the U.S. War in Southeast Asia." *Theatre Journal* 46(3):385–98.

Meyerowitz, Joanne, ed. 1994. *Not June Cleaver: Women and Gender in Postwar America, 1945–1960.* Philadelphia: Temple University Press.

Miller, Arthur. 1953. *The Crucible, A Play in Four Acts.* New York: Viking Press.

Parsons, Talcott. 1955. "Family Structure and the Socialization of the Child." In *Family Socialization and Interaction Process,* ed. Talcott Parsons and Robert F. Bales, 25–131. Glencoe, Ill.: Free Press.

Poovey, Mary. 1989. "The Anathematized Race: The Governess and Jane Eyre." In *Feminism and Psychoanalysis,* ed. Richard Feldstein and Judith Roof, 230–54. Ithaca, N.Y.: Cornell University Press.

Spigel, Lynn. 1992. *Make Room for TV: Television and the Family Ideal in Postwar America.* Chicago: University of Chicago Press.

———. 2001. *Welcome to the Dreamhouse: Popular Media and Postwar Suburbs.* Durham, N.C.: Duke University Press.

Spock, Benjamin. 1954. *The Pocket Book of Baby and Child Care. New Edition.* New York: Duell, Sloan and Pearce.

———. 1962. *Problems of Parents.* Boston: Houghton Mifflin.

Stevenson, Robert. 1964. *Mary Poppins*. Burbank, Calif.: Walt DisneyProductions. Motion picture.

Toby, Mark. 1961. *The Courtship of Eddie's Father*. New York: Random House.

Umansky, Lauri. 1996. *Motherhood Reconceived, Feminism and the Legacies of the Sixties*. New York: New York University Press.

United States Interdepartmental Committee on the Status of Women.1968. *American Women, 1963–1968, Report*. Washington, D.C.: U.S. Government Printing Office.

Watson, John. 1928. *Psychological Care of Infant and Child*. New York: W. W. Norton.

Wise, Robert, dir. 1965. *The Sound of Music*. Beverly Hills and Los Angeles, Calif.: 20th Century Fox Film Corp. and Argyle Enterprises Inc. Motion picture.

Wolf, Stacy. 1996. "The Queer Pleasures of Mary Martin and Broadway: *The Sound of Music* as a Lesbian Musical." *Modern Drama* 39(1):51.

Wylie, Philip. 1942. *Generation of Vipers*. New York: Farrar & Rinehart.

CHAPTER FIVE

# Millions "Love Lucy": Commodification and the Lucy Phenomenon

LORI LANDAY

"You need a pretty girl in your act to advertise the sponsor's product. She eats it, or drinks it, or waxes the floor with it, or cuts potatoes with it, or drives off in it . . . or smokes it!" Lucy Ricardo's line from the March 1951 pilot episode of *I Love Lucy* underscores a key aspect of the connections between women, television, and commodification. The "pretty girl" is the woman-as-spectacle who gains the attention of the consumer and, by embodying the exchange value of the sponsor's product, creates the associations that advertise it. The line demonstrates how women in performance are valued primarily for their appearance, and makes a joke based on the audience's knowledge that the sponsor of *I Love Lucy* was Philip Morris, the brand of cigarettes Lucy and Ricky Ricardo—or is it Lucille Ball and Desi Arnaz—smoke on the show.

The blurring of the boundaries between whether it is Lucy and Ricky or Ball and Arnaz smoking Philip Morris cigarettes suggests some of the issues surrounding commodification and the Lucy phenomenon. Ultimately, commodification is about transforming reality, selfhood, and experience into quantifiable products of mass consumer culture, and situating those fetishized commodity-forms in a social context in which people define things in terms of themselves and themselves in terms of things. "Individuality" is secured from the goods and the appearance of the goods people consume; discursive and social practices reinforce the notion that a person's character is based on the commodities consumed rather than on anything internal or intrinsic. The Lucy phenomenon is a triumph of commodification; the television series, the merchandise, and the character are all aspects of one of the most successful products television and postwar American society has ever manufactured. Today, Nick at Nite reruns, websites, fan conventions, collectibles, television specials, books, videotapes, laserdiscs, the merchandising, and the recent popular vote to put Lucy on a U.S. postage stamp commemorating the 1950s are all evidence of the contemporary Lucy phenomenon.

Since 1951, *I Love Lucy* has been one of the most enduring and influential transformations of a public persona in American culture. In the 1950s, *I Love Lucy* addressed the central ideological concerns of the postwar period within the emerging medium of television situation comedy in a show that climaxed with a performance by perhaps the most brilliant

Originally published in the Summer 1999 issue of the *NWSA Journal*.

physical comedienne on film. Of course, *Lucy*'s continuing success hinges on this comic genius. However, the resonance and relevance of *Lucy* is due to the way the series and the character dramatized and personified cultural conflicts about gender, marriage, and commodification caused by the legitimation crisis that emerged in postwar America and remains pertinent throughout the twentieth and into the twenty-first centuries.

One explanation for the centrality and significance of the Lucy phenomenon is Lucy's embodiment of one of the most beloved and central cultural figures: the trickster (Landay 1998, 160–95). A trickster is a subversive, paradoxical fantasy figure who does what we cannot or dare not by moving between social spaces, roles, and categories that the culture has deemed oppositional. When faced with a situation that appears to have only two choices, the trickster is the kind of hero/ine who creates a third possibility. But the trickster's chicanery often backfires on him or her, and then the trickster becomes the dupe. Like other tricksters, Lucy Ricardo fuses the most exalted and base aspects of human nature into an engaging character who remains true to her mixed nature. As Walter Matthau remarked in explaining the universal appeal of Lucy, "There's no dream she wouldn't reach for, and no fall she wouldn't take" (Sanders and Gilbert 1993, 368).

Because the straightforward path to satisfying her desires is barred in some way, Lucy turns to trickery to get what she wants. Lucy's ambitions are thwarted in part because of her status as a woman, particularly as a married woman without financial or creative autonomy, so the object of her trickery is often to subvert her husband's authority through the covert tactics of "feminine wiles" available to her. Lucy is specifically a female trickster because her attempts to circumvent the limitations of the feminine mystique of postwar domesticity oscillate between "masculine" and "feminine" social roles, spaces, practices, and metaphors. In a rapidly changing postwar society when the gap between the ideology of polarized gender roles clashed so powerfully with the social experience of American men and women, Lucy's inability to reconcile her ambitions and her social position articulated increasing tensions about gender.

By calling attention to the power relations of the sexes in everyday domestic life, *I Love Lucy* participated in a proto-feminist current building in American culture. To be sure, Lucy's desire was to escape the confines of domesticity, to be autonomous and public instead of dependent and private, ridiculed and usually ineffectual. However, the glimmers of equality in the Ricardo marriage, combined with the audience's extratextual knowledge of the real-life Ball and Arnaz marriage/creative partnership, posited the hope of a collaborative marriage alongside a dramatization of the conflicts of the 1950s ideal of the companionate marriage.

Although Lucy's dissatisfaction with being a housewife was couched in layers of contradictions, and the character's incompetence was comic fodder, the series incorporated cultural contradictions and anxieties about women's participation in the public sphere. A consumer good installed in the home that brought representations of other consumer goods into the home, the postwar television was literally and metaphorically a bridge between the public and private, dissolving some of the sexual division of labor in those spheres. Although postwar ideology clung to polarized gender roles in its impetus to be "homeward bound," the number of women in the workforce in 1952 exceeded the largest female workforce during the war (May 1988). In this context, we can interpret Lucy's botched attempts at paid labor outside the home as addressing both men's and women's fears about women's increased involvement in the public sphere.

Moreover, the Lucy phenomenon articulated both the fantasy of the good life central to the situation of the sitcom and the dissatisfaction bred by commodification, the very condition consumerism is supposed to quell. As a kind of postwar domestic realism, *I Love Lucy*'s comic representation of everyday life placed a romantic, yet screwball comedy version of the battle of the sexes into a more intimate, private setting than any other medium—written, stage, film, or radio; the Ricardo living room was literally in the living rooms of America. The setting and props—the furniture, clothes, room layouts, cigarettes–became intertwined in a commodified fantasy and a fantasy of commodification in a new, more powerful way. Not only did a vision of the good life provide the cultural context and setting of the series, but the plots often revolved around Lucy's insatiable desire for what she doesn't have, whether that is a role in Ricky's show or a new freezer.

What cultural work did *I Love Lucy* perform and how was and is it shaped by the cultural and social contexts in which it is created and reprised? *I Love Lucy* emerged as a central story cycle concerned with the major cultural preoccupations of the postwar era: marriage, domesticity, and the attainment of a middle-class lifestyle. It did so because of the particular historical conditions, the newness of television programming and the genre of the situation comedy, Lucy's function as a trickster figure, and the extraordinary creative and business talents of Ball, Arnaz, and their collaborators.

One of the attractions of *I Love Lucy* was its blend of reality and fiction, or "real life" and "reel life," as a 1953 *Look* article called it. Self-reflexive jokes like Lucy's statement that Ricky needs a "pretty girl" in his act bisociate[1] inept housewife Lucy Ricardo and TV star Lucille Ball, calling attention to how she both is and is not the "pretty girl" in the various narrative frames of the *I Love Lucy* phenomenon. Interwoven are the episode, the advertisements during the episode, knowledge about the series and its stars from secondary texts, the cultural contexts that inflect the combinations of private housewife/public pretty girl and femininity/comedy with contradictions, and the ideology of the feminine mystique.

The ideology of mass consumer culture is central to all the levels of the Lucy phenomenon: in the sponsor's framing of episodes; in the self-reflexivity of the episode "Lucy Does a TV Commercial" and other episodes that revolve around commodification; in the "good life" portrayed in the series; in Ball's public persona as "just a housewife"; in the myriad of products tied to the series in the 1950s (furniture, clothes, dolls); as a syndicated series; in the Lucy collectibles popular today; and in the continuation of the Lucy phenomenon on the internet and in fan gatherings. At the core of the phenomenon is a juxtaposition of reality and artifice, of advertising and programming. Individual episodes offer commodities including household appliances (a freezer, television set, washing machine), apparel (dresses, a fur coat), and furniture as the solution to Lucy's dissatisfaction, an example of the consumerist ethos that presented private solutions to public problems. However, at the same time that *I Love Lucy* participated in the mass consumer economy, the series' comedy played on conflicts and anxieties about commodification, domesticity, and the culture industries.

## Making Memories

Why does *I Love Lucy* persist in its popularity today? What cultural work does it continue to perform? One function *Lucy* performs is found within the concept of "memory as misappropriation" that George Lipsitz locates in the popularity of the early television series *I Remember Mama* (1949–56). Lipsitz argues that *Mama*'s appeal might have been because it *didn't* depict the past accurately (it was set at the turn-of-the-century), and *did* represent the past as people wished it had been. One view of "memory as misappropriation" is compensatory fantasy, but Lipsitz also suggests some liberatory facets:

> It enables us to see beyond our own experience, rendering the oppressions of the past as contingent and unnecessary while modeling an alternate past, one as responsive to human wishes and desires as to the accidents of history. . . . If our own personal pasts cannot be venerated as moral guides for the present, we must choose another from history or art and embrace it as our own. But such leaps cannot be fashioned purely from the imagination; the past has more informative power and more relevance to the present if we believe that it is what actually happened, because what people have done before they can do again, while what they imagine may never be realized. (1990, 80)

From this perspective, contemporary audiences' delight in *I Love Lucy* may very well be due to the series' portrayal of the 1950s. It offers contemporary audiences a misappropriated memory of the past that is a fitting vanguard of the many advancements gained by the women's movement in the past 30 years. The more Lucy's antics are recast in the past, the funnier her trickery becomes because the social conditions that necessitated her trickery have changed. Actually, some of those conditions have changed and others persist, such as Lucy's concern with her attractiveness and her desire to be treated as an equal. Like Coyote, Brer Rabbit, the con-man, and other incarnations of the trickster, Lucy can withstand historical and cultural changes and remain a central figure in the culture's mythos.

## Making Merchandise

*I Love Lucy* reached an unprecedented level of popularity as a successful commodity in itself and excellent advertising for its sponsor. After the Ricardo and Ball-Arnaz babies were born almost simultaneously in January 1953, it spawned merchandising tie-ins that exceeded $50 million. As Ball explains in her autobiography, "In addition to the production company, we also had a merchandising business. It was possible to furnish a house and dress a whole family with items carrying our *I Love Lucy* label" (Ball 1996, 224). Desilu, the Ball-Arnaz production company, received 5 percent of the gross earnings of the products the stars endorsed; beginning in October 1952, there were 2,800 retail outlets for Lucille Ball dresses, blouses, sweaters, and aprons as well as Desi Arnaz smoking jackets and robes. There were pajamas for men and women like the ones Lucy and Ricky wore and a line of dolls. In one month in late 1952, 30,000 "Lucy" dresses, 32,000 heart-adorned aprons, and 35,000 dolls were sold. The pajamas sold out in two weeks, and the Christmas rush sold 85,000 dolls. In January 1953, the first month of selling a line of bedroom suites, $500,000 in sales in two days were reported. As of January 1953 there were layettes and nursery furniture, Desi sport shirts and denims, Lucy lingerie and costume jewelry, and desk and chair sets ("Desilu Formula" 1953, 58; Andrews 1985, 108). There were also *I Love Lucy* albums, sheet music, coloring books, and comic books.

A month after 44 million people watched the episode "Lucy Goes to the Hospital," Ball and Arnaz signed a contract for $8 million with Philip Morris and CBS, the largest contract ever written for a television series to date. In describing the contract, the Philip Morris president explained:

> This show is the all-time phenomenon of the entertainment business. On a strictly dollars-and-cents basis, it is twice as effective as the average nighttime

> television show in conveying our advertising message to the public. . . . It is probably one of, if not the most efficient advertising buys in the entire country. In addition, we derive many supplementary merchandising and publicity benefits from the show. As you can see, we love "Lucy." (Andrews 1985, 107–8)

Of course Philip Morris loved Lucy; what's not to love?[2] The phenomenon exemplified the symbolic motives of advertising. Advertising seeks to create a web of associations that allows the consumer to justify purchasing a specific consumer product in terms of abstract social goals. A hit show like *I Love Lucy* provides those associations, as articulated in a 1953 furniture ad that proclaimed "Live Like Lucy!" Frankfurt School critics Max Horkheimer and Theodor Adorno noted this trend: "Advertising and the culture industry merge technically as well as economically" (1944, 163). Indeed, in an era characterized by the idea of consensus, everyone seemed to agree. As *New York Times* television critic Jack Gould wrote, " 'I Love Lucy' is probably the most misleading title imaginable. For once, all the statistics are in agreement: Millions love Lucy" (quoted in Andrews 1985, 109). Horkheimer and Adorno also provide a more somber interpretation of the success of popular texts like *I Love Lucy,* asserting, "The deception is not that the culture industry supplies amusement but that it ruins the fun by allowing business considerations to involve it in the ideological cliches of a culture in the process of self-liquidation" (1944, 142–3). However, there is much more to be learned about the role popular culture plays in the process of commodification. As George Lipsitz comments, many critics of popular culture "are so eager to tell us what popular culture does not do (advance the agenda of the Enlightenment) that they fail to tell us what popular culture actually does or how it is shaped by the economic and social matrix in which it is embedded" (1990, 18).

## Making "Lucy"

At the center of the Lucy phenomenon is "Lucy," that combination of Lucille Ball and the series of screwy redheaded heroines she infused with a life of their own. The red hair is one of the most fetishized aspects of the Lucy icon, ironic since *I Love Lucy* was, of course, in black and white. Ball stopped bleaching her hair blonde and shifted to red hair in the mid-1930s when she was working in mostly B-movies at RKO. She chose the pink-orange hue, called "Tango Red," when she went to MGM in 1943 because it added to the spectacle of the Technicolor musicals Ball made between 1943 and 1946. Ball recalled, "It gave me just the right finishing touch before the cameras. Maybe I didn't look so good in person, but I wasn't worrying about that" (Doty 1990, 6; Ball 1996, 156). That the "finishing touch" on her self-commodification was purely for the camera, not for "real life," and that the artificial color of her hair was widely publicized and known, show how much artifice was a part of Ball's star persona.

That women's hair color was commodified and fetishized was certainly nothing new in the mid-1930s. By choosing red hair over blonde, Ball eschewed the well-established golddigger/dumb blonde image in favor of the unconventional, individualistic, and vibrant redhead. "Madame" Elinor Glyn, a celebrity writer and film producer, always sought opportunities to mythologize her own preferred hair color: "titian" red. *It* (1927) and *Red Hair* (1928), Glyn's movies starring Clara Bow, the most famous redhead before Ball, advanced her agenda into mass consumer culture. In 1932, famous blonde Jean Harlow shunned platinum for red and questioned gentlemen's preference for blondes in the Anita Loos–scripted *Red-Headed Woman*.

By connecting herself with unconventional redheaded comic heroines, Ball put herself in the tradition of screwball heroines, who had moved from film to radio to television, and in shifting media, had become increasingly domesticated. The resolution to the film screwball comedy of the 1930s and early 1940s was marriage (sometimes remarriage); acts one and two dealt with courtship staged as a comic, slapstick battle of the sexes. For serialized programs in the "homeward bound" postwar era, the comic terrain shifted to married life. Nevertheless, two lines from *Bringing Up Baby* (1938) articulate the principles of the screwball comedy, and then the radio and television situation comedy: "The love impulse in man frequently reveals itself in terms of conflict" and "Everything's gonna be alright." In *My Favorite Husband*, Ball's radio situation comedy, Ball played Liz Cooper, whose schemes for helping her banker husband's career led her into funny mishaps. In radio, Ball found the fame and recognition that eluded her in film. The radio show set up much of the narrative and ideological groundwork for *I Love Lucy*. It led to comic climaxes with exaggerations of everyday life that reflected and parodied the cultural ideals of the postwar period: domesticity; polarized gender roles; material acquisition; attaining a successful, white, middle-class lifestyle. When *Husband* writers Jess Oppenheimer, Madelyn Pugh, and Bob Carroll Jr. became the writers for *I Love Lucy*, they recycled many of the radio plots, facilitating the development of Lucy Ricardo, postwar domesticity's inheritor of the legacy of screwball heroines.

Ball's red hair almost had a very different—and career ending—connotation. At one point in the House Un-American Activities Committee (HUAC) hearings, Ball was questioned about a 1936 registration card on which she had declared that she intended to vote for the Communist Party's candidates. At the second closed hearing in 1953, Ball was cleared of suspicion when she explained she did it only to please her grandfather and that she had little interest in politics herself. Yet somehow the news leaked out, leading to a *Los Angeles–Herald Express* headline in three-inch red letters: "LUCILLE BALL NAMED RED." That night, at the filming of the 1953–54 season premiere, Arnaz warmed up the studio audience as usual, but he gave a serious speech denouncing communism and labeling the rumors lies. The crowd cheered. He ended with, "And now, I want you to meet my favorite wife" (a play on Ball's successful 1940s radio show *My Favorite Husband*), and then he continued, "my favorite redhead—in fact, that's the only thing red about her, and even that's not legitimate—Lucille Ball!" (Brady 1994, 220; Ball 1996, 231–2; Sanders and Gilbert 1993, 81).

## Making Reality

This question of reality and artifice characterized early television in general and *I Love Lucy* in particular. The medium of television had an immediacy and sense of presence that far outstripped radio and film. Whether live or, like *I Love Lucy*, filmed "live," the discursive patterns of early television encouraged viewers to feel like they were actually present at the event or performance. In his discussion of the changes television wrought on American political and social life, historian David Halberstam summarizes, "People now expected to *see* events, not merely read about or hear them. At the same time, the line between what happened in real life and what people saw on television began to merge. . . . Nothing showed the power of this new medium to soften the edge between real life and fantasy better than the coming of Lucille Ball" (1993, 195–6).

The on-screen chemistry of Ball and Arnaz, the combination of the familiar (screwball and situation comedy conventions, show business couples) with the innovative (a Cuban-American marriage), and Ball's superlative abilities at physical comedy all created a context for the success of *I Love Lucy*. However, most likely the cultural movement toward domesticity was the biggest factor in creating the Lucy phenomenon. The situation of *I Love Lucy* articulated the contradictions of marriage, gender, the battle of the sexes, and middle-class life: the things of concern to a majority of television buyers and television watchers. Ball attributed the series' success to how it made comedy out of everyday life:

> We had a great identification with millions of people. They could identify with my problems, my zaniness, my wanting to do everything, my scheming and plotting, the way I cajoled Ricky. People identified with the Ricardos because we had the same problems they had. Desi and I weren't your ordinary Hollywood couple on TV. We lived in a brownstone apartment somewhere in

> Manhattan, and paying the rent, getting a new dress, getting a stale fur collar on an old cloth coat, or buying a piece of furniture were all worth a story.
>
> People could identify with those basic things—baby-sitters, traveling, wanting to be entertained, wanting to be loved in a certain way—all the two couples on the show were constantly doing things that people all over the country were doing. We just took ordinary situations and exaggerated them. (quoted in Andrews 1985, 225–6)

Note that all the things Ball lists as ordinary problems deal with domestic, private life. Episodes most often ended with temporary truces between Ricky and Lucy (articulated in lines like "Now we're even" and an embrace), but sometimes the episode ended with the reassertion of control by Ricky or another authority figure, or sometimes by simply breaking off the action at the height of comic chaos. In any case, the problem solving leads back to the core of the show: the "love" between the couple. As May summarizes, "In the postwar years, Americans found that viable alternatives to the prevailing family norm were virtually unavailable. Because of the political, ideological, and institutional developments that converged at the time, young adults were indeed homeward bound, but they were also bound to the home" (1988, 15). In the world of *I Love Lucy,* home meant the "love" that Ricky had for Lucy no matter what odd, property damaging, career jeopardizing, financially threatening thing she did. *I Love Lucy* assured viewers that with "love," everything would turn out all right. And that "love" could be yours in the form of his and her pajamas for only $5.95.

Television brought the world into the home and the home into the world. Because American culture was engrossed in the ideas and commodification of domesticity, postwar society was a fertile field in which television expanded. In her excellent study, *Make Room for TV: Television and the Family Ideal in Postwar America*, Lynn Spigel explores the development of television as a commodity and as an institution, discussing the rhetorical strategies advertisers and programmers used to promote television as an essential part of family life in the context of increased consumer spending, which rose 60 percent in the five years after World War II. Spending on household furnishings and appliances rose a staggering 240 percent (May 1988, 165), including the televisions that were in .02 percent of homes in 1946 and in 9 percent of homes in 1950; by 1955, 65 percent of homes had televisions. When the young couples who were homeward bound created homes, they put televisions in the center of them, and when they gathered around the television in the family "togetherness" touted by television advertisements, they saw shows like *I Love Lucy* that dramatized the "good life." Perhaps, as the work of May and Spigel suggests, television was particularly influential to the postwar generation who left neighborhoods comprised of several generations for single-family detached houses in the suburbs. "Postwar Americans—particularly those being inducted into the ranks of middle-class home ownership—must, to some degree, have been aware of the theatrical, artificial nature of the family life. For people who had lived through the Depression and the hardships of World War II, the new consumer dreams must have seemed somewhat synthetic or, at least, unorthodox. Leaving ethnic and working class areas for mass-produced suburbs, these people must have been cognizant of the new roles they were asked to play in a prefabricated social setting" (Spigel 1992, 163).

The paradox of isolation within idyllic suburban communities was particularly difficult for women, and it contributed to the problems of the feminine mystique. A series of magazine ads for silverware named "Community" unironically portrayed this contradiction by commodifying the desire for a sense of community; the ads featured young brides who desired "Community" to make their wedded bliss complete. On *I Love Lucy*, when Lucy and Ricky moved to the Connecticut suburbs in 1956, they found congenial new neighbors, but still missed the Mertzes so much that eventually Fred and Ethel moved into the house next door and they all took up raising chickens. Postwar consumer culture attempted to fill the need for community with the intimacy and immediacy of television and the neighbors on the other side of the "window on the world."

The families portrayed on television modeled an everyday life in which television was an integral part; this self-reflexivity characterized shows like *Lucy, Burns and Allen, The Goldbergs*, and *Ozzie and Harriet*, among others. The self-reflexivity of people on television going on television, or watching television, was a characteristic of the situation comedy in the genre-forming years of 1950–1955. In *I Love Lucy*, this tendency manifested most clearly in the many episodes in which Lucy and Ricky appeared on television, but television also figured prominently as a consumer item. In "The Courtroom," the Ricardos and their neighbors Fred and Ethel Mertz end up in court over damage done to the television the Ricardos gave the Mertzes for their wedding anniversary. In self-reflexive episodes like "Lucy Does a TV Commercial," "Fred and Ricky are TV Fans," "The Million Dollar Idea," "Home Movies," and "Mr. and Mrs. TV Show," televisions and being on television are central to the plot.

Although televisions were a special consumer item, other consumer items propelled conflict and plot. In addition to presenting the Ricardo home (with many items available for purchase), the majority of Lucy's schemes concerned acquiring commodities—a freezer, fur coat, furniture, dresses, washing machines, vacuum cleaner, cars, wigs, pearls, and a twenty-five pound rare Italian cheese that Lucy passes off as a baby—or enough money to buy them. Lucy's material desires get the better of her, and often lead her into more trouble than they could ever be worth. Always sparked by the unequal economic power relation between Ricky and Lucy, Lucy often ended up in a jam because she had already spent her "allowance" and Ricky wouldn't give her the money she wanted.

As Fred Mertz quipped, "When it comes to money, there are two kinds of people: the earners and the spenders. Or as they are more popularly known, husbands and wives." This consumerist ethos of gender, wryly articulated by Fred Mertz (played by William Frawley) in a 1952 episode of *I Love Lucy*, gets a big laugh from the studio audience. The joke recognizes a key facet of postwar ideology, a cluster of ideals and expectations at the crossroads of mainstream representations of gender roles, marriage, domesticity, and consumerism. "People" are divided into two types, each defined by their relationship to mass consumer culture, and that division of labor is sexual. One of the ironies of the postwar era is that the ideology of separate spheres and polarized gender roles was strongest at a time of increasing permeability of the boundaries of those spheres and roles. The promise of the "good life" of home ownership and the exhortation to "Live Like Lucy" often necessitated that women get a paid job in the public sphere, which challenged the gendered separation of the "earners and the spenders."

For good reason, the postwar consumer unit was thought of as the married couple, and in Fred's joke at least, women were responsible (or in Lucy's case irresponsible) for translating the husband's income into commodities. Advertisers had long targeted women as the primary decision makers in consumption, and television, often thought of as a feminized medium, was no exception. As Mary Ann Doane contends, "The increasing appeal in the twentieth century to the woman's role as perfect consumer (of commodities as well as images) is indissociable from her positioning *as* a commodity and results in the blurring of the subject/object dichotomy" (1987, 13).[3] The comedy of *I Love Lucy* draws attention to and, simultaneously, parodies and reifies the veiling of that dichotomy.

A quick analysis of the title of the show demonstrates this conflation. "I" is nominally Ricky, but it also refers to the viewer who, individualized, loves Lucy, too. Lucy is clearly the object of the love, not the subject who loves. By watching the show, the viewer participates in the act of loving Lucy and voyeuristically enjoys the love between Ricky and Lucy, Arnaz and Ball; the viewer also enjoys the advertising presented as entertainment (discussed below).

Love and commodification: these key facets of the Lucy phenomenon are inexorably linked in what historian Carolyn Johnston calls the love *economy*:

> Excluded from most forms of public power until recently, women have primarily operated in the "love economy" of motherhood, housework, and vol-

> untarism; although millions of women have been employed, they have still exercised power only covertly in their homes through emotional and sexual influence. Such covert sexual power relies on persuasion, manipulation, giving and withholding sex; it may be exerted in the nurturing of children and in making men dependent on women for daily needs of all kinds. Sexual power may be used to acquire material possessions, to influence family decisions, and generally get one's way. Covert sexual power works only when it is unseen and undetected, like any subversiveness. (1992, ix)

The love economy fosters women's use of covert tactics, reinforcing woman's place in the private sphere. If husbands are the earners and wives are the spenders, then the only way for women to get their hands on the money necessary to participate in mass consumer culture is through the exercise of covert sexual power, or through circumventing masculine authority, both of which were enacted comically in *I Love Lucy*.

As an influential representation of the love economy, *I Love Lucy* made this self-perpetuating circle of domesticity and female trickery seem cute, essential, even lovable. Everything about the series—the title of the series, the production company name "Desilu," the heart that encloses the names of the stars, the *mise en scène* that creates such a desirable image of "home"—reinscribes the centrality of the couple, the irreducible place of the "love" that motivates Lucy's machinations and Ricky's forgiveness of her covert tactics. That the love economy is part of mass consumer culture is the central tenet of the Lucy phenomenon: a swell of popularity still growing unabated in the realms of syndicated television, the Internet, and the commodity culture of collectibles.

## Making Money

Television in the 1950s was a consumer product for the home and, simultaneously, an advertising showroom for consumer products. Television advertising was especially effective in preselling the brand recognition that resulted in "reflex buying": unplanned purchases that, according to a 1952 NBC report, accounted for one-third of all food purchases, 40 percent of drugstore sales, and half of all nonfood supermarket purchases (Boddy 1990, 157). Television series producer Frederick Ziv illuminated the process: "We did material that would appeal to the broadest segment of the public. And they became the big purchasers of television sets. And as they bought television sets, the beer sponsors began to go on television. And the beer sponsors, for the most part, wanted to reach the truck and taxi driver, the average man and woman" (quoted in Boddy 1990, 72).

Substituting "cigarette" for "beer" in Ziv's statement reveals the bottom-line function of the *I Love Lucy* series: to sell Philip Morris cigarettes.

Television advertising was the perfect medium for small-ticket, everyday items like cigarettes. The marketing director for Johnson Wax Company explained, "The medium is extremely suited to low interest products because it is such an intrusive medium. Products can be injected where they are not wanted—which doesn't sound very moral but which is a fact of life with television. . . . Television is the medium which depends least on consumer cooperation to develop a rich response to symbolic stimulation" (Boddy 1990, 156).

Considering the series *I Love Lucy* as advertisements for cigarettes instead of as a text shifts the meaning we ascribe to *I Love Lucy.* In *fin de millennium* America, on the brink of what might be a post-cigarette culture, the recognition of cigarettes as an ultimate commodity—so addictive, so fetishized, so easily packaged and advertised, such revenue—can color perceptions of the Ball-Arnaz Philip Morris ads with an ironic distance akin to, but far more cynical than, the rhetorical strategies of Nick at Nite. The print ads for Philip Morris featured photographs of Ball and Arnaz smiling, with lit cigarettes in hand; the slogan reads "Smoke for Pleasure *today*—No Cigarette Hangover *tomorrow*!" This and other print ads reinforced the Philip Morris sponsorship that framed the audience's experience of watching the show.

The first episode of the series, aired on October 15, 1951, began with an announcer standing in the Ricardo living room and saying,

> "Good evening and welcome. In a moment we'll look in on Lucille Ball and Desi Arnaz. But before we do that, may I ask you a very personal question? The question is simply this—do you inhale? Well, I do. And chances are you do, too. And because you inhale you're better off—much better off—smoking Philip Morris and for good reason. You see, Philip Morris is the one cigarette proved definitely less irritating, definitely milder than any other leading brand. That's why when you inhale you're better off smoking Philip Morris. . . . And now Lucille Ball and Desi Arnaz in *I Love Lucy.*" (Halberstam 1993, 197–8)

This announcement clouds the boundaries that exist between the sponsor's product, the series, the actors, and the viewing audience. By standing in the living room set, the announcer places himself in the fictional world of the Ricardos, greeting and welcoming the viewer as a guest visiting the Ricardo home, yet his words move out of the fictional set and into "your" living room, as he first allies himself with the viewer ("In a moment *we'll* look in") and then hails the viewer directly with the attention-getting implied dialogue made familiar by radio advertising ("may I ask you a very personal question?"). The rhetorical set-up of the series, then, presents the product, the cigarette advertised with the slogan, "Smoke for Pleasure *today*—No Cigarette Hangover *tomorrow!*" as what is "real," as the ultimate reference point that joins the viewer's everyday experience of smoking with the world of the series.

In addition to the announcer, *I Love Lucy* used animated openings to the series to break down the barriers between the advertising, the diegesis (the fictional world created within the narrative), and the world of the viewing family. The now-familiar satin heart inscribed with "I Love Lucy" and the four stars' names did not appear until 1957, when CBS started to rerun the series and Philip Morris was no longer its sponsor. The heart motif was present from the beginning, but in animated form. The first opening shows the Philip Morris cigarette pack, zooms in on the pack and then to the cigarettes, cuts to the Philip Morris boy dressed in his bellhop uniform, and zooms in on the pack he is holding. Then an animated Lucy, holding her purse (apparently she goes nowhere without it), saunters up to the pack, and spins it around so that it reveals Desi (or Ricky?) in an elevator car. They ride up to the roof of their apartment building and we see a billboard that first reads "Philip Morris presents," then "Lucille Ball and Desi Arnaz," and then a heart drawn around the title, "I Love Lucy." The two stick figures run in front of the billboard, and the show begins. These animated figures also introduced commercials and provided a closing frame at the end of the episode leading to Ball and Arnaz in a heart-shaped frame plugging Philip Morris cigarettes once more.

Every week's episode featured a different opening animated by Gene Hazelton and the Hanna-Barbera unit at MGM,[4] similar to *The Simpsons'* weekly family run to the couch in front of the television set. Lynn Spigel describes the opening of "Lucy Does a TV Commercial" as a particularly good example of how "the sponsor's product literally served as the stage of representation of the narrative" (1992, 168). In this animated opening, the cigarette pack turns into a stage as the two cartoon figures approach it. The cigarette wrapper, which has changed into a curtain, lifts to show Lucy sitting in the Ricardo living room. By blending these different diegetic spaces, the framing device functions to both highlight and dim the boundaries between real life and reel life.

The self-reflexivity does not stop there. The content of the episode "Lucy Does a TV Commercial" that opens with the cigarette pack uncovering Lucy in her living room adds to and complicates the fusion of reality and artifice, and raises questions about the series' portrayal of commodification. "Lucy Does a TV Commercial" plays on the same principle expressed in Lucy's line about Ricky needing a "pretty girl" to advertise the sponsor's product; as usual, Lucy wants to be on television, and Ricky, as usual, wants a wife who just wants to be a wife, but he's got this screwy redhead . . . and this time he comes home and there she is in the television set! Lucy has taken out the TV and, dressed as the Philip Morris boy in a bellhop hat, and holding a pack of Philip Morris cigarettes, mimics the opening of the shows. "Presenting the Lucy Ricardo show!" she exclaims, but not before dropping the pack of cigarettes. She leans out of the television frame to pick them up, and the first principle of *I Love Lucy* is dramatized. Lucy exceeds the boundaries of whatever structure momentarily contains her; she will cajole, impersonate, use "feminine wiles," team up with other women, lie, or steal to get to the goal whose straightforward attainment has been blocked—often but not always—by Ricky. When she reaches out of the television frame, it seems spontaneous, yet the gag has been clearly set up. As always, Ball's physical comedy and timing are brilliant. She pauses long enough for us to get it before completing the gag.

Ricky then enters the frame and there is a power struggle as Lucy tries to continue proving that Ricky should hire her to do the sponsor's commercial for his television show. Ricky picks up the television's electrical plug and, with the logic of the absurd that propels comedy, shocks Lucy when he plugs it in, rapidly ending her presentation. Lucy gets the last laugh, or maybe it is only the butt of the last laugh, depending on the viewer's interpretation of the ambiguous image of Lucy bringing out the dismantled, chaotic guts of the television set she took apart in order to put herself in the console.

This scene offers viewers a parody of television sponsorship. If part of the cultural work of early television was being an advertisement for the spread of television, then this scene advertises advertising. Lucy, the ordinary person who, although untrained and of questionable talent, desires strongly to be in the act, is positioned where the viewer is. Of course Lucy can climb inside the television set in her living room; she's in yours, isn't she? The paradox of this works, as Spigel notes, in two directions that seem antithetical: "On the one hand, self-reflexivity provided viewers with critical distance from everyday life; the ability to laugh at the stagy artifice of domesticity. On the other hand, it encouraged viewers to feel closer to the scene of action, as if they had an intimate connection to the scene" (1992, 165). Similarly, the *mise-en-abyme* of living rooms and Lucys and televisions makes television sponsorship seem both domestic and individualized. Television and commodification are equated, and the advertising is part of the entertainment. As a 1960 NBC audience research report concluded: "The viewer watches commercials in the same way that he watches programs—in fact he looks for the same things in commercials that he seeks in programming. He does *not* think of commercials as something different and apart from programs" (Boddy 1990, 156). The comic intrusion of Lucy Ricardo in Ricky's TV set, in his living room, and in the viewer's TV set and living room dramatizes the commonality between commercial and program. Commodification emerges as the one constant in all the different discursive and diegetic realms.

The scene from "Lucy Does a TV Commercial" also dramatizes Spigel's point about American families making "room for TV." The lines between domestic and theatrical space, between everyday life and artifice, are easily crossed in the Ricardo living room, just as they can be crossed to replace the hearth with the box. The self-conscious recognition that gendered middle-class life is performance, that the standards and values emulated by the "homeward bound" postwar couples necessitated a theater of the domestic, is facilitated by the oscillation between reality and fantasy. The *I Love Lucy* bedroom suites, pajamas, clothes, aprons, and baby bottle bags are the props both the stars and the audience need to make the dramatization real.

In the second half of "Lucy Does a TV Commercial," Lucy does a television commercial, but this time she will be on "real" rather than "pretend" television. Although Ricky had already hired a "pretty girl" for the commercial, Lucy answers the phone when the girl calls and, instead of passing on the message about the time and place of the live broadcast, tells her she's not needed and shows up in her place. This is the set-up for the famous Vitameatavegamin sequence, in which Lucy gets hilariously (and inadvertently) drunk on the tonic that is actually 23 percent alcohol. Rehearsing for the commercial entails drinking spoonful after spoonful of the stuff. The line between the "reality" of the awful taste of the tonic and the scripted reaction of pleasure plays on audience knowledge that advertising is, at best, hyperbole, and at worst, lies. And whatever else is in Vitameatavegamin, the audience knows it's the alcohol that makes this snake oil do its "magic."

Moreover, the connection to tonic swindles is particularly interesting in terms of "the feminine mystique," which provides the context for Lucy's frustrations with domesticity and femininity. "Hello friends. I'm your Vitameatavegamin Girl. Are you tired, run down, listless? Do you poop out at parties? Are you unpopular? The answer to all your problems is in this little bottle." Like the Rolling Stones' "Mother's Little Helper," the only solution Vitameatavegamin provides is to mask the fatigue and dissatisfaction of domestic containment with a drug. Furthermore, Lucy parodies how advertising stimulates demand for the commodities proliferating in mass consumer culture, how television advertising intrudes, asking if you can be asked a "personal question." In the conclusion of the episode, the product, which has caused Lucy to become drunk, leads Lucy to disrupt Ricky's act. She sings and dances along drunkenly, tries to kiss him, embarrassing him as once again she participates in the realm of performance to which she was barred, the public sphere of "show business" she continually crashes.

Of course, the pleasure in this episode, as in all *I Love Lucy* episodes, is the comic climax that showcases Ball's genius at physical comedy to which the show builds. All else is set-up—albeit ideologically revealing set-up—and, as critic Patricia Mellencamp argues, "if Lucy's plots for ambition and fame *narratively* failed . . . *performatively* they succeeded" (1986, 88). We want and need Lucy to "fail" so that Ball can triumph.[5] The secondary texts, such as the many magazine and newspaper stories about Ball, contributed to "Lucy's" embodiment of the contradictions of postwar femininity and commodification. For example, the first in *Cosmopolitan* magazine's series of cover stories on "America's Top Saleswomen" quotes Ball as saying, "I'm just a typical housewife at heart" (Morehead 1953, 19). The conflation of "typical housewife" and "top saleswoman" is emblematic of the way that Lucy and early television obfuscated the lines between fiction and reality, between program and commercial, through commodification. As a trickster in the story cycle of *I Love Lucy*, Lucy called attention to the boundaries of gender roles, of appropriate and inappropriate middle-class behavior. The points at which her escape attempts from domesticity fail disclose the blocks to women's emancipation, and provide a map of the contested terrain on which the battle of the sexes took place in the postwar era. Through the comic bisociation of reality and artifice, of typicality and stardom, of prescriptive definitions of femininity and human ambition, *I Love Lucy* shaped and refracted the context in which American culture redefined ideals of gender in the women's liberation movements of the 1960s and 1970s.

## Lucy Today

*I Love Lucy* not only persists but also reigns in what the cable television channel Nickelodeon calls "TV land." More than other modes of syndicated reruns, Nick at Nite's self-reflexive programming of "classic TV" offers collective memories of American life—misappropriated images of how family life never really was—that we see depicted again and again. Likewise parodic features like the "Why We Watch" spots of the early 1990s with Dr. Will Miller offered up "academic" readings of the television texts that both mock and confirm the idea that television shows are powerful articulations of cultural fears and fantasies. Nick at Nite's recent addition of "retrommercials" also documents the history of commodification at the same time that it perpetuates the blurring of programming and advertising.

Nostalgia and the collector's desire to acquire and own parts of a cultural phenomenon make for a brisk market in Lucy collectibles: memorabilia from Ball's various series, photographs, and the tie-in items. *TV Guide* covers featuring Ball continue to increase in value, and the most valuable *TV Guide* of all, vol. 1, no. 1, has the Ball-Arnaz baby on its cover.[6] A plethora of Lucy merchandise produced today includes greeting cards, videotapes, magnets, t-shirts, posters, ceramic teapots, salt and pepper shakers, and bookends. The Viacom Store in Chicago contains an impressive range of items from the aforementioned stuff to fashionable and pricey clothing items like smoking jackets, aprons, leather jackets, negligees, shirts, and dresses. If it can be thought of, someone somewhere has put Lucy on it, and someone else has bought it. Participation through purchasing, the internal logic of commodity capitalism, prevails in the Lucy merchandising marketplace today as it did in the 1950s: if you "love" it, you want to own it.

Lucy also has found a home in the newest cultural medium: the internet. In the past year, Lucy websites have proliferated. There are episode guides, scanned pictures of private Lucy collections, biographies, sources for videotapes, links to pages that sell Lucy merchandise, homages, a fanclub site, lists of Arnaz's recordings, the original animated *I Love Lucy* opening, and a site for the Lucy-Desi museum.[7] The web seems to have given new life to a growing fan club, whose third annual convention occurred in July 1998. Amid the collectibles, merchandising, public appearances of cast and crew members, and trivia, there was a special session on *My Favorite Husband,* which celebrated its fiftieth anniversary in 1998 by recreating two of the radio segments with a Lucy impressionist and some of the original cast members. All ticket proceeds went to the Elizabeth Glaser Pediatric AIDS Foundation.

Could there be a new market opening up for recreations of aspects of the Lucy phenomenon? There have been rumors that husband and wife Tea Leoni and David Duchovny are interested in doing a new *I Love Lucy* series (and many suggestions online that they leave *Lucy* alone). Universal Studios Hollywood has created "A Tribute to Lucy," a walk-through tourist attraction with footage, memorabilia, a game, and recreations of the *I Love Lucy* set.[8] Will there soon be virtual reality programs so you "really" can live like Lucy? I imagine that into whatever new realms popular culture and commodification take us, Lucy will be there, and for constantly shifting reasons, millions will continue to love Lucy in their hearts, and with their pocketbooks.

## Acknowledgments

I'd like to thank Chris Anderson, David Bogen, and Susan Gubar for insightful feedback on the various stages of my work on the Lucy phenomenon. The *NWSA Journal* readers and editorial staff were also helpful.

## Notes

1. "Bisociation," or the clash between two distinct associative contexts or planes of discourse, is the term coined by Arthur Koestler to describe the

sudden jolt involved in the creation and interpretation of a joke (see Landay 1998, 24–6).

2. In 1954, Philip Morris gave up half the sponsorship of the increasingly expensive show to Procter & Gamble. In 1955, Philip Morris relinquished the sponsorship of *I Love Lucy* because cigarette sales had fallen despite the show's success. Mark Crispin Miller argues that *Lucy* failed to be a profitable advertisement for Philip Morris because the show was "too exciting to complement the ads" (1986, 191). However, the relationship between the show's popularity and the sponsor's product sales—and advertising and television in general—is more complicated. At the end of 1954, *Lucy* had slipped from its top-rated spot to third and then sixth place, but by mid-1955, the Hollywood episodes brought the series back to first place. More importantly for Philip Morris's decision to back out, there was a "cancer scare" that lowered sales, and even Philip Morris's direct appeal to viewers to buy more cigarettes to support the series was ineffective. *Variety* suggested that the Desilu–Philip Morris split was due to "conflict" and "difference of opinion." General Foods picked up Philip Morris's half sponsorship, acting on the industry belief that a family-oriented, domestic show would be more cost-effective for a company that made home-based products (Sanders and Gilbert 1993, 99–102).

3. See Joyrich (1996) for a discussion of this point.

4. The openings are available on the *I Love Lucy* laser disc from Criterion Television Classics, Voyager Catalog # CTC1000L, and on The Toon Tracker Animated Lucy Page (http://members.tripod.com/~mrstoon/lucy.htm).

5. Critic Alexander Doty also discusses this paradox, but in his view, the "tensions between [television character] 'Lucy Ricardo' and [composite film image] 'Lucille Ball' in Ball's televisual star image often threaten to disrupt the series' sitcom characterizations and narrative development" (1990, 4). See also Andrea Press's ethnographic viewer reception study that argues that "the social class of female viewers makes a difference in the way the character of Lucy is perceived. While middle-class women move out of the diegetic space in describing Lucy as a character, working-class women rarely do this" (1991, 134). The ironic, self-reflexive rhetorical contexts provided today by Nickelodeon, merchandising, and nostalgia encourage the current generation of viewers to revel in the unreality appreciated by the middle-class viewers in Press's study and disliked by the working-class viewers. The commodification of Lucy positions viewers as middle class, and thus continues the hegemonic function implicit in its original broadcast. Commodification makes us all middle class.

6. It's hard to think of a better symbol of television's role in the commodification of postwar life than the most famous product of the baby boom, Desi Arnaz Jr., on the cover of the first *TV Guide*, an important source of extratextual knowledge about television schedules and programming.

7. For books about Ball and Arnaz: do an Internet search for *I Love Lucy* and find the hundreds of pages that come up.

8. See www.universalstudios.com/unicity/attractions/lucy.html.

## References


Andrews, Bart. 1985. *The "I Love Lucy" Book*. New York: Doubleday.

Ball, Lucille, with Betty Hannah Hoffman. 1996. *Love, Lucy*. New York: G. P. Putnam's Sons.

Baron-Smith, Camille. 1992. *Enterprising Women: Television Fandom and the Creation of Popular Myth*. Philadelphia: University of Pennsylvania Press.

Bartky, Sandra Lee. 1990. *Femininity and Domination: Studies in the Phenomenology of Oppression*. New York: Routledge.

"Beauty into Buffoon." 1952. *Life*, 18 February , 93–7.

Boddy, William. 1990. *Fifties Television: The Industry and Its Critics*. Urbana and Chicago: University of Illinois Press.

Brady, Kathleen. 1994. *Lucille: The Life of Lucille Ball*. New York: Hyperion.

Chafe, William H. 1991. *The Paradox of Change: American Women in the Twentieth Century*. New York: Oxford University Press.

"Desilu Formula for Top TV: Brains, Beauty, Now a Baby." 1953. *Newsweek*, 19 January, cover, 56–9.

Doane, Mary Ann. 1987. *The Desire to Desire: The Women's Film in the 1940s*. Bloomington and Indianapolis: Indiana University Press.

Doty, Alexander. 1990. "The Cabinet of Lucy Ricardo: Lucille Ball's Star Image." *Cinema Journal* 29:3–22.

Halberstam, David. 1993. *The Fifties*. New York: Fawcett Columbine.

Horkheimer, Max, and Theodor Adorno. (1944) 1995. *Dialectic of Enlightenment*. Trans. John Cumming. Reprinted. New York: Continuum.

Johnston, Carolyn. 1992. *Sexual Power: Feminism and the Family in America*. Tuscaloosa: University of Alabama Press.

Joyrich, Lynne. 1996. *Re-Viewing Reception: Television, Gender, and Postmodern Culture*. Bloomington: Indiana University Press.

Landay, Lori. 1998. *Madcaps, Screwballs, and Con Women: The Female Trickster in American Culture*. Philadelphia: University of Pennsylvania Press.

Lipsitz, George. 1990. *Time Passages: Collective Memory and American Popular Culture*. Minneapolis: University of Minnesota Press.

May, Elaine Tyler. 1988. *Homeward Bound: American Families in the Cold War Era*. New York: Basic Books.

Mellencamp, Patricia. 1986. "Situation Comedy, Feminism, and Freud: Discourses of Gracie and Lucy." In *Studies in Entertainment: Critical Approaches to Mass Culture*, ed. Tania Modleski, 80–95. Bloomington: Indiana University Press.

Miller, Douglas T., and Marion Nowak. 1977. *The Fifties: The Way We Really Were*. Garden City, N.Y.: Doubleday.

Morehead, Albert. 1953. "'Lucy' Ball." *Cosmopolitan*, January, cover, 15–9.

Oppenheimer, Jess. 1953. "Lucy's Two Babies." *Look*, 21 April, 20–4.

Pateman, Carole. 1988. *The Sexual Contract*. Stanford, Calif.: Stanford University Press.

Press, Andrea L. 1991. *Women Watching Television: Gender, Class, and Generation in the American Experience*. Philadelphia: University of Pennsylvania Press.

Sanders, Coyne Steven, and Tom Gilbert. 1993. *Desilu: The Story of Lucille Ball and Desi Arnaz*. New York: William Morrow.

"Sassafrassa, the Queen." 1952. *Time*, 26 May, cover, 62–8.

Silvian, Leonore. 1952. "Laughing Lucille." *Look*, 3 June, 7–8.

Spigel, Lynn. 1992. *Make Room for TV: Television and the Family Ideal in Postwar America*. Chicago: University of Chicago Press.

"There's No Accounting for TV Tastes." 1953. *TV Guide*, 4 September, 20.

# PART II Explicit Selves, Explicit Bodies

CHAPTER SIX

# Fractured Borders: Women's Cancer and Feminist Theater

MARY K. DeSHAZER

> I have stage four metastatic ovarian cancer. There is no stage five. Oh, and I have to be very tough. It appears to be a matter, as the saying goes, of life and death.
>
> —Margaret Edson, *Wit* (1999, 12)

> I am a One-Breasted, Menopausal, Jewish Bisexual Lesbian Mom and I am the topic of our times. I am the hot issue. I am the cover of *Newsweek*, the editorial in the paper. I am a best-seller. And I am coming soon to a theatre near you.
>
> —Susan Miller, *My Left Breast* (1995, 219)

The women's cancer movement is indeed the "topic of our times" after decades—some would say centuries—of silence and denial by many physicians, researchers, and sometimes women themselves. "THE NEW THINKING ON BREAST CANCER," screams the 18 February 2002 cover of *Time* magazine, "The Smartest Drugs/The Gentlest Treatments/The Latest on Mammograms" (Gorman 2002). Inside, the article reports that 200,000 U.S. women will learn each year that they have breast cancer, double the number from 1980. Forty thousand will die from it. The article acknowledges that the American Cancer Society's emphasis on mammograms might have resulted in overdiagnoses, causing thousands of women who might otherwise live long and healthy lives to undergo invasive radiation and chemotherapy treatments for microscopic cancers and even precancerous conditions. The article further claims that Tamoxifen, hailed in the early 1990s as an estrogen-based drug that could both treat breast cancer and reduce the risk of contracting it, may increase the risk of uterine cancer. At the same time, the author hails new research methods in the battle against breast cancer and glibly promises readers "a guide to saving lives" (50).[1]

As media headlines and research technologies have proliferated, so have works of literature by women about their carcinomas. Although breast cancer has attracted the most media attention, women contract the same cancers that men do, as well as a few that are gender-specific. Breast, uterine, and ovarian diseases account for 43 percent of all women's cancers (Proctor 1995); they thus provide the primary subject matter for the hundreds of cancer narratives, memoirs, and poems written by North American women. The late 1970s and 1980s produced such important

Originally published in the Summer 2003 issue of the *NWSA Journal*.

cancer narratives as Rose Kushner's *Breast Cancer* (1975), Betty Rollin's *First, You Cry* ([1976] 2000), Susan Sontag's *Illness as Metaphor* (1977), and Audre Lorde's *The Cancer Journals* (1980). Some of this literature was not feminist; rather, it contributed to what Barbara Ehrenreich describes as an "ultrafeminine" cancer marketplace:

> In the mainstream of breast-cancer culture, one finds very little anger, no mention of possible environmental causes, few complaints about the fact that, in all but the more advanced, metastasized cases, it is the "treatments," not the disease, that cause illness and pain. The stance toward existing treatments is occasionally critical . . . but more commonly grateful; the overall tone, almost universally upbeat. (2001, 48)

Certainly mainstream approaches to cancer literature and activism have been fruitful; they have brought valuable research and federal budget dollars as well as awareness to the cause of women's health. But early feminist approaches to cancer such as Sontag's and Lorde's questioned the equation of illness with femininity and the pathologizing of cancerous bodies; examined the politics of mastectomy, reconstructive surgeries, and prosthesis; and documented the power of feminist communities to resist society's discipline and punishing of ill bodies (Foucault 1977). These narratives thus provided vital critiques of what Ehrenreich terms "the Cancer Industrial Complex" (2001, 52).

The four plays under consideration here—Margaret Edson's *Wit* (1999), Susan Miller's *My Left Breast* (1995), Maxine Bailey and Sharon M. Lewis's *Sistahs* (1998), and Lisa Loomer's *The Waiting Room* (1998)—offer trenchant feminist perspectives on cancer and embodiment. Written and produced in the 1990s, these plays express outrage at the disease and its invasive treatments, examine environmental and cultural factors that may cause cancer, challenge the medical establishment, and foreground links between the personal and the political. In the words of Nancy Datan, a feminist psychologist who died of breast cancer, "It is a central tenet of feminism that women's invisible and private wounds often reflect social and political injustices. It is a commitment central to feminism to share burdens. And it is an axiom of feminism that the personal is political" (Wilkinson and Kitzinger 1994, 124). Theorist and breast cancer survivor Zillah Eisenstein similarly politicizes her mastectomy through a feminist lens: "Feminism's brilliance is found in this recognition that the body is not simply personal, that there is a politics to sex, that personal and political life are intermeshed. . . . Maybe it is this feminist autonomy of the body that has allowed me to live fully without all my body parts" (2001, 3). These plays engage postmodern feminisms as well by interrogating the body's cultural history, exploring such concepts as the politics of appearance, the body in pain, and the privilege of the temporarily able-bodied. Theatrical representations of women's cancer thereby enrich and complicate "our understandings of social justice, subject formation, subjugated knowledges, and collective action" (Garland-Thomson 2002, 1).

The saga of English Professor Vivian Bearing's unsuccessful struggle to overcome advanced ovarian cancer in the face of increasingly invasive medical treatments, *Wit* is the best-known play about a woman's cancer. First performed in 1997 at Long Wharf Theatre in Connecticut, it moved to New York's Union Square Theatre and won the Pulitzer Prize for Drama in 1999. *My Left Breast*, which premiered at Actors Theatre in Louisville in 1994, features a lesbian's account of the effects of her mastectomy on her family and her sense of self. *Sistahs*, first produced at Poor Alex Theatre in Toronto in 1994, explores the nurturing aspects of soup-making and women's friendships for a woman with advanced uterine cancer who has refused further chemotherapy. And *The Waiting Room*, performed in Los Angeles in 1994 at the Mark Taper Forum and in 1996 at the Vineyard Theatre in New York City, spans history and cultures to join women suffering from footbinding in eighteenth-century China, "hysteria" in Victorian England, and breast cancer in the contemporary United States. Two of the protagonists in these plays are lesbians, two are women of color—facts that signify the diversity of feminist perspective and acknowledge the increased risks for African American women and lesbians. As contributors to the women's movement, and as "illness testimonials," such plays constitute "counter-authoritative text[s], a revisionary genre, and a call to activism" (Schmidt 1988, 73).[2]

In offering a feminist analysis of women's performance narratives, I argue that they differ from other cancer narratives in three significant ways. First, these plays employ what Rebecca Schneider has called "the explicit body in performance" to mark women's cancerous breasts, ovaries, and wombs as sites of social meaning that transgress from the "rules" of normative female bodies and convey powerful embodied histories (1997, 2). As Schneider notes, explicit body theater aims to

> explicate bodies in social relation . . . to peel back layers of signification that surround [them] like ghosts at a grave. . . . A mass of orifices and appendages, details and tactile surfaces, the explicit body in representation is foremost a site of social markings, physical parts and gestural signatures of gender, race, class, age, and sexuality—all of which bear ghosts of historical meaning. (2)

Second, women's theatrical narratives challenge the capacity of a spectatorial, consuming "male gaze" to appropriate, fetishize, or otherwise sexualize women's bodies (Mulvey 1975). As the protagonists touch, flaunt, inspect, or bare their bodies in pain, they enact on stage what Schneider describes as "an in-your-face literality, a radical satiability that thwarts the consumptive mantra of infinite desire" (1997, 8). Third, these plays invite empathy and activism on the part of readers/theater-goers by fostering a complex sense of intimacy among playwrights, actors, and audience, each of whom becomes a "penetrating witness to extreme rites" (Renner 1999, 3–4). While women read most cancer literature in private spaces, theater offers a public space at which audiences can reckon with the physical and emotional ravages as well as the politics of the disease. Although voyeurism remains a potential response, feminist performance narratives strive to evoke a "complicit, satiable reciprocity between viewer and viewed rather than the traditional perspectival one-way-street relationship" (Schneider 1997, 8).

In the sections that follow, I explore the diverse representations of *body politics* and *medical politics* in these four plays. An analysis of body politics demonstrates how the protagonists view their breasts, uterus, and ovaries; how they cope with their disease and the accompanying fear, loss, and rage; and how they survive or prepare for their deaths. An exploration of medical politics reveals how the playwrights interrogate the behavior and discourse of medical practitioners and the complex problem of debilitating cancer treatments. In probing how the graphic representations of suffering women, who nonetheless claim agency, provide these works with dramatic urgency, I examine the source and nature of the plays' narrative coherence. As Laura K. Potts has noted, many cancer texts by women follow a formal patterning of structure that she labels the "proairetic code," shaped by such common points of reference as "discovery, diagnosis, decisions about treatment, confronting possible death and life after treatment" (2000, 114)—yet the plays under consideration here tend to depart from this model, and I explore why. Finally, I consider the tension between voyeurism and empathic witness and the forms of reciprocity that audiences may experience while viewing these plays. The ways in which feminist plays about women's cancers can activate their audiences provides a rich area of theoretical exploration.

## Body Politics: From Anguish to Autonomy

> My breast cancer body does not say enough about how other body demands have choreographed my life. Although breast cancer has often suffocated me . . . my body has had other selves. I am never simply my cancer because I have other bodies *and* I am something besides my body struggles.
>
> —Zillah Eisenstein, *Manmade Breast Cancers* (2001, 42)

Feminist theories of the body illuminate theatrical representations of women's cancers by foregrounding the body's materiality, its erotic force, its subjugation, and its politics. In the 1970s and 1980s, French feminist theory offered creative women many reasons to write: to disrupt and subvert patriarchal definitions of "the feminine," to reconstruct a fluid yet forceful female identity, to locate women's subjectivity centrally in the realm of the body. Luce Irigaray (1981) argued that woman's sexuality and creativity emerge through her totality of body, a huge erotic field that brings her *jouissance*—a term that suggests both sexual satisfaction and the pleasure of the written text. The practice of the woman scribe "inscribing woman" Irigaray called *parler femme*, Hélène Cixous *l'écriture féminine* (Cixous and Clément 1975). U.S. feminists inscribed their own bodily manifestoes; Adrienne Rich, for instance, defined the body as "the geography closest in," that territory which women have a right to claim and settle on their own terms (1986, 212). However liberating Rich's metaphor might seem, considering women's embodiment in geographical terms reminds us of how often women's bodies, particularly those of women of color, have been raped, plundered, and colonized. For many women writing the body, autonomy is impossible until violation and its aftermath have been painfully inscribed.[3]

Postmodern theory from the 1990s has demonstrated that raced and gendered bodies are never fixed but ever in process, multiple, contingent, and fluid. This theory posits that since the body is both material and discursive, any feminist understanding of its corporeality must be constantly mediated by its spoken contexts. In Judith Butler's words, "There is no reference to a pure body which is not at the same time a further formation of that body" (1993, 10). How women's bodies have been constructed and politicized, therefore, becomes a central question for contemporary feminism and its textual representations. Indeed, the constructions of gender and embodiment found in women's performance narratives of cancer draw important links between "the everyday body as it is lived, and the regime of disciplinary and regulatory practices that shape its form and behaviour" (Shildrick and Price 1999, 8).

It is with these theoretical contexts in mind that we must consider contemporary playwrights' liberatory strategies for writing about cancer. As Sontag has noted, in traditional literary representations "the person dying of cancer is portrayed as robbed of all capacities of self-transcendence, humiliated by fear and agony" (1977, 17). Feminist dramatists' portrayals of cancer bear the weight of such condescending representations even as they attempt to upend them. They depict the bodily betrayal and suffering of women diagnosed with cancer but present as well their struggles for autonomy, their multiple subjectivities. Furthermore, they often do so with outrageous humor, evoking in audiences astonished laughter, itself a healing force, and employing transgressive discursive strategies to represent cancer. For example, the fact that cancers are diagnosed in stages one through four provides an opportunity for self-referential punning. Edson's protagonist in *Wit* acknowledges this when she explains wryly that "there is no stage five" (12). Similarly, the speaker in Miller's *My Left Breast* foregrounds cancer's pervasiveness with comic irony, claiming that women's cancer is "coming soon to a theatre near you" (219). Such meta-commentary reveals the playwrights' valorization of the power of theater to promote feminist awareness and lead to social change.

The medicalized body is clearly on display in *Wit*, as Vivian Bearing appears on stage emaciated, bald, and hooked up to an intravenous pole. She is eight months into her cancer, hospitalized and terminal; thus the play begins not with her diagnosis, as Potts's proairetic code would dictate, but with the inevitability of her death. As a distinguished scholar of seventeenth-century poetry, however, Vivian remains authoritative; indeed, she couches her cancer confessional in the terms of textual criticism. "*Irony* is a literary device that will necessarily be deployed to great effect," she tells the audience.

> I ardently wish this were not so. I would prefer that a play about me be cast in the mythic-heroic-pastoral mode; but the facts, most notably stage-four metastatic ovarian cancer, conspire against that. *The Faerie Queen* this is not.
>
> And I was dismayed to discover that the play would contain elements of . . . *humor.* I have been, at best, an *unwitting* accomplice. (*She pauses.*) It is not my intention to give away the plot; but I think I die at the end. (6)

In contradiction to the predictable opening of many cancer narratives—a traumatic diagnosis, subsequent despair, and a loss of grounding—Vivian's initial self-presentation exudes confidence. She banters with the audience, acknowledges the dramatic dimensions of her struggle, and employs irony to distance herself from her disease, even as she predicts her imminent demise. Accustomed to scholarly detachment, Vivian remains impassive as she recounts the diagnosis of her "insidious adenocarcinoma" by a physician who, like herself, hides behind a professorial mask. Indeed, they debate the meaning of "insidious," with the surgeon defining it as undetectable at the source, the patient as "treacherous" (8).

As the disease progresses and the treatment fails to provide a cure or eliminate her pain, Vivian uses irony as a shield: "One thing can be said for an eight-month course of cancer treatment: it is highly educational. I am learning to suffer" (31). Ultimately, however, she reveals her vulnerability, as she moves from discomfort to agony:

> Yes, it is mildly uncomfortable to have an electrocardiogram, but the . . . agony . . . of a proctosigmoidoscopy sweeps it from memory. Yes, it was embarrassing to have to wear a nightgown all day long—two nightgowns!—but that seemed like a positive privilege compared to watching myself go bald. . . . Oh, God. . . . Oh, God. It can't be. (32)

A former healthcare worker in a hospital cancer unit, Edson refuses to downplay the anguish of the dying patient. As Vivian's condition deteriorates, her doctor's initially inane question—"Dr. Bearing, are you in pain?"—becomes cruel:

> Vivian: (*Sitting up, unnoticed by the staff*) Am I in pain? I don't believe this. Yes, I'm in goddamn pain. (*Furious*) I have a fever of 101 spiking to 104. And I have bone metastases in my pelvis and both femurs. (*Screaming*) There is cancer eating away at my goddamn bones, and I did not know there could be such pain on this earth. (71)

This play is not for the squeamish; Vivian does not mince words about her misery. Indeed, Edson herself has described *Wit* as "ninety minutes of suffering and death, mitigated by a pelvic exam and a lecture on seventeenth-century poetry" (Zinman 1999, 25). Moreover, Vivian's suffering is psychological as well as physical, since she faces her cancer alone.

Like *Wit*, *Sistahs* violates the proairetic code by skipping over the cancer patient's discovery and diagnosis. This play, too, features a professor with metastatic cancer who is grappling with her own death; however, Sandra Grange-Mosaku teaches history, not English, and her cancer is uterine rather than ovarian. "I carry my story in my womb," she admits in the play's initial scene. "Most women do, but not all" (4). In contrast to the friendless Vivian Bearing, Sandra boasts a kitchen full of loving friends as well as an attentive female partner and a concerned, if truculent, teenaged daughter. The presence of these supporters is insufficient, however, to quell Sandra's wrath at the ravages of her disease, a wrath that she unleashes on her loved ones when they fail to adhere to her script for preparing West Indian soup and making peace with one another:

> You couldn't make an effort to get along this one time? A lot to handle? I wanted a dinner, one dinner with the people that I care about. Try waking up each morning, deciding whether or not to be drugged up, or sit with the pain all day. Getting needles stuck in you. It took me three hours to get off the bed this morning. A lot to handle? Fuckery! Pure fuckery running through my blood. (47)

Like Vivian, Sandra rages at the attack of her body by renegade cells and at her subsequent loss of control. As she stirs the soup, blood runs between her legs, forcing her to change her skirt and hide the ruined garment so that her daughter will not see. Although Sandra initially feels humiliated—the female body, after all, has been culturally constructed as "unpredictable, leaky, and disruptive" and therefore shameful—she finds comfort in the soothing touch of her sister (Shildrick and Price 1999, 2). Nonetheless, both cancer patients find appalling the invasion of their bodies: having destroyed her ovaries, cancer "eats away" at Vivian's bones; it "runs through" Sandra's blood and assaults her womb—insistent, ghastly.

Both Sandra in *Sistahs* and Vivian in *Wit* employ battle imagery, a conventional cancer trope, and each woman perceives herself as losing the contest. Although Sontag has justly critiqued the oppressive use of battle metaphors in medical discourse (1977, 68–71), in feminist performance narratives such metaphors can be liberatory—perhaps because the spectacle of ill women angrily resisting bodily appropriation has been so rarely visible. Sandra approaches her defeat head-on and blames herself for having misplaced her rage and striking her daughter:

> I lost my temper. I lost control. Casualties. I lost control of the situation. . . . I've LOST! This war. Fighting, and trying to control my child. I've hit her. Fighting. This gift from my womb, and . . . this thing in my womb. I have done something terrible. (48)

Both the violence of "this thing in [her] womb" and her own internal violence horrify Sandra. Vivian, in contrast, is a measured combatant who initially claims to be destined for fame, if not victory, by "distinguishing [her]self in illness." Yet she realizes that becoming the subject of a scholarly article in a medical journal does not prevent her objectification:

> I have survived eight treatments of Hexamethophosphacil and Vinplatin at the *full* dose, ladies and gentlemen. I have broken the record. I have become something of a celebrity.
>
> But I flatter myself. The article will not be about *me*, it will be about my ovaries. It will be about my peritoneal cavity, which, despite their best intentions, is now crawling with cancer. (53)

Such are the fears of many women cancer patients on and offstage: that they have become merely the sum of their body parts, and of parts that fail to comprise a whole. They feel no longer themselves, indeed, no longer human. "What we have come to think of as *me*," Vivian muses, "is, in fact, just the specimen jar, just the dust jacket, just the white piece of paper that bears the little black marks" (53).

Despite this apparent loss of autonomy, both Vivian in *Wit* and Sandra in *Sistahs* experience a transformation that allows them, at least in part, to reclaim their intellectual and bodily selves. It is significant that Edson and co-authors Bailey and Lewis create characters that are university professors, since in their subject matter lie the protagonists's intellectual passion and life's meaning. In retrospective scenes in which each woman lectures to a roomful of engaged, if mystified, students, these playwrights offer insights that characterize their philosophical vision. Edson has claimed that *Wit* is "about redemption"; for Vivian, the vehicle of redemption is John Donne's poetry, with its emphasis on paradox and its intricate punctuation: "And Death—*capital* D—shall be no more—*semicolon*! Death—*capital* D—*comma*—thou shalt die—*exclamation point*!" As Vivian's graduate school mentor, the renowned scholar E. M. Ashford, explicated the poem years earlier, life and death exist on a continuum; what divides the two states of being are "not insuperable barriers, not semicolons, just a comma"—a belief to which the dying Vivian holds tenaciously (14–5). For Sandra, the possibility of redemption is cultural rather than individual. In her classes she lectures on the horrible realities of slavery—"the middle passage . . . the surgical removal of female reproductive organs" (24)—topics that evoke her racial history as well as the loss of her own uterus to a different invading force. But she also teaches her students about cultural survival by urging them to redefine family—not as a patriarchal unit but as "a recipe to survive genocide" (38).

Both Vivian and Sandra find a reconciled peace, and in each woman's transformation her body figures prominently. Near the end of *Sistahs*, Sandra asks her partner Dehlia, her sister Rea, and her friend Cerise to care for her daughter, Assata, after Sandra's death. However, the play's denouement focuses not on her demise but on the healing properties of the communal soup. "It's alchemy," claims Dehlia; "it's magic," intones Rea. "It's voodoo," insists Cerise; "it's Obeah," chimes Assata. "It's soup," concludes Dehlia, demystifying the healing brew that Sandra has requested. "Sistahs" is the last word Sandra utters, naming the source of the strength she conjures, even as her body continues to suffer. "Sandra *doubles over in pain,*" proclaims the final stage direction. "*Lights come down onstage*" (61). This stage direction undermines the potentially transcendent discourse of healing potions, since Sandra's leaky body continues to cause her agony. Yet in doubling over—enfolding her wounded belly—she affirms the resilience of still-living flesh, a site of power for African women ravaged by disease or cultural genocide. As Bibi Bakare-Yusuf notes, because African women during slavery often perceived their flesh as their own, "hidden from the violations of the body," the embrace of one's own flesh can serve as a liberatory gesture for postcolonial women (1999, 321). As a source of "counter-memory" and strength, flesh "retrieves, recovers the memory of the body's capacity for resistance, for transformation, for healing" (321).

*Wit* ends with Vivian's death and one final violation, as doctors attempt to resuscitate her, and in so doing ignore her request that no life-prolonging treatment be administered. Despite this ultimate invasion, Edson preserves her protagonist's dignity. As the doctors recognize their error and grapple with possible repercussions, the dying Vivian rises from her hospital bed, "*attentive and eager, moving slowly toward the light.*" The stage directions reveal that as Vivian strips off the cap that hid her baldness and the bracelet that provided her hospital name and number, she is luminous, in control of her body and its movements, whole:

(*She loosens the ties and the top gown slides to the floor. She lets the second gown fall. The instant she is naked, and beautiful, reaching for the light—Lights out*). (85)

This nude, ghostly Vivian "doubles back" to reveal an absent presence, a transgressive strategy that is characteristic of explicit body performance. According to Schneider, "the subject returns for a second time in relation to its own death, as if beside itself . . . exposing the historical mechanisms of a social drama which has parsed its players, by bodily markings, into subjects and objects" (1997, 180–1). As Vivian, newly dead, moves toward the light, she assumes what Schneider calls "the guise of subjectivity," an uncanny "second sight/site" (180).

*My Left Breast* and *The Waiting Room*, both of which address breast cancer, also move between anguish and autonomy. In *My Left Breast* the narrator, Susan, has lived for more than a decade since her mastectomy, though she is aware that she might not remain cancer-free. In *The Waiting Room*, Wanda flaunts her prosthetic body, especially her enormous breasts, the products of cosmetic surgery, until she learns that a faulty implant may have caused or hidden an incipient cancer. While her diagnosis is unnerving and several lymph nodes are involved, Wanda grapples with the tough decision of conventional versus alternative treatment, not with the immanence of her death. Controlling one's own body, rather than confronting death, constitutes the dominant motif in these two plays. Both plays disrupt the proairetic code, however, by denying the closure that reconstructive surgery or even death provides.

The celebratory tone of *My Left Breast* is evident when the play begins, as Susan comes out dancing. Indeed, her liberated movement mirrors her frank speech, as she confronts the audience immediately with the reality of her amputated body through a defiant juxtaposition of a "real" and a prosthetic breast: "The night I went to the hospital, that is what I did. I danced. (*Indicates breasts*) One of these is not real. Can you tell which?" (214). Later she shows the audience her prosthesis, using it to expound upon the commercial spectacle and emotional vulnerability of cancer patients:

> Don't worry. It's a spare. When you go for a fitting, you can hear the women in the booths. Some of them have lost their hair and shop for wigs. Some are very young and their mothers are thinking: why didn't this happen to me, instead? (215)

Contrasted with the insistent presence of the prosthesis is the poignant absence of the breast itself—an absence the protagonist notes but refuses to find mournful. Like Eisenstein, who claims herself as "something besides my body struggles" (2001, 42), Miller's speaker defines her missing breast as beloved but expendable:

> I miss it but it's not a hand. I miss it but it's not my mind. I miss it but it's not the roof over my head. I miss it but it's not a sentence I can't live without. I miss it but it's not a conversation with my son. It's not my courage or my lack of faith. (215)

In addition to assertions of bodily autonomy, Miller foregrounds the epidemic of breast cancer, thus politicizing her play overtly. Specifically, Miller's narrator challenges two cultural stereotypes: that women's illnesses matter little in light of AIDS and that women who contract breast cancer somehow bring it on themselves. Regarding the first stereotype, it is useful to contextualize Miller's play in an early 1990s timeframe, when breast cancer research dollars were sorely lacking and activists yearned to have physicians and government leaders use the term "epidemic" as a measure of public accountability comparable to that which AIDS was finally receiving. The tensions that occurred between certain lesbian and gay male health activists are reflected in this monologue:

> A man I know said to me, Lesbians are the chosen people these days. No AIDS. I said, Lesbians are women.
>
> Women get AIDS. Women get ovarian cancer. Women get breast cancer. Women die. In great numbers. In the silent epidemic. He said, I see what you mean. (218)

In a play characterized by rapid-fire monologues, this passage stands out for its staccato language and strategic repetition. Susan unpacks two false assumptions: that lesbians are not "real women," and that women, lesbians included, are less vulnerable to fatal diseases than men are.

The second cultural stereotype, that women cause their own cancers by living unhealthily or internalizing their emotions, also enrages Miller's protagonist. Debunking this stereotype lets Miller critique a variety of social ills: violence against women everywhere; racism in nineteenth-and early-twentieth-century America; ethnic cleansing in Bosnia, Somalia, the Middle East, and Cambodia. She therefore offers not the liberal feminist perspective of Edson and Bailey and Lewis but a global feminist perspective that links the women's cancer movement to other struggles for human rights.

> There are those who insist that certain types of people get cancer. So I wonder, are there certain types of people who get raped and tortured? Are there certain types who die young? Are there certain types of Bosnians, Somalians, Jews? . . . Is there a type of African American who is denied, excluded, lynched? Were the victims of the Killing Fields people who couldn't express themselves? Are one out of eight women—count 'em, folks—just holding onto their goddamned anger? (219)

Susan's use of urgent repetition, rhetorical questions, and direct challenge to the audience reveals her outrage at the presumption of a "blame the victim" mentality.

This emphasis on global feminist politics in *My Left Breast* intersects powerfully with the experience of one woman, Susan, who recognizes that her body carries political as well as personal signification: "This is my body—where the past and the future collide. This is my body. All at once, timely. All at once, chic" (219). Both grateful for societal recognition and resentful of her commodification, Susan determines to display her body on her own terms. The primary insignia of Susan's newfound subjectivity is her mastectomy scar, which serves as an erogenous zone and a marker of survival. The amputated breast thus becomes not a site of marginalization due to its difference from the normate body, but instead a site of pleasure and power. Indeed, a prominent theme in both *My Left Breast* and *The Waiting Room* is the effect of cancer on women's sexuality and body image. For Miller's protagonist, the loss of her breast pales next to the loss of her lover, Franny, which occurs not because of Susan's cancer but because their relationship is long-distance and troubled. A recurring erotic memory for the bereft Susan involves the sexualization of her scar: "Skinnied on the left side like a girl, I summon my breast and you there where it was with your mouth sucking a phantom flutter from my viny scar" (215). At the end of the play, when Susan has healed from the shock of her cancer and the end of her relationship, she reinvokes her scar, this time as "a mark of experience" to be "cherished":

> It's the history of me, a permanent fix on the impermanence of it all. A line that suggests that I take it seriously. Which I do. . . . There is no other sign on my body that repeats the incongruity and dislocation, the alarm. A scar is a challenge to see ourselves as survivors, after all. Here is the evidence. The body repairs. And the human heart, even after it has broken into a million pieces, will make itself large again. (236)

Such capacity for regeneration provides hope for all women with cancer, to whom Susan refers metonymically as "the women in the changing booths." Her message to them is simple but profound: "we are still beautiful, we are still powerful, we are still sexy, we are still here" (236). To document her/their resistant subjectivity, Susan opens her shirt and reveals her mastectomy scar.

*The Waiting Room* interweaves the cancer motif with feminist themes of sexuality and autonomy. As the play opens, three women meet in a doctor's clinic: Forgiveness from Heaven, an eighteenth-century Chinese woman whose bound feet have become infected; Victoria, a nineteenth-century Englishwoman seeking treatment for "shrunken" ovaries; and Wanda, a modern American woman whose breast implants are malfunctioning. None of these women initially claims bodily autonomy. Forgiveness and Victoria are bound by the judgments of their husbands: the apologetic Forgiveness would like to wash her stinking feet, "but my husband, he's crazy for the smell" (14); the corseted Victoria enjoys romantic novels but has been forbidden to read them, since her husband thinks that reading causes ovarian atrophy. Wanda at first appears to be independent; she is single, flamboyant, mouthy. As she confesses to her nurse, Brenda, however, Wanda received silicone breast implants for her thirtieth birthday as a gift from her father and has since had plastic surgery on everything else: nose, chin, cheekbones, stomach, thighs. Thus, Loomer conflates history to satirize patriarchal control of women's bodies across time and cultures, as well as women's complicity in the multibillion-dollar beauty industry.

With the support of Brenda, however, Wanda approaches her biopsy and cancer on her own terms. In scene nine of Act I, Brenda uses humor to calm Wanda's fears: "We don't even know you got cancer. Where you goin' get cancer? You don't have a single body part that's real" (40). Those silicone body parts, of course, are the *cause* of Wanda's cancer, diagnosed in Act II, scene iv, as a malignant tumor so large that lumpectomy is not an option; only mastectomy will suffice. In the recovery room after surgery, Wanda appears to have accepted the recommended treatment passively. When Victoria asks how she's doing, she replies: "I don't know. I guess that's for the doctor to say. They took a—they took my breast. . . . And my tits, of course. . . . And they took some lymph nodes to see if they're . . . 'clear'" (60). The repetition of "they took" illustrates Wanda's lack of agency, intensified by the fact that the pronoun "they" has no clear antecedent and "took" bears the connotation of theft. But when her doctor later reports on Wanda's "bad" lymph nodes and recommends aggressive chemotherapy, she refuses both his condolences and his treatment: "Don't be sorry, doc. 'Cause you're not shooting me up with a goddamn thing" (64). From telephone calls to her insurance agent and her boss at work, she has learned that her surgery isn't covered and her job is no longer hers; from Brenda she has learned about alternative cancer treatments available in Mexico. What she *can* control, Wanda finally determines, is the body that her cancer inhabits: "This cancer is . . . mine. For better or worse, till death do us part, it's about the one thing I got left that's all—mine. And if I want to take it to Tijuana or Guadafucking-lajara—I've never been out of the tri-state area!" Although her defiance diminishes as Wanda realizes the enormity of her plight, she continues to assert that "it's MY BODY! MINE" (70)!

Even feminist theater, however, does not escape entirely the cultural edict that cancer is the female patient's fault—that she ate too much or too little, neglected to seek medical care or sought the wrong kind. In all four plays the protagonists blame themselves, at least momentarily, for their cancer. Vivian, in *Wit,* blanches when she admits to Jason, her intern, that she drinks "two . . . to six" cups of coffee daily: "But I don't really think that's immoderate." She responds more defensively when he inquires how often she has had "routine medical checkups":

> VIVIAN: Well, not as often as I should, probably, but I've felt fine, I really have.
> JASON: So the answer is?
> VIVIAN: Every three to . . . five years. (26)

Sandra in *Sistahs* laments the time she spends "cursing myself each day for not being more careful," although she fails to explain in what way she has been careless (56). Wanda in *The Waiting Room* implies that her "lousy screwed up life" has led her to the operating table (70). Even Susan in *My Left Breast,* arguably the most feminist of these protagonists, infuses her probe of environmental causes with an implicit self-critique:

> When I was pregnant, I took something called Provera. Later it was shown to cause birth defects. So, when I got breast cancer I wondered, was it the time someone sprayed my apartment for roaches? Or too much fat in my diet? Was it the deodorant with aluminum, or my birth control pills? Or was it genetic? (228)

That such anguished questions abound among women diagnosed with cancer, on stage or in life, is undeniable. As Lorde has noted, however, blaming cancer patients for their illness is "a monstrous distortion of the idea that we can use our strengths to help heal ourselves" (74–5). Unfortunately, these otherwise feminist playwrights at times perpetuate that distortion, although Miller counters it more effectively than do the others.

Nonetheless, these dramatic representations of women's cancers successfully foreground four transgressive forms of embodiment that reveal women's ill bodies as disciplined but not subjugated—as subjected to the "stare" that tracks disabled persons but is not undone by it (Garland-Thomson 1997). The *medicalized* body, most notably Vivian's in *Wit,* experiences poisonous treatments and public violations, but resists appropriation. The *leaky* body, exemplified by Sandra's in *Sistahs,* spurts bloody fluids at embarrassing moments yet asserts authority through its flesh. The *amputated* body, particularly Susan's in *My Left Breast,* speaks through its scar, the lost breast mourned but lovingly re-membered. And the *prosthetic* body, exemplified by Wanda's in *The Waiting Room,* embraces contradiction, "posthuman" in its alienation from itself but powerful in its hybridity (Herndl 2002, 150–1). Ultimately these protagonists insist on self-determination, if not self-healing. They break silence about their illnesses, assume the right to control their bodies, live with missing breasts and wombs, or die with dignity. Embodying cancer on stage, they "take the power of words, of representation, into their own hands" (Friedman 1988, 91).

## Medical Politics: Contested Sites of Meaning

> The body and the *identity* of the woman with breast cancer become contested sites of meaning between the hegemony of the discourse of medical practice and her own sense of the disease and her relationship to it, the meaning she generates through the process.
>
> —Laura K. Potts, *Ideologies of Breast Cancer* (2000, 117)

The authors of these four plays offer a profound indictment of callous physicians, hospital personnel, and pharmaceutical companies. These professionals are typically represented as inept or arrogant—at best, uncomprehending of women cancer patients' fears and needs; at worst, dismissive of them. Nurses (who are all women in these plays) generally fare better than doctors (who are almost all men), though occasionally a doctor is presented as empathic. Not only do nurses give care and comfort to the traumatized women, they often question the physicians' ethics and defy their orders. Yet even nurses are sometimes represented as apathetic or abusive. As their primary recourse, the protagonists struggle to comprehend and acquire a complex, ominous, and closely guarded medical vocabulary. These women work to bridge the gap between what Potts calls "the hegemony of the discourse of medical practice" and their own comprehension of their disease (2000, 117). In the doctor's office or the hospital room, they often suffer physical, verbal, and psychological indignities. Moreover, they face invasive treatments with painful side effects and uncertain outcomes rivaling the malignancy of the cancer itself. At times they experience or resist the disposition of their bodies for medical experimentation. Consequently, these cancer patients challenge the medical establishment even as they envision little alternative to seeking its assistance.

Both *Sistahs* and *My Left Breast* contain pivotal scenes in which the protagonist questions the effectiveness of her prescribed treatment. *Sistahs* explores Sandra's reasons for rejecting further treatment once chemotherapy and radiation have failed to prevent metastasis. This exploration occurs primarily through the tension that exists between Sandra and her frightened daughter, who desperately wants her mother to resume treatment. When Sandra complains about weariness and asks Assata to do more housework, her daughter rages: "Well maybe you wouldn't be so tired if you would go back to the doctor and get that stupid ciscarbplaytane" (7). Sandra's only response is to implore Assata to "make peace" with her. Later in the play, when the angry daughter accuses her mother of a defeatist attitude, Sandra's sister echoes her niece's criticism: "The last time we talked, Sandy, I thought you were trying alternative methods; now it seems you're not trying anything" (44). Impervious to such attempts at intervention, however, Sandra stands her ground. When Assata inquires a final time why her mother is "giving up," Sandra claims her right to protect her body from further invasion:

> I'm not, Assata. I'm fighting with everything I have left. Cutting and more cutting until there is nothing left of my womb. Three years of cutting and slicing, and pricking and burning. . . . It didn't feel like *my* body anymore. So many things in my life have been beyond my control. *I'm* doing the . . . cutting, chopping, and slicing. With help from my daughter. (56)

Ultimately Assata comes to accept, if not understand, her mother's reasons for facing her death unimpeded by medical intervention.

In *My Left Breast* the condemnation of inadequate medical personnel is overt. Early in the play Susan recounts implacably one doctor's misdiagnosis of benign fibroadenoma and her initial acceptance of that diagnosis. Months later and in pain, she seeks an opinion from a second physician, who biopsies her breast and confirms that she has cancer. Mistakes she can tolerate, but Susan is moved to resist what she perceives as malice:

> There were two positive nodes. I went through eleven months of chemotherapy and I had only one more month to go. But at my next to the last treatment, after they removed the IV, the oncologist and his nurse looked at me with what I distinctly recognized as menace. I thought, they're trying to kill me. If I come back again, they'll kill me. I never went back. (219)

Although some might describe Susan's reaction as paranoid, her act of resistance has worked to her benefit, since she has survived for twelve years without a recurrence of her cancer.

Susan's survival, however, occurs at the cost of her bones. Thrown into early menopause by estrogen-depriving chemotherapy, she develops osteoporosis in her thirties and is driven to consult a bone specialist whom she detests. The subsequent consultation scene reveals Miller's frustration at the imperiousness of some physicians, the imprecision of their treatments, and the economic injustices of the breast cancer industry:

> "Here are your choices," the bone specialist in L.A. said. "Pick one. A shot every day of Calcitonin, which costs a fortune. I wouldn't do it. Etidronate, which can cause softening of the bones. Or Tamoxifen, an antiestrogen that acts like an estrogen."
>
> I really hate this arrogant, out of touch, son of a bitch specialist, you know? But my internist concurs, and him I love. So, I take the Tamoxifen.
>
> Side effects: Increase in blood clots, endometrial cancer, liver changes. (229)

While Susan's worst side effect from the Tamoxifen is aching ovaries, her ribs continue to fracture when she maintains the prescribed exercise regimen. Hence, she consults a gerontologist and experiences this "gracious woman" as impatient and incompetent. "Tired of hearing me whine," Susan explains, the doctor asks her patient to experiment: "All right, look, I know this sounds like I'm waffling, but I think I want to put you on Etidronate. . . . We'll follow you closely for a year" (229–30). Although Susan takes the prescription, she decides not to fill it, having maintained little confidence in medical authority.

As might be expected since they take place in hospital settings, *Wit* and *The Waiting Room* provide especially ferocious interrogations of medical politics and women's cancers. Unlike *Sistahs* and *My Left Breast*, whose casts are women only, *Wit* and *The Waiting Room* feature male doctors and researchers whose own words and actions call their motives into question. Jason, the self-absorbed resident who treats Vivian Bearing at the teaching hospital where she is a patient, has a laughable bedside manner. "Why don't you, um, sort of lie back, and—oh—relax," he urges Vivian, as if women whose feet are in stirrups can ever relax (28). Their doctor-patient relationship is further complicated by the fact that he was her student just a few years ago. "Yes," Vivian assures the audience, "having a former student give me a pelvic exam was thoroughly degrading—and I use the term deliberately" (32). No longer in awe of his teacher, Jason uses her body as a text, pointing to various parts and speaking to medical students about and over her still form. Vivian recognizes the irony of her situation. "They read me like a book," she tells the audience during one all-too-public medical exam. "Once I did the teaching, now I am taught" (37).

In his lectures, moreover, Jason employs medical jargon designed to exclude the layperson. The medication Vinplatin becomes "Vin," tumors are "de-bulked," patient charts are "I & O sheets" (36–7, 47). Vivian, however, refuses to be excluded: "My only defense is the acquisition of vocabulary" (44). As illustration, she riffs on the medical term "neutropenia," likening it to a series of philosophical words on which *she* is the expert: "ratiocination, concatenation, coruscation, and tergiversation"—terms that connote a movement from logical reasoning to glittering insight to strategic evasion. Surely words in "Cancerland" are often used to obfuscate rather than to clarify, as Vivian is fully aware.

Edson uses the technique of simultaneous discourse to give Vivian's voice equal weight to the voices of her doctors. On stage, Vivian often muses aloud as Jason and her other physician, Dr. Kelekian, instruct their students. Stage directions reveal that the men's words are "barely audible," though their gestures are clear; Vivian's words provide an authoritative voiceover:

VIVIAN: "Grand Rounds." The term is theirs. Not "Grand" in the traditional sense of sweeping or magnificent. Not "Rounds" as in a musical canon, or a *round* of applause (though either would be refreshing at this point). Here, "Rounds" seems to signify darting around the main issue . . . which I suppose would be the struggle for life . . . *my* life . . . with heated discussions of side effects, other complaints, additional treatments.

JASON: Very late detection. Staged as a four upon admission. Hexamethophosphacil with Vinplatin to potentiate. Hex at 300 mg. per meter squared. Vin at 100. Today is cycle two, day three. Both cycles at the *full dose.* (*The* FELLOWS *are impressed.*) The primary site is—*here (He puts his finger on the spot on her abdomen)*, behind the left ovary. Metastases are suspected in the peritoneal cavity—here. (36)

Vivian does not lie in silence as she is displayed and probed, nor does she fail to note the competitive atmosphere that Jason's classroom manner fosters—partly because she recognizes it as a style she once employed with her own students. "Full of subservience, hierarchy, gratuitous displays, sublimated rivalries," she observes of her physician's performance; "I feel right at home. It is just like a graduate seminar" (37).

Although Vivian identifies to some degree with Jason's pedagogical pretensions, Edson ultimately presents this young physician not merely as arrogant but as irresponsible. He consistently privileges his own career goals over Vivian's care and rights, an attitude that costs him dearly when he calls in an emergency team to revive the dying woman, having ignored the fact that she has signed a "Do Not Resuscitate" (DNR) order. When the nurse grabs Jason and shouts, "She's DNR!" the doctor shoves her away: "She's Research" (85)! Thus Edson dramatizes the extent to which the cancer patient risks becoming dehumanized in the modern teaching hospital. The Code Team whom Jason erroneously summons, however, hold him responsible for his mistake: "It's a doctor fuckup.—What is he, a resident?" As the dying Vivian leaves her bed, "naked, and beautiful," Jason laments, "Oh, God"—bemoaning not her death but the blemish on his record (85).

The objectifying characters in *The Waiting Room* include Douglas, a surgeon who is "excellent with bodies, and befuddled by the people who inhabit them"; Larry, the vice-president of a drug company and board member of the cancer center where Douglas works; and Ken, a Food and Drug Administration (FDA) official described as "a scientist turned bureaucrat" (7). Loomer uses ironic dialogue to reveal these men's condescension toward cancer patients. "You know how vulnerable these people are—they're like children," claims Larry to Ken (47). She also exposes the men's unwillingness to acknowledge flaws in their treatment methods, their dismissal of alternative treatments, and their complicity in a multibillion-dollar cancer industry. Of the four playwrights under consideration, only Loomer takes on the FDA and the pharmaceutical companies, and she does so with a vengeance. In Act I, scene ii, for example, Wanda explains to Douglas that her breast implants have malfunctioned: "The foam broke down. The casing hardened. It's funny, I can keep a couch six years, I can't keep a pair of tits six months" (17). Unmoved by her attempts to use self-deprecating humor as a relaxation tool, the doctor replies by spouting the party line: "Well, the FDA believes there is not enough evidence to justify having silicone implants removed if the woman is not having symptoms" (18). When Wanda expresses relief that her implants are not harming her, however, Douglas acknowledges that "unfortunately, there is no sure way to monitor for bleed, leakage, rupture" (18). Women and their physicians must obey FDA guidelines, he insists, even if those guidelines are potentially harmful.

Another political topic on which Loomer focuses is the FDA's refusal to make a successful Jamaican-based cancer treatment, Carson's serum, available to patients in the United States. Although Douglas's nurse, Brenda, who is from Jamaica, attests to the viability of this serum, the male researchers dismiss her as an unreliable source. Several scenes in the play take place in the steam room of a local health club, where Douglas, Larry, and Ken are pampered by Asian women they call "hon" and where they discuss the latest clinical trials. To his credit, Douglas hopes that his hospital will test the serum, given its success rates in Jamaica; Larry, however, prefers another drug:

> LARRY: Well, I love Jamaica . . . (*Lightly*) And you know, from what I've heard, Carson's serum isn't really all that different from INT-2, which Jones Pharmaceuticals is working on at Smith Memorial right now. And doing quite well with actually.
> DOUGLAS: But INT-2 is toxic, isn't it?
> LARRY: All drugs have side effects—
> DOUGLAS: Not Carson's serum apparently.
> LARRY: (*Elbows Douglas*) According to your nurse?
> DOUGLAS: The girl's had two years of medical school, Larry.
> LARRY: You boning her?
> DOUGLAS: Am I—? No. I just thought it would be interesting for us to give this a try, Larry. And I'd think you'd be interested too, as a member of the board of Smith Memorial . . . if not as a vice president of Jones Pharmaceuticals—which stands to make a killing on INT-2. (32–3)

The playwright uses Douglas to unmask the real reason Larry resists allowing clinical trials of Carson's serum: it is not to his economic advantage. We later learn that the FDA resists it too, on the grounds that the serum is "unproven." Furthermore, the above scene reveals that if Douglas takes his nurse seriously, he must be sleeping with her—or so runs patriarchal logic.

Ironically, Nurse Brenda emerges as Loomer's spokesperson on behalf of economic justice and fairness in research of women's cancer. Brenda's case in point regarding the viability of Carson's serum is her own mother in Jamaica, as she later explains to Douglas: "My mother . . . got cancer. And she couldn't scare it away. Hmmmm-hmmmm. Doctors took a breast; it jumped to the other one. They took that, it jumped to the bones. Like a lizard with little feet. Quick little fucker. Doctors chasing it all over her body." Thanks to Carson's serum, however, she is doing well, "back at work cleaning houses" (42). Such testimonials have little impact, however. In Act II, scene iv, an enraged Brenda, frustrated by the intransigence of the doctor for whom she works, exposes his motive:

> BRENDA: (*Quietly.*) Maybe you good people just don't want to fix cancer. Maybe there's a cancer industry out there and it does not want to die. After all, no one is in business for their health.
>
> DOUGLAS: (*Voice rising*) Oh fine. Now we are getting hysterical.
>
> BRENDA: I am a hysterical woman, Douglas—I'm *stressed*!—forty-six thousand women died last year—we don't even put their names on a quilt! (58)

Traditionally considered a sickness of the womb, hysteria emerges as a condition Brenda wants to claim—on her own behalf and that of other outraged women. What does it mean to live in a society in which women's cancers receive too little in research money, where alternative treatments proven effective in other countries are denied to women? The playwright ultimately indicts the U.S. cancer industry for its arrogance and greed. In this indictment, Loomer echoes the viewpoint of radical feminist activists, who expose the hypocrisy of "the multinational corporate enterprise that with the one hand doles out carcinogens and disease and, with the other, offers expensive, semi-toxic pharmaceutical treatment" (Ehrenreich 2001, 52).

## Conclusion: Bearing Witness

> For the testimonial process to take place there needs to be a bonding, the intimate and total presence of an *other*—in the position of one who hears. Testimonies are not monologues; they cannot take place in solitude. The witnesses are talking to *somebody*: somebody they have been waiting for for a long time. . . . Knowledge in the testimony . . . is not simply a factual given that is reproduced and replicated by the testifier, but a genuine advent, an event in its own right.
>
> —Dori Laub, Testimony (Felman and Laub 1992, 62)

> It is arguably the current project of postcolonial and cultural critical studies to ask: What can reciprocity look like? How can we *do* it? How do we access

> reciprocity in our approach to alterity, our approach to "objects" of study as well as our approach to our "selves"?
>
> —Rebecca Schneider, *The Explicit Body in Performance* (1997, 177)

The testimonies of Holocaust survivors that Dori Laub recorded are, of course, different in nature and historical context from the testimonies of cancer patients. Certainly vital distinctions exist between the witnessing of Jewish survivors offered in the semiprivate "safe space" of the therapist's office and the witnessing of women's bodily traumas offered in the gaudy public space of the contemporary theater. Yet both types of testimonies, I propose, are "genuine advents," advents that herald the possibility of resistance and transformation. Although the theater has a set of frameworks and conventions that audiences and actors must observe, and thus as spectators we "know" we are watching not actual events but performances, we are nonetheless called upon to experience empathically the cancer patient's hybrid reality of pain and redemption. Acknowledging the suffering of women whose bodies have been invaded by cancer, and applauding those courageous enough to write about such invasions and present them, become the playgoers' charge.

To be sure, some audience members are uncomfortable with representations of women's cancers. Despite rave reviews, for example, *Wit* evoked ambivalence from viewers unprepared to bear witness to such raw suffering. As one reviewer noted, this play "was considered so much of a downer that it was originally rejected by almost every theatre that read it" (Martini 1999, 23). Similarly, for many there occurs a tension between witness and spectacle when, in *Sistahs*, Sandra wipes her vagina, strips off her bloody skirt, and hides it behind the sofa. *Must* we witness this private ritual in a public space? Yet audiences in New York came in droves to see *Wit*, as they did in Toronto to see *Sistahs*, in Louisville to see *My Left Breast*, and in Los Angeles to see *The Waiting Room*. To understand why, we must consider a question that theorist Jackie Stacey poses: "What is the particular appeal of these cancer narratives in contemporary culture" (1997, 21)?

Certainly, it is the actors' job as well as the playwrights' to convince spectators of the power of witness. Indeed, actors are the primary agents of embodied consciousness:

> For the playwright, the actor's body is, of course, the channel through which the play comes to life, but at a time when physicality is of such significance in theatre and cinema, it is not surprising that there should be a strong emphasis on the body in the work of many playwrights. No longer merely a vehicle for speaking the words written in the script, the body becomes the site of another theatrical language. (Bassnett 2000, 79)

In women's performance narratives of cancer, women's ruptured bodies "speak" in ways that many theater-goers have not previously experienced.

Graphic depictions of suffering move most members of an audience, reminding them that everyone has lost some beloved woman to cancer, or fears doing so, and that all women are at risk. Moreover, the protagonists' outrage and the plays' "in your face" humor call spectators to awareness and action. This "language" of female embodiment often creates a collaborative knowledge and ethos that evokes reciprocity, which Schneider describes as "a project of recognizing the ricochet of gazes, the histories of who-gets-to-see-what-where" (1997, 184). Theatrical representations of women's cancers appeal in part because historically the one-dimensional perspectival gaze has been predictable and overcirculated, thus fostering a distorted audience-actor dynamic by which "masculinized producers are delineated from feminized consumers, just as the masculinized viewer is dislocated from the feminized view" (8). Women's cancer plays enrich viewers by presenting them with new forms of embodied knowledge via illness testimonies rarely before recounted in public but available to be witnessed now in innovative theatrical productions. These plays further enrich viewers by investing in them the power of a reciprocal gaze that ricochets daringly rather than targeting them through a linear gaze that narrows and delimits.

Another possible reason for the popularity of these plays, at least among feminist viewers, is that the theatrical foregrounding of women's cancer-affected bodies refuses to reinscribe patriarchy. This is not easy to do. Indeed, one risk that feminist playwrights take in producing cancer narratives for the stage is that some audience members will respond as voyeurs rather than as compassionate witnesses. Certainly feminist scholars are aware that a problem with women's onstage reclamation of their bodies, especially their unclothed bodies, is that there can be no guarantee that the naked body in this "woman-identified model" will subvert the sign of the feminine in dominant systems of gender representation. As art historian Griselda Pollock explains, the "attempt to decolonise the female body [is] a tendency which walks a tightrope between subversion and reappropriation, and often serves rather to consolidate the potency of signification rather than actually to rupture it" (Aston 1999, 9).

I argue, nonetheless, that patriarchal signification *is* ruptured when the naked body displayed is bald and shriveled yet luminous, as is Vivian's in *Wit*—or when the breast displayed is missing, marked by a puckered horizontal scar, yet eerily present, as is Susan's in *My Left Breast*. Signification is ruptured because the onstage presentation of such forbidden images as a wrinkled female corpse or a flat, scarred breast disrupts the all-too-familiar spectacle of women's sexualized bodies on prurient display, vulnerable to masculinist appropriation. As Garland-Thomson has argued, feminist counter-representations "produce a powerful visceral violation by exchanging the spectacle of the eroticized breast, which has been desensationalized by its endless circulation, with the medicalized image of the scarred breast, which has been concealed from public view," thereby challenging "oppressive representational practices" (2002, 12). Ultimately, therefore, women's performance narratives of cancer participate in feminist decolonization by offering, in Elin Diamond's words, "a female body in representation that resists fetishization and a viable position for the female spectator" (1997, 44).

Thus envisioned, the plays of Edson, Miller, Loomer, and Bailey and Lewis contribute significantly to a feminist theatrical praxis that Schneider has termed "inspecting the cracks": countering patriarchal representations of women's bodies as "always already different, aberrant, cracked," yet "courting aberrance" by featuring onstage explicit bodies, ill, "stretched across this paradox like canvases across the framework of the Symbolic Order" (1997, 184). Elaine Aston has described feminist theatrical praxis similarly, claiming that it operates "formally and ideologically as a 'sphere of disturbance' "—a sphere in which audience ambivalence can, for many viewers, be transformed into a desire to participate in cancer activism (1999, 17). Such activism may be mainstream—racing for the cure, wearing a pink ribbon—or it may be radical: tattooing one's scar, acting up, engaging in guerrilla warfare. Such is the power of feminist theater. As audience members, potential activists, and intimate Others, we bear witness to the fractured borders that women with cancer negotiate.

## Notes

1. Similar accounts of research, risks, and possible cures have abounded since the women's health movement began in the 1970s, when feminists first promoted self-help, organized cancer support groups, challenged paternalistic physicians, and criticized the disabling Halsted mastectomy (Ehrenreich 2001). Women's cancer advocacy continued in the 1980s, most notably with the establishment of the Susan G. Komen Breast Cancer Foundation in Texas in 1982 and the Mautner Project for Lesbians with Cancer in Washington, D.C., in 1989 (Klawiter 2000; Brownsworth 2000). However, feminist cancer activism entered the political mainstream with full force during the 1990s. In 1991, Dr. Susan Love, with Susan Hester and Amy Langer, founded the National Breast Cancer Coalition (www.natlbcc.org), a lobbying group dedicated to increasing research funds. On 15 August 1993, Susan Ferraro analyzed "the anguished politics of breast cancer" and helped to popularize the well-known statistic that one in eight U.S. women will experience this disease in their lifetimes (24–5). "Breast Cancer Risk in Lesbians Put at 1 in 3," proclaimed an article in the *Boston Globe* later that year (Boehmer 2000). "Deadliness of Breast Cancer in Blacks Defies Easy Answer," asserted another *New York Times* headline (Kolata 1994).

2. It is important to note that these plays address topics other than cancer. *Wit* offers a philosophical lens for examining mortality, death, and dying:

"Nothing but a breath—a comma—separates life from life everlasting" (14). *My Left Breast* traces the bonds of affection between a lesbian and her son: "Now he is twenty and I am still his mother. I am still here. We are still arguing" (215). *Sistahs* celebrates chosen family as a vehicle of resistance: "When I say family, I mean it in the biggest sense. A complex, extended, nontraditional family, with its own secret language, a recipe to survive genocide" (38). *The Waiting Room* explores how women reject the temptation of negative body image: "But the sisters kept saying, 'You're beautiful.' . . . And eventually the women started to buy it" (75).

3. Although Irigaray, Cixous, and Rich offer embodiment and sexuality as sources of empowerment, their analysis raises the question of why writing about bodies has been difficult for many women historically. The belief in a mind/body dichotomy has characterized Western philosophy from Plato to Descartes to Nietzsche, and church fathers such as Augustine and Jerome have presented the body as the enemy of both spirituality and reason. Moreover, in this conception of body and mind as inimical, women have been identified with the bodily sphere and thus devalued, while men have been posited as rational and superior beings. The female body has been seen as fundamentally passive yet paradoxically dangerous, which has led to its social devaluation and, in turn, to the oppression of women (Grosz 1994).

## References

Aston, Elaine. 1999. *Feminist Theatre Practice: A Handbook*. New York: Routledge.

Bailey, Maxine, and Sharon M. Lewis. 1998. *Sistahs*. Toronto: Playwrights Canada Press.

Bakare-Yusuf, Bibi. 1999. "The Economy of Violence: Black Bodies and the Unspeakable Terror." In *Feminist Theory and the Body: A Reader*, ed. Margrit Shildrick and Janet Price, 311–23. Edinburgh, U.K.: Edinburgh University Press.

Bassnett, Susan. 2000. "The Politics of Location." In *The Cambridge Companion to Modern British Women Playwrights*, ed. Elaine Aston and Janelle Reinelt, 73–81. Cambridge, U.K.: Cambridge University Press.

Boehmer, Ulrike. 2000. *The Personal and the Political: Women's Activism in Response to the Breast Cancer and AIDS Epidemics*. Albany: SUNY Press.

Brownsworth, Victoria, ed. 2000. *Coming Out of Cancer: Writings from the Lesbian Cancer Epidemic*. Seattle, Wash.: Seal Press.

Butler, Judith. 1993. *Bodies That Matter: On the Discursive Limits of "Sex."* New York: Routledge.

Cixous, Hélène, and Catherine Clément. 1975. *The Newly Born Woman*. Trans. Betsy Wing. Minneapolis: University of Minnesota Press.

Diamond, Elin. 1997. *Unmaking Mimesis*. New York: Routledge.

Edson, Margaret. 1999. *Wit*. New York: Faber and Faber.

Ehrenreich, Barbara. 2001. "Welcome to Cancerland." *Harper's Magazine*, November:3–53.

Eisenstein, Zillah. 2001. *Manmade Breast Cancers*. Ithaca, N.Y.: Cornell University Press.

Felman, Shoshana, and Dori Laub. 1992. *Testimony: Crises of Witnessing in Literature, Psychoanalysis, and History*. New York: Routledge.

Ferraro, Susan. 1993. "The Anguished Politics of Breast Cancer." *New York Times Magazine*, 15 August:24–7, 58–62.

Foucault, Michel. 1977. *Discipline and Punish: The Birth of the Prison*. Trans. Alan Sheridan. London: Allen Lane.

Friedman, Susan Stanford. 1988. "Women's Auto-Biographical Selves: Theory and Practice." In *The Private Self*, ed. Shari Benstock, 34–42. Chapel Hill: University of North Carolina Press.

Garland-Thomson, Rosemarie. 1997. *Extraordinary Bodies: Figuring Physical Disability in American Culture and Literature*. New York: Columbia University Press.

———. 2002. "Integrating Disability, Transforming Feminist Theory." *NWSA Journal* 14(3):1–32.

Gorman, Christine. 2002. "Rethinking Breast Cancer." *Time*, 18 February: 50–8.

Grosz, Elizabeth. 1994. *Volatile Bodies: Toward a Corporeal Feminism*. Bloomington: Indiana University Press.

Herndl, Diane Price. 2002. "Reconstructing the Posthuman Feminist Body Twenty Years after Audre Lorde's *Cancer Journals*." In *Disability Studies: Enabling the Humanities*, ed. Sharon L. Snyder, Brenda Jo Bruggemann, and Rosemarie Garland-Thomson, 144–55. New York: Modern Language Association of America.

Irigaray, Luce. 1981. "This Sex Which Is Not One." In *New French Feminisms*, ed. Elaine Marks and Isabelle de Courtivron, 99–106. New York: Schocken Books.

Klawiter, Maren. 2000. "Racing for the Cure, Walking Women and Toxic Touring: Mapping Bay Area Cultures of Action." In *Ideologies of Breast Cancer: Feminist Perspectives*, ed. Laura K. Potts, 63–97. London: Macmillan Press.

Kolata, Gina. 1994. "Deadliness of Breast Cancer in Blacks Defies Easy Answer." *New York Times*, 3 August:A1.

Kushner, Rose. 1975. *Breast Cancer: A Personal History*. New York: Harcourt Brace.

Loomer, Lisa. 1998. *The Waiting Room*. New York: Dramatists Play Services.

Lorde, Audre. 1980. *The Cancer Journals*. San Francisco: Spinsters Ink.

Martini, Adrienne. 1999. "The Playwright in Spite of Herself." *American Theatre*, October:22–5.

Miller, Susan. 1995. *My Left Breast*. In *The Breast: An Anthology*, ed. Susan Thames and Marin Gazzaniga, 214–36. New York: Global City Press.

Mulvey, Laura. 1975. "Visual Pleasure and Narrative Cinema." *Screen* 16:6–18.

Potts, Laura K. 2000. "Publishing the Personal: Autobiographical Narratives of Breast Cancer and the Self." In her *Ideologies of Breast Cancer: Feminist Perspectives*, 98–127. London: Macmillan Press.

Proctor, Robert N. 1995. *Cancer Wars: How Politics Shapes What We Know and Don't Know about Cancer.* New York: Basic Books.

Renner, Pamela. 1999. "Science and Sensibility." *American Theatre,* April:34–6.

Rich, Adrienne. 1986. "Notes toward a Politics of Location." In *Blood, Bread, and Poetry: Selected Prose, 1979–1985.* New York: W. W. Norton.

Rollin, Betty. (1976) 2000. *First, You Cry.* New York: Quill Press.

Schmidt, Maia Saj. 1988. "Literary Testimonies of Illness and the Reshaping of Social Memory." *a/b: Auto-Biography Studies* 13(1):71–91.

Schneider, Rebecca. 1997. *The Explicit Body in Performance.* New York: Routledge.

Shildrick, Margrit, with Janet Price. 1999. "Openings on the Body: A Critical Introduction." In their *Feminist Theory and the Body: A Reader,* 1–14. Edinburgh, U.K.: Edinburgh University Press.

Sontag, Susan. 1977. *Illness as Metaphor.* New York: Farrar Straus Giroux.

Stacey, Jackie. 1997. *Teratologies: A Cultural Study of Cancer.* New York: Routledge.

Wilkinson, S., and C. Kitzinger. 1994. "Toward a Feminist Approach to Breast Cancer." In their *Women and Health, Feminist Perspectives.* London: Taylor and Francis.

Zinman, Toby. 1999. "Illness as Metaphor." *American Theatre,* October:25.

CHAPTER SEVEN

# Representing Domestic Violence: Ambivalence and Difference in *What's Love Got to Do with It*

DIANE SHOOS

> Does it seem late in the day to be writing about abused women? Hasn't the subject filled our newspapers and magazines and talk shows? Haven't we seen enough battered women, enough psychologists, enough lawyers, on "Donahue" and "Oprah" and "Sally"? Haven't we watched those terrible stories dramatized often enough on the TV Movie of the Week?
>
> —Ann Jones (1994, 5–6)

One of the most disturbing scenes in director Brian Gibson's 1993 biopic, *What's Love Got to Do with It,* occurs more than halfway through the film when for the first time we see Tina Turner (Angela Bassett) assaulted by her husband Ike Turner (Laurence Fishburne). Knocked off-balance by the force of Ike's slap, Tina lands on a nearby couch and falls behind it in a frantic attempt to escape. In the next shot, Ike, arm flexed and fist balled up, bends over Tina, and pausing between hits, punches her twice in the face. As he does, however, the camera remains fixed in front of the couch in a low-angle medium shot, thereby obscuring the sight of Ike's fist coming into contact with his wife's body.

The moment is an unusual one for Hollywood cinema, renowned for its ongoing love affair with jaw-breaking, eye-popping, gut-spilling violence. Within the context of an otherwise graphic depiction of the brutality of wife abuse as experienced by one of its real-life victims, this literal if momentary "punch pulling" has the quality of an unconscious lapse or omission. For film and media critics, such a textual lapse evokes questions of the visual as evidence ("seeing is believing") and intersects with ongoing debates about the representation of, especially, the violated female body. Viewed within a larger context, this omission is an uncanny metaphor for what battered women advocates like Ann Jones have argued is the continued invisibility of battering in the United States. Following on this claim, in this paper I interrogate the problem of visibility/invisibility as it relates to our ways of "seeing" domestic abuse. I re-view the film *What's Love Got to Do with It* in order to consider how the complexities of gender, race, and class construct popular representations of abusive relationships and how these popular representations can offer us

Originally published in the Summer 2003 issue of the *NWSA Journal.*

comfortable positions from which to see what we already assume about men as abusers, women as victims, and the racial and class politics of violence.

Considering the events of the past decade, it may seem paradoxical to argue that we still do not see abuse. Certainly this is a social problem that, following the broadcast of the O. J. Simpson double murder trial in 1995, has received increasing attention from the U.S. media, and appears to be widely condemned. Yet the trial's controversial verdict and the racial and class tensions that it evoked are manifestations of the complexity of domestic violence as well as our reactions to it. Jones herself comments in her powerful book *Next Time She'll Be Dead*, published the year before the Simpson trial:

> A great many people now agree that men who beat up their wives or girlfriends do a bad thing. Many understand that children who witness such violence against their mothers can only be harmed by the experience. Many sympathize with battered women, and hardly anyone any more—apart from religious fundamentalists—seems to think that women should put up with abuse. . . . But no matter how you interpret the numbers it's clear that male violence is not going *down*. . . . Why, when things seem to have changed so much for the better, do they seem so much the same? Why, when we actually keep score, do they seem *worse*? (1994, 6–7)

Part of the answer, Jones suggests, is the simple but still compelling point that awareness is not always the same as understanding: the ubiquity and visibility of battering has not fundamentally changed our attitudes or altered our denial about certain aspects of abuse. Having heard the voices of battered women and seen their photos, many people—including many feminists—still have only a superficial knowledge of the emotional labyrinth of the lived experience of domestic violence. We thus fail to comprehend the scope and depth of the abuser's control, which may assert itself through physical, psychological, social, and financial means; the variety of strategies through which this control is maintained; or the loving behavior that is part and parcel of the cycle of abuse. Our sympathy notwithstanding, we may underestimate the terrible dilemmas that a battered woman faces, the serious risks she takes, and the price she pays no matter what choices she makes—even those that seem to be for her ultimate good. As a result, we may minimize or discount (if no longer label masochistic) the victim's powerful emotional attachment to the abuser, which researchers note exists "not because of the violence, but in spite of it" (Jacobson and Gottman 1998, 51). As private individuals who witness or suspect battering, we may still succumb to the temptation to remain silent out of embarrassment or respect for privacy. As public citizens—police officers, judges, and jury members—we may still lean toward treating abuse as a family matter rather than a criminal act and thus fail to pursue and prosecute abusers to the full extent of the law.

As Jones argues, above the veneer of awareness and *zero tolerance* hover the ghosts of old attitudes about abuse. They haunt us especially in the form of latent ambivalence about battered women, embodied in the persistent question that we know we shouldn't ask but that revisits us nonetheless, if only in our minds: "Why does she stay?" On some level we may continue to condemn abused women, if not for the battering itself, for their bad choices or their failure to terminate abusive relationships.[1] Speaking about what she calls our "pernicious habits of mind," Jones comments:

> Whether we blame battered women or pity them for their plight, we tend to think of them as a kind of pariah group, rather like prostitutes, who apparently choose to live "abnormal" and dangerous lives because of some peculiar kinks of background and personality. (After all, we think, she *could* leave.) (1994, 14)

As Jones notes, even more pernicious is the fact that it is these very attitudes that often cause abused women to keep silent, "out of shame and a fear of being blamed, thereby appearing to acquiesce to violence" (14).

Other ghosts inhabit our attitudes toward batterers. In her pioneering 1979 work *The Battered Woman*, Lenore Walker enumerated not only myths about abused women but those surrounding the motivations and characteristics of the abuser, such as "batterers are unsuccessful and lack resources to cope with the world," "batterers are psychopathic personalities," "the batterer is not a loving partner," "batterers are violent in all their relationships" (24–8). Although Walker's study is twenty-three years old at this writing, only within the last eight years have there been any significant challenges to these myths in the form of sustained research on the methods, motives, and psychology of batterers.[2] Indeed, some of our most harmful habits of mind have manifested themselves not in what we think about batterers but in our failure to think about them. In popular as well as clinical discourses on domestic violence, the place of the batterer has been virtually empty, causing two male researchers to remark: "It is sometimes forgotten that men's violence is men's behavior. . . . What is surprising is the enormous effort to explain male behavior by examining characteristics of women" (quoted in Jones 1994, 153). Statements like the one from an American Medical Association report issued in the mid-1990s—"Each year, 4 million women are battered in the United States" (quoted in Felder and Victor 1996, 69)—point to the continued tendency to treat abuse as something that happens to women rather than something that a current or former intimate partner does to them.[3]

In sum, if some of our previous habits of mind seem to have changed, others have simply gone underground or, to use the term Stuart Hall has applied to a kind of invisible or naturalized racism, become "inferential": that is, they have "premises and propositions inscribed in them as a set of unquestioned assumptions," making them more difficult to identify and address (1981, 36). Current ideas about domestic violence have also been complicated and ambivalence compounded by often competing contemporary discourses on victims and victimization, sexual politics in/after feminism, theories of female subjectivity and agency, and the meaning and politics of difference. As a result, responses to domestic violence in the new millennium are at once reformed and recidivist, outwardly resolute yet internally conflicted, more open yet just as frequently displaced and/or repressed.

A case in point is the representation of abuse in popular culture, specifically popular visual media. No longer relegated to daytime talk television and self-proclaimed women's channels like Lifetime and Oxygen, or social documentaries shown primarily on public broadcasting channels or in art cinemas, the topic of abuse has been embraced by primetime television and the Hollywood movie industry. In 2002, for instance, domestic violence was featured on multiple episodes of the perennially popular television dramas *ER* and *NYPD Blue* and the much-lauded HBO series *Six Feet Under* and *The Sopranos*. The same year it was one of the subjects of the Academy Award–nominated film *In the Bedroom* (Field 2002), starring Sissy Spacek and Marisa Tomei, as well as the Jennifer Lopez vehicle *Enough* (Apted 2002). These productions followed in the footsteps of earlier films such as *Sleeping with the Enemy* (Ruben 1991), *What's Love Got to Do with It* (Gibson 1993), and *Dolores Claiborne* (Hackford 1995) in positioning abuse at the center rather than the periphery of the narrative.

This list suggests that representations of domestic violence, like women directors and producers, seem to have finally broken through the celluloid ceiling. Yet, as I propose in the pages that follow, despite their increased number and accessibility, there are nonetheless modes of invisibility at work in many of these representations. These modes include the tacit denial of the many complexities and contradictions of abuse, to which there are no easy Hollywood solutions; the continued if continually disavowed construction of abused women and abusive men as the Other; and, most significantly, the linking of this Otherness to particular categories of race and class.

*What's Love Got to Do with It* is one of the best-known and most commercially successful of the "new wave" of Hollywood films on domestic violence, due perhaps to Turner's status as a black female star who survived an abusive relationship and went on to become a solo Grammy Award–winning rock and roll artist. *What's Love* sets itself apart from other recent film representations of abuse by offering audiences a powerful, nuanced portrait not only of a battered woman but of the complex psychology and tactics of a male batterer. Most importantly, the film's focus on a black man and woman whose musical success became their ticket out of poor, working-class families provides the opportunity for an analysis of the ways in which larger ambivalences about race and class become caught up with and support those that circulate within discursive formulations of abuse.

The primary goal of this discussion, then, is to re-view Gibson's film through a variety of intersecting discursive lenses, including that of the growing literature by both researchers and victims of abuse.[4] Admittedly, it has become almost a critical cliché to argue that representations not only reflect but help to shape social experience. Yet, particularly in the case of domestic violence, it bears repeating, as Joan Scott reminds us, that experience itself is not a natural or transparent category and that simply bringing hitherto invisible experiences to light is not a productive end in itself:

> Making visible the experience of a different group exposes the existence of repressive mechanisms, but not their inner workings or logic. . . . For that we need to attend to the historical processes that, through discourse, position subjects and produce their experiences. It is not individuals who have experience, but subjects who are constituted through experience. (1992, 26)

For my purposes here, then, experience is defined not in opposition to discourse or representation, but as Teresa de Lauretis has proposed as "a complex of habits resulting from the semiotic interaction of 'outer world' and 'inner world,' the continuous engagement of a self or subject in social reality," a reality that increasingly includes visual texts (1984, 182).

At the same time, the material and social consequences of experience mean that it cannot be reduced to mere discourse. Indeed, I want to suggest that examining the complex of discourses that constitute subjectivity may be particularly crucial in the case of a form of violence whose victims are psychologically and often physically isolated from society and which, as one of the most underreported crimes in the United States, is less likely to be the subject of open discussion. In other words, what we see in the widely available popular culture representations of domestic violence may have serious implications for our ability to recognize and intervene in abuse.

## Domestic Violence and Difference

> No one has to "provoke" a wife-beater. He will strike out when he's ready and for whatever reason he has at the moment. I may be his excuse, but I have never been the reason.
>
> —Letter excerpt from an abused woman (quoted in Martin 1981, 3)

> The first I heard of women's lib was when *Time* magazine ran this picture of some women waving their bras in the air. Great picture, but I didn't really get it. . . . They were talking about "liberation"—but liberation from, like, housework. That was the least of my problems. My problem was simply survival.
>
> —Tina Turner (1986, 170)

As I have noted, the concept of difference/Otherness is mobilized in multiple ways in discourses on domestic violence. Canadian psychologist and researcher Donald Dutton comments, for instance:

> A woman returning to an abusive relationship represents a salient example of what, to common sense, is unusual or counter-normative behavior. In other words, outside observers, be they male or female, believe that they and others would act differently than does the assaulted woman. Furthermore, from their perspective, there do not appear to be tangible impediments to her leaving: she is not physically confined, imprisoned, under constant surveillance. When we observe behavior that appears unusual and is not externally determined, we tend to attribute it to a trait indigenous to the person who performs the behavior and overlook the impact of subtle situational forces on his/her behavior. (1995, 169)

Such reasoning allows us to retain our conviction that, despite its apparent ubiquity, domestic violence is an aberration. Most importantly, it erects a mental wall around abuse, marking both batterers and victims as Other and reassuring us that we could never be them. Jacobson and Gottman pinpoint this often hidden anxiety:

> When we first started our research one question we heard frequently was, Why do battered women stay in these abusive relationships? This question implies an accusation, namely, what is wrong with these crazy women for staying with these awful men? Often what the questioner really means is, "They are not like me. I would never stay. It's their own fault, and don't ask me to care about them. Serves them right for not getting out." (1998, 136)

Similarly, referring to the deep divide among feminists in the 1980s about the Hedda Nussbaum case,[5] Gloria Steinem observed, "Either you allow yourself to realize that it could have happened to you or you're so invested in making sure it couldn't have been you that you reject the victim" (quoted in Jones 1994, 176). Yet for those who assume the latter stance some of the research on trauma is less than reassuring. Judith Lewis Herman, for example, has noted that survivors of trauma attribute their survival primarily to good luck rather than any particular mental or emotional strength (quoted in Jones 1994, 174). Such a perspective flies in the face of our collective idea that we would not succumb to abusive behavior or tolerate its continuation.

The need to see ourselves as above and beyond the reach of domestic violence also resonates in our definitions of abuse. It is well established among researchers that physical battering is a very small part of an abuser's tactics and that, correspondingly, emotional or psychological abuse is the primary form of domestic violence. Jacobson and Gottman observe, "Emotional abuse is so common in batterers that, in the majority of instances, emotional abuse is *not* followed by physical abuse" (1998, 62). They go on to note that this form of abuse persists after physical abuse subsides and that it is often the most important factor in a woman's decision to leave (148). Commenting on the persistence in popular imagination of the notion that only physical battering merits the designation abuse, Felder and Victor remark, "There are very few individuals who are immune to or exempt from becoming either a victim or a batterer, and those who claim that they have never been in an abusive relationship might change their minds if they were to learn all the different forms that kind of relationship can take" (1996, 204).

This reluctance to accept broader, more complex definitions of domestic violence may be even more acute for feminists in the new millennium. Acknowledging that even in a Western democratic country like the United States women are still subjected to such a heinous form of sexism may seem to call into question the very achievements of feminism and undermine conviction about the possibility of female agency within patriarchy. So-called anti-victim feminists such as Katie Roiphe, Naomi Wolf, and Camille Paglia may be especially resistant to calling attention to abused women as an oppressed group with special needs, since from this perspective doing so seems to define these women as passive or weak, and thus, may encourage them to abdicate responsibility for their own welfare and independence. Yet, as Alyson Cole points out in her excellent article on the rhetoric of anti-victim feminism:

> Women's liberation can be neither properly conceived nor actualized if women are considered nothing more than victims. But as formidable as this problem is, it is unlikely to be resolved by ignoring women's oppression. Women have been and continue to be discriminated against as women, despite their great advancement over the course of the last quarter of a century. (1999, 90)

Popular and clinical discourses about abused women have also been structured, often in conflicting ways, by issues related to racial and class differences. On the one hand, beginning with Lenore Walker and Del Martin in the 1970s, battered women researchers have struggled to counter the myth that abuse occurs only in relationships between low-income, working-class men and women of color, pointing to evidence that neither race, education, or financial or professional status guarantee women immunity from domestic violence. Indeed, testimonies and exposés of abuse in middle-class, professional households suggest that humiliation and fear of exposure—which compound the problem of underreporting—may be especially acute for these women, who believe that they should be *above* the abuse or able to control it and whose careers and professional reputations may also be at risk.[6] On the other hand, just as mainstream feminism's emphasis on commonality and unity long suppressed crucial discussions of the diversity of female experience (a diversity evident in the citation from *I, Tina* [1986] that describes Tina Turner's reaction to "women's lib"), focus on the widespread occurrence of abuse has contributed to a tendency to theorize domestic violence outside of social categories or to underplay its significance. Recently, however, advocates and researchers have underlined the importance of balancing an under-standing of the ways in which abuse cuts across lines of difference with analysis of the particular social, racial, and economic contexts in which it occurs. Felder and Victor comment, "While economic or social status does not eliminate certain men from becoming batterers, the techniques they use to control their partners can reflect their level of education or sophistication. In all cases, however, without exception, the batterer uses whatever means are within his social, financial, and emotional power to control his partner" (1996, 205).

The lived social experience of race and class and the racist and classist meanings all-too-frequently assigned to them are central to an analysis of the politics and representation of violence against women, including domestic violence. Susan Bordo's (1997) observations about the decision in the O. J. Simpson case foreground this point. Bordo suggests that the verdict of the Simpson jury points to an "intellectual failure to *think* race and gender at the same time, let alone to analyze the interrelations between the two," a failure that she describes, in language that recalls that of Ann Jones, as "more indicative of contemporary habits of thought than unique" (103). She goes on to comment, "Popular culture provides virtually no models of such multidimensional, analytic thinking but instead continually encourages us to take sides, assign villains and victims, come to the 'bottom line' and so forth" (103). Given Bordo's claim, it seems particularly important to closely examine popular culture texts such as *What's Love Got to Do with It* that mobilize and condense the multiple meanings of difference.

## Representing Domestic Violence

> It was like a horror movie. That's what my life had become: a horror movie, with no intermissions.
>
> —Tina Turner (1986, 138)

Based on a screenplay by Kate Lanier, *What's Love Got to Do with It* has many of the characteristics of other performance musical bio-pics, whose codes and conventions consequently structure the experience of domestic violence as it takes place on screen. The film's narrative, for instance, has a rise-fall-rise line that alternates between private moments that reveal Ike's increasingly abusive treatment of Tina and performances and interviews that portray an apparently happy, successful professional couple. This counterpoint between public *niceness* and private *roughness* is ironically echoed in Tina's stage introduction to the song "Proud Mary," where she tells the audience: "We never ever do nothin' nice and easy; we always do it nice and rough." *What's Love,* however, ultimately reveals the destructiveness of this cycle even as it effectively demonstrates that violence and coercion are completely compatible with the abuser's conception of love. Furthermore, by foregrounding the socio-cultural and ideological contexts in which Ike's abuse of Tina takes place, including the tacit acceptance of his behavior by her family and most of her friends and colleagues, the film not only avoids the temptation to blame the victim but also reveals the many subtle but powerful pressures and deterrents that work to keep women imprisoned in abusive relationships.

In his introduction to the collection *Mythologies of Violence in Postmodern Media,* Christopher Sharrett remarks, "The belief in violence as an aberration is a prominent aspect of American ideology" (1999, 12). The narrative of domestic violence in *What's Love* presents an important challenge to this ideology through its emphasis on battering, not as an involuntary or aberrant reaction to stress or anger, but as one point along an extended continuum of male dominance. Similarly, the film does not focus solely on instances of physical violence but situates these along an ever-escalating trajectory of abuse that includes a broad range of controlling behaviors that exert their own psychological damage. The beginning of *What's Love,* for instance, chronicles more subtle forms of manipulation in the form of Ike's comments to young Anna Mae (Tina Turner's birth name) about her behavior and personal appearance. In one early scene he asks Anna Mae to open her mouth; when she obeys, anticipating a kiss, he inspects her teeth as if inspecting a horse and promptly orders her to go to the dentist. In the film, Ike's attentiveness carries with it the threat of disapproval and rejection that itself can function as a form of control: when he comments that Anna Mae is "putting on some pounds," she nervously begins to apologize until he expresses his approval.

As the film's narrative progresses, such controlling tactics, camouflaged as affection and concern, evolve into more overt instances of dominance that prioritize Ike's welfare and needs over Anna Mae's. After the birth of their first child, Ike kidnaps an anemic Anna Mae from the hospital in order to avoid canceling a series of important concert dates that will further his career. When she objects that she is seriously ill, Ike plays on her sense of guilt and loyalty and asks whether she is going to listen to the doctor or to her "man." Saying that he wants to take her to Mexico to marry her because he "can't wait any longer," Ike skillfully transforms abduction into seduction through song: leaning toward Anna Mae and holding out a wedding ring as a bribe, he croons "You're just a fool, you know you're in love." A reverse shot of Anna Mae shows her face softening as she then responds with the rest of the musical phrase.

The abduction scene is framed on either end by home movie footage, two in a series of such scenes that serve as temporal transitions in the first half of the film. The first home movie shows Ike filming his newborn son in the nursery and then Anna Mae in her hospital bed, surrounded by her mother and sister and a disapproving doctor who tells Ike that Anna Mae is too sick to be discharged. The grainy black and white images of the wailing baby and Anna Mae's wan, exhausted face stand in sharp contrast to the ostensibly happy occasion. Similarly, the home movie of the Mexican wedding scene, accompanied on the soundtrack by Ike and Tina singing "It's Gonna Work Out Fine," concludes with a mock fight in a limousine, foreshadowing the later ride to the Hilton where, subjected once more to Ike's beatings, Anna Mae fights back in self-defense and shortly thereafter makes her escape. The home movies function, then, as an inadvertent visual record of the violent underside of marital bliss.

The music that punctuates the film's narrative also serves to deconstruct Ike and Tina's relationship. Many of the song lyrics suggest that certain controlling behaviors are not only socially acceptable but desirable, the mark of true passion. The title and words of the first number that the young Anna Mae rehearses with Ike's band, "I Wanna Be Made Over," make explicit both the power that Ike already exerts over her and her own vulnerability to his obsessive attention. A sequence of her performing "A Fool in Love," with the lines "You know you love him, you can't understand / Why he treat you like he do when he's such a good man," follows immediately on a scene of verbal and psychological abuse. Shortly after Ike beats Anna Mae and she blames herself for criticizing him and then pledges to take responsibility for getting the relationship "back on track," we see her in the studio recording "River Deep," whose second verse compares the woman in love to a "faithful puppy" who always follows her lover around. Such musical cues are reinforced at strategic moments by the film's visuals. During the "faithful puppy" line, for instance, the camera cuts pointedly to a shot of a stony-faced Ike, angered by Anna Mae's first solo venture.

*What's Love* counters the myth that domestic violence is an individual pathology and identifies it instead as the product of a set of culturally sanctioned attitudes about men and women, attitudes supported on multiple levels by a range of institutions, including popular culture. The point here is not to condemn popular culture as a *bad object* but to understand how it functions and participates in the particular ideological climate that the film delineates. In this context, scenes like the "I Wanna

Be Made Over" sequence, while seemingly unremarkable in the larger flow of the story, are in fact narratively overdetermined. The montage of Anna Mae's physical transformation from innocent girl into sexual seductress operates most obviously to connect the film with other star and "overnight success" narratives: the specifics of Anna Mae's transformation—we see her modeling outfits for Ike's approval and later dying her hair blond at his request—recall other male-orchestrated makeovers such as Kim Novak's transformation in *Vertigo* (Hitchcock 1958). *What's Love,* however, explicitly links male obsession to a media-perpetuated female ideal. In the scene where Ike tells Anna Mae to get a bleach job, he first states that he wants her to look like Marilyn Monroe and then, gesturing to a large billboard featuring a blond woman, commands, "Make her look like that." Perhaps most striking is the racial specificity of this ideal, its coding of femininity as necessarily white. Significantly, Ike later gives Anna Mae the stage name "Tina" because of its resemblance to "Sheena" and the names of other white jungle goddesses from the Saturday matinee movie serials.

By the time Ike's control finally explodes into the physical assault supposedly provoked by Anna Mae's comment that his songs "all sound the same," the beating, although shocking, seems not an exception to but a logical extension of his already abusive behavior. Anna Mae's plea during the attack ("You promised you wouldn't hit me.") and a later comment by her friend and back-up singer Jackie ("You can't keep hiding those black eyes from us.") indicate that this is not the first instance of physical violence but a pattern of mounting tension, followed by abuse, apology, and increased attention, one that echoes the by now well-documented cycle of violence first identified by Lenore Walker in *The Battered Woman* (1979). Tellingly, after the first scene of physical abuse we see Ike leave a gift on Tina's bed. Immediately following the vicious verbal battering that ends with Ike calling Tina a "sorry mother-fucker," he makes a show of delaying the opening number of their concert in order to move downstage and gently kiss Tina's tear-stained cheek. The staging of this scene in particular brings home the pain of emotional abuse as well as the covert dynamics of domestic violence, in the context of which even apparently loving behavior can be abusive. Jones reminds us, "Those seductive periods of male contrition . . . are not respites from battering, as they appear, but part of the coercive process, pressuring women to forgive and forget, to minimize and deny, to *submit,* and thus to appear complicitous: they *are* battering" (1994, 93).

The sequence where Anna Mae records her song "Nutbush City Limits" and Ike brutally rapes her serves as the turning point in the narrative, a moment of horrific violence after which she tries to commit suicide and then decides to leave the relationship. The scene is set in Ike and Tina's home recording studio, suggesting, as Yvonne Tasker remarks, that work and marriage function together to maintain the image of Ike and Tina (1998, 190). The strong association of "Nutbush" with Anna Mae/Tina—the song is her solo composition about her hometown—gives the scene its centrality in terms of the real motivation for Ike's battering. Tasker notes, "The violence of their fight over this song, that she has written, comes to signify their struggle over creativity, popularity and her independence" (190). Thus, rather than a momentary loss of control, Ike's battering is symptomatic of his need to manipulate all aspects of Anna Mae's life, from her emotions and her personal life to her work and professional achievements. This need in turn stems from Ike's fear of abandonment, suggested in the film through his repeated comment to Tina, "I suppose you gonna leave me now," which itself becomes a self-fulfilling prophecy and has its parallel in Tina's own abandonment by her mother.

*What's Love Got to Do with It* challenges some of the most common misconceptions, prejudices, and myths surrounding domestic violence. Like *Sleeping with the Enemy* (Ruben 1991) and *Enough* (Apted 2002), which portray abused women who terminate abusive relationships only to be stalked and threatened by their abusers, *What's Love* makes the important point that the story isn't over and women aren't safe just because they leave. At the point when Anna Mae escapes from Ike in their hotel room and runs to a nearby Ramada Inn, it would have been narratively convenient to abandon the domestic violence plot for the more upbeat rock star success story. Instead, in tacit response to the question "Why doesn't she just leave?" the film relates the experience of not only Tina Turner, but many abused women who find themselves more rather than less endangered when they finally break away from their abusers (Jones 1994, 149–50; Jacobson and Gottman 1998, 239). Significantly, in the final scene of *What's Love,* as Tina is about to go on stage for her comeback solo concert, Ike sneaks past security and enters her dressing room, brandishing a gun and threatening her life.

Yet there are, equally, tensions and splits in this text that are emblematic of those found in discourses on domestic violence more broadly. Indeed, this scene sends another, dangerous message. When Ike threatens her, Anna Mae dares him to shoot her, recalling the earlier limousine scene where she beats him back. Such moments seem to imply that the ultimate solution to domestic violence—rather than to seek help or to make a plan to achieve safety—is to simply stand up to the abuser, a tactic that may put women at increased risk (Jacobson and Gottman 1998, 252–3).

Furthermore, in spite of the fact that, through the character of Jackie, the film acknowledges the importance of informal support systems for abused women, it fails to address the role that institutions such as the police and the legal system play in either intervening in, or in some cases, facilitating and perpetuating domestic violence. Thus, just as its star narrative and performance numbers foreground Turner's phenomenal talent and her superstar potential, the film's portrayal of Turner as a fighter, who through her newfound religious faith succeeds in saving herself, comes perilously close to suggesting that the responsibility for the abused woman's fate begins and ends with her. To put it another way, although *What's Love* doesn't blame the victim for the abuse itself, it continues to place the burden of change solely on her shoulders. In this way, the film conforms to Hollywood's much-analyzed penchant for narratives of individual triumph over those that chronicle collective action or the possibility of social intervention or systemic change. In a similar way, the film's focus on a celebrity figure obscures the problems of material resources, childcare, and custody that confront many victims of abuse, and serve as powerful obstacles to leaving.

Other tensions in this film relate specifically to interrelated issues of performance and spectacle, stardom, and race. Yvonne Tasker notes that performance as a cinematic mode has allowed black women, in particular, movement, however limited, into films. She goes on to comment on the double edge of this mode: "Performance has long been a Hollywood staple, allowing the production of both female flesh and women's work as sexual spectacle, whilst simultaneously evoking women's strength through the very power of the performance" (1998, 184). Such a tension is evident in Turner's representation in *What's Love.* There is no doubt that in many ways Turner's image in and out of the film intersects with stereotypical representations of woman as fetishized sexual object (her ad campaign for Hanes stockings is a striking example). However, the power of her voice on the soundtrack and the incredible energy of the musical performances in the narrative in many ways make it difficult to come away from *What's Love* with anything other than an impression of strength and independence. The disjunction between sound and image in the performance sequences of the film—the use of the real Tina Turner's voice over Angela Bassett's body—may unconsciously enhance this effect.

Along with Tina Turner's career as a successful black vocal artist, her previous film appearance as the matriarch Auntie Entity in George Miller's 1995 film *Mad Max 3: Beyond the Thunderdome,* and her ongoing construction as a star are of course important as contexts for *What's Love.* Many critics and theorists have observed that a star's image is never homogeneous or complete, but dynamic, incorporating diverse and conflicting elements. Tasker's comments about the complex layering that characterizes the construction of the star are relevant here:

> The star's body, worked out/on, transformed or preserved by surgery as it is, both offers and undermines a guarantee of authenticity, that of the "naturalness" of the star herself (whether this is in terms of natural talent or natural beauty). Ultimately the body itself, the supposed ground of what it is to be

> sexed and raced, for example, a body which is only ever experienced by an audience as an image in any case, provides just one more layer to the star image, operating as another component that is worked over. (1998, 180)

Clearly, *What's Love*'s final sequence, consisting of a direct cut from Bassett to a shot from behind of Turner performing, is meant to mend the film's voice/body split and authenticate what we have just seen as *real*. Yet Tasker's analysis of the paradoxical way in which the changeability of the star's body undermines as well as supports authenticity—contributes to an awareness of the body *as* (mere) image—seems particularly significant for a film whose audience may be, first, mentally resistant or unprepared to confront the reality of domestic violence and, second, conscious of the performance/artifice that structures the film's diegesis. Although I do not wish to push this analysis too far by suggesting that these factors completely discredit the abuse we see on screen, it is nonetheless possible that for some viewers they may work subconsciously to undermine the portrayal of Turner's victimization, making the abused body in effect just another layer or role.

Turner's identity as not only a female performer but a black female performer is of prime importance here. In *Cinema and Spectatorship* Judith Mayne argues that "for white audiences, one of the most stereotypical and therefore comforting relationships between black and white is that of performer and onlooker" (1993, 154). Her comments suggest that the very fact of Turner's race may potentially distance as well as engage the audience. Such a possibility leads to larger questions about spectatorship and difference as crucial components of the representation of domestic violence.

## Domestic Violence, Spectatorship, and Difference

At the beginning of this discussion I suggested, perhaps rather naively, that the question of how domestic violence is portrayed in film and television might be particularly important because of the ubiquity of these media and their potential access by a large number of viewers, including abused women, many of whom are physically and psychologically isolated by their abusers and for whom external validation is one of the most important factors in deciding to leave the abusive relationship (Jacobson and Gottman 1998, 140). Certainly, however, as cultural critics of all kinds have noted, identification or even what is more mundanely termed "viewer response" is a many-layered and dynamic process rather than a static, unified position, and one constructed by gender, race, class, age, ethnicity, and a multiplicity of factors.[7] In some ways *What's Love Got to Do with It* goes out of its way to point out that abuse cuts across these lines—for example, by noting that Anna Mae, like the real-life Turner, had nothing but a Mobil card and 36 cents when she escaped. Yet these issues are much more complex and intertwined than the flat, one-dimensional treatment that the narrative gives them: for example, despite Ike's control of her finances and the fact that she has only 36 cents in her pocket, Turner's position is not equivalent to, for instance, that of working-class women; certainly the white Ramada Inn manager who takes Turner in, for instance, recognizes her not simply as an abused woman, but as a (presumably wealthy) celebrity.

In a similar and equally intricate way, Tina Turner's position as a black woman from a Southern working-class background is undoubtedly a central factor in the film's reception as well as its production and marketing. As the shots of the horrified white mother and children who see Ike abuse Tina in a restaurant or those of the white clientele who witness the couple's bloody entrance into the Hilton lobby suggest, many spectators will associate the abuse in the film with particular class and racial stereotypes like those Tina Turner herself confronted when she sought help. In an interview in *Vanity Fair,* she comments, "In those days, believe me, a doctor asked you what happened and you say, 'I had a fight with my husband,' that was it. Black people fight. They didn't care about black people" (Orth 1993, 172). Similarly, scenes of Ike's drug use and womanizing may allow spectators to attribute his behavior to his cocaine habit or see it as a natural part of the degenerate lifestyle of sixties (especially black) R & B musicians. And, while the graphic sounds and images accompanying Ike's rape of Tina in the sound studio convey the inhumanity and degradation of domestic violence, they are also consistent with the racial stereotype of the black man as savage animal. On this level, what the film tells us is what we already assume about the volatility and violence of black heterosexual relationships. Perhaps it is not surprising, then, that the predominantly white viewers who made up the audience when I saw the film laughed during the scene where Tina returns Ike's blows as the limousine speeds past their names on the marquee.

Black feminist critic bell hooks's reaction to *What's Love* brings home the fact that spectator response is based on a complex of elements and does not divide neatly along, for example, gender or racial lines (1994). Speaking of the film in the course of an interview, hooks remarks, "What I kept thinking about was why this culture can't see a serious film that's not just about a black female tragedy, but about a black female triumph. It's so interesting how the film stops with Ike's brutality, as though it is Tina Turner's life ending. Why is it that her success is less interesting than the period of her life when she's a victim" (41)? In this way, hooks rightfully insists that the narrative's portrayal of abuse be considered not in isolation, but rather in the historical context of the representation of black women within Hollywood cinema. In the same way, a full analysis of *What's Love* would need to consider the often-contradictory Hollywood film representations of black men.

hooks's comments suggest that the fact that abuse does indeed occur across lines of difference makes its representation and corresponding issues of spectatorship more rather than less complex, the need for a diversity of representations and spectators more and not less urgent. In addition, it calls for divergent critical methods and perspectives that attempt to identify, confront, and analyze rather than dismiss or reconcile the contradictions of difference. As hooks states, it demands a focus on, precisely, "the question of representation, what function it serves, whose interests" (1990, 71). In the case of *What's Love Got to Do with It*, it entails open acknowledgement of the functioning of gender with and through race and class and rigorous dialogue about the ways in which a film that condemns domestic abuse in the black community can at the same time perpetuate racist ideas about both black men and black women. Ultimately, an examination of the intersections of abuse and difference requires a radical reconceptualization of both terms, a rewriting of difference itself, as Linda Gordon (1991) has so eloquently argued, not as separation or immobilizing pluralism, but as a series of relationships of power that have repercussions for all subjects.

Like the moment in the film where Anna Mae confronts her own bruised and bleeding face in the hotel mirror, the release of *What's Love Got to Do with It* marks a shift in cinematic representations of domestic violence. In its foregrounding of abuse as a spectrum of controlling behaviors bolstered by popular culture's image of passionate love, this film deconstructs many of the habits of mind that have functioned to keep abuse invisible. Nevertheless, another moment from the film sticks in the mind: that of the look of desperation on Tina Turner's face as she is raped by her husband inside the transparent walls of the recording studio. Through its lack of acknowledgement of the need for systemic support and fundamental institutional change for battered women, along with its failure to directly confront the racism and classism that inform our attitudes about domestic violence, *What's Love* also serves as a barometer of our denial and ambivalence, our failure to contend with the continued invisibility of abuse.

## Acknowledgments

I would like to thank Marilyn Cooper, Judith Mayne, and Cindy Selfe for their insightful comments on early drafts of this article, and Vicky Bergvall, Heidi Bostic, Elizabeth Flynn, Diana George, Stephen Pluhacek, and Patty Sotirin, for their generous intellectual and moral support during the later stages of revision.

## Notes

1. Deborah Sontag notes in her cover story in the 17 November 2002 *New York Times Magazine* that "abused women often make calculated decisions to stay with their partners. Sometimes a woman really has no choice; she's scared that leaving would make him more dangerous, or she doesn't think she can survive financially on her own. But other times she stays for the same reasons that people in other kinds of imperfect relationships do: because of the kids, because of her religion, because she doesn't want to be alone or simply because she loves him" (54).

2. See the work of Donald Dutton (1995) and Neil Jacobson and John Gottman (1998).

3. As Jones has remarked, the term *domestic violence* is itself a euphemism, since all available data indicates that men are overwhelmingly the major perpetrators of this crime. I have retained this term in my discussion because of its common usage, along with *abuse* and *battering*. Although my focus here is exclusively on domestic violence in heterosexual relationships, I wish to emphasize the importance of acknowledgement and analysis of abuse that occurs in same-sex relationships.

4. These categories often literally overlap. The first chapter of Ann Jones's *Next Time She'll Be Dead*, for instance, recounts the author's own abuse at the hands of her father (1994).

5. Nussbaum was a battered woman who testified against her partner Joel Steinberg after he beat to death their six-year-old illegally adopted daughter Lisa. For a detailed account of the controversy surrounding Nussbaum, see Jones's articulate analysis in chap. 6 of *Next Time She'll Be Dead: Battering and How to Stop It* (1994).

6. See, for instance, Hillary Johnson's article "The Truth about White Collar Domestic Violence" (1995), part I of Ann Goetting's book *Getting Out: Life Stories of Women Who Left Abusive Men* (1999), and Susan Weitzman's *"Not to People Like Us": Hidden Abuse in Upscale Marriages* (2000).

7. For a critical discussion of cinematic theories of spectatorship see Mayne (1993).

## References

Apted, Michael, dir. 2002. *Enough*. New York: Sony Pictures. Motion picture.

Bordo, Susan. 1997. *Twilight Zones: The Hidden Life of Cultural Images from Plato to O.J.* Berkeley: University of California Press.

Cole, Alyson M. 1999. "'There Are No Victims in This Class': On Female Suffering and Anti-'Victim Feminism.'" *NWSA Journal* 11(1):72–96.

de Lauretis, Teresa. 1984. *Alice Doesn't: Feminism, Semiotics, Cinema*. Bloomington: Indiana University Press.

Dutton, Donald G. 1995. *The Domestic Assault of Women*. Vancouver: UBC Press.

Evans, Patricia. 1992. *The Verbally Abusive Relationship*. Holbrook, Mass.: Bob Adams.

Felder, Raoul, and Barbara Victor. 1996. *Getting Away with Murder: Weapons for the War against Domestic Violence*. New York: Simon and Schuster.

Field, Todd, dir. 2002. *In the Bedroom*. New York: Miramax Films. Motion picture.

Gibson, Brian, dir. 1993. *What's Love Got to Do with It*. Burbank, CA: Touchstone Pictures. Motion picture.

Goetting, Ann. 1999. *Getting Out: Life Stories of Women Who Left Abusive Men*. New York: Columbia University Press.

Gordon, Linda. 1991. "On Difference." *Genders* 10(1):91–111.

Hackford, Taylor, dir. 1995. *Dolores Claiborne*. New York: Castle Rock Entertainment. Motion picture.

Hall, Stuart. 1981. "The Whites of Their Eyes: Racist Ideologies and the Media." In *Silver Linings: Some Strategies for the 80's*, ed. George Bridges and Rosalind Brunt, 28–52. London: Lawrence and Wishart.

Hitchcock, Alfred, dir. 1958. *Vertigo*. Universal City, Calif.: Universal Studios. Motion picture.

hooks, bell. 1990. *Yearning: Race, Gender and Cultural Politics*. Boston: South End Press.

———. 1994. *Outlaw Culture: Resisting Representations*. New York: Routledge.

Jacobson, Neil, and John Gottman. 1998. *When Men Batter Women: New Insights into Ending Abusive Relationships*. New York: Simon and Schuster.

Johnson, Hillary. 1995. "The Truth about White Collar Domestic Violence." *Working Woman* March:54–7; 92–6.

Jones, Ann. 1994. *Next Time She'll Be Dead: Battering and How to Stop It*. Boston: Beacon Press.

Martin, Del. 1981. *Battered Wives*. Volcano, Calif.: Volcano Press.

Mayne, Judith. 1993. *Cinema and Spectatorship*. New York: Routledge.

Miller, George, dir. 1985. *Mad Max 3: Beyond Thunderdome*. Burbank, Calif.: Warner Brothers. Motion picture.

Orth, Maureen. 1993. "The Lady Has Legs." *Vanity Fair* 56(May):114–21, 166–77.

Ruben, Joseph, dir. 1991. *Sleeping with the Enemy*. Los Angeles: Twentieth Century Fox. Motion picture.

Scott, Joan W. 1992. "Experience." In *Feminists Theorize the Political*, ed. Judith Butler and Joan W. Scott, 22–40. New York: Routledge.

Sharrett, Christopher. 1999. *Mythologies of Violence in Postmodern Media*. Detroit: Wayne State University Press.

Sontag, Deborah. 2002. "Fierce Entanglements." *New York Times Magazine*, 17 November:52–7, 62, 84.

Tasker, Yvonne. 1998. *Working Girls: Gender and Sexuality in Popular Cinema.* New York: Routledge.
Turner, Tina, with Kurt Loder. 1986. *I, Tina.* New York: Avon Books.
Walker, Lenore E. 1979. *The Battered Woman.* New York: Harper Perennial.
Weitzman, Susan. 2000. *"Not to People Like Us": Hidden Abuse in Upscale Marriages.* New York: Basic Books.

CHAPTER EIGHT

# The Missing Story of Ourselves: Poor Women, Power, and the Politics of Feminist Representation

VIVYAN C. ADAIR

> Until the missing story of ourselves is told, nothing besides told can suffice us / We shall go on quietly craving it / In the missing story of ourselves can be found all other missing stories.
>
> Laura Riding Jackson (1973, 111)

In the spring of 1986 I awoke in a shelter for battered women. I had four missing teeth, a broken clavicle, and bruised ribs; in the small cot next to me lay my 8-month-old daughter, Heather, still traumatized by the brutalization we had suffered at the hands of her own father. With scant education and family support, few resources, and no job, I had little reason for hope.

That morning we boarded a public bus to find our way to the welfare office where I had hoped to secure support with which we might begin to rebuild our lives. As we somberly boarded the bus, passengers recoiled, reacting to my wrinkled and still vaguely blood-stained clothing, unwashed hair, bruised and deformed face. I am quite sure that even my beloved and beautiful child startled them with her blank and oddly aged gaze. As I held up the line by stumbling to count out my change, the bus driver looked from the infant in my arms down to the worn-out shoes I had purchased at the Salvation Army a week before, shook his head and raised his voice, painstakingly enunciating his words. "Don't bother," he shouted, perhaps confusing my tattered footwear and missing teeth for a loss of hearing and/or common sense, "the welfare office is only a few stops away. Sit down and get out of the way."

At the Department of Health and Human Services I was met with similar looks of disdain mingled with uneasy pity. Only my caseworker was clear and unequivocal. It would take at least two weeks to reopen my case and process my request for assistance; I could not apply for food stamps unless I had a rent receipt in my own name (which of course I did not); and state-issued medical coupons would only cover the repair of my one missing front tooth. The others—a bicuspid and two molars—he explained with unintended irony, were not considered medically necessary for someone "feeding at the public trough."

---

Originally published in the Spring 2008 issue of the *NWSA Journal*.

I was ashamed and humiliated. In that moment, however, I understood quite clearly that the bus driver, the caseworker, and those I came into contact with were all literally reading our bodies like texts, somehow finding my infant daughter and I pathological and aberrant and in need not of support or assistance, but of control, regulation, punishment, and discipline. Further, the policy that this reading of the bodies of poor women and children assured, nay determined, that I would be destined to walk through the world with inadequate clothing, missing teeth, a distanced and shell-shocked child, and a body that would, as a result, continue to both evoke and justify fear and further punishing judgments. In that moment I came to appreciate the complexity of the circuit through which bodies are represented and understood in ways that reflect the dominant ideology. (See diagram below.) That ideology in turn determines, shapes, and reinforces public policy; and public policy leaves its marks on the bodies of poor single mothers of all ages, races, sexualities, and nationalities. These women are then interpreted endlessly as broken, scarred, dangerous, and illegitimate others in need of further public and material control (Adair 2002).

My intimate understanding of this inviolate and closed cycle helped me to reframe childhood memories of being marked as "trash," "unworthy," "dirty," and "illegitimate." I became convinced that if I could only go back to school, I might be better able to understand, contextualize, and counter this cycle; and that through higher education I could acquire the knowledge, skills, and the authority needed to disrupt this ubiquitous, self-replicating, and nearly impenetrable cyclical force of power. I imagined that with this power I might additionally begin to redirect, or at least to impact, the policy that had such a profound and devastating impact on my life and on the lives of other poor women and children in the contemporary United States.

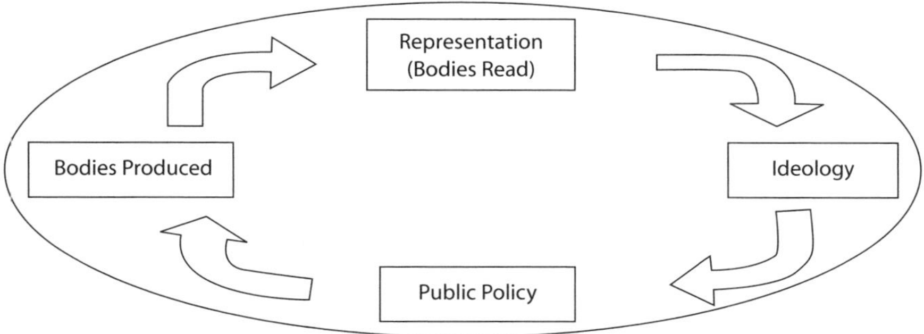

## Poverty and the Promise of Higher Education

I returned to the shelter on that spring afternoon without help or hope. However, with a newfound and passionate desire to go to college so that I might come to understand and mitigate my place in the circuit of power, and with the assistance of kind, loving, and patient women in the shelter—who had themselves been victims of both poverty and domestic violence—I began to intervene, to work to rewrite my own life and value in the world, to tell different stories to/of myself and others, and to dedicate myself to helping other poor women with a similar empowerment through higher education.

At the age of 32, after leaving the shelter, I enrolled in General Education Degree (GED) classes at a local community college. I entered school as a single mother, welfare recipient, and fragile student. Undoubtedly I lacked the skills, knowledge, self-esteem, and/or vision necessary to glean the full benefits of a liberal arts education and to earn a college degree that might enable me to work productively and to support and nurture my family.[1] Yet, at North Seattle Community College, and later at the University of Washington, Seattle, I was supported and challenged by dedicated, able, and patient instructors who encouraged me to transform my life positively through the pathway of higher education. My passage was guided by those teachers whose feminist classrooms became places where I was able to build bridges connecting my own knowledge of the world to crucial new knowledge, skills, and methodologies. Dedicated faculty created exciting, engaging exercises and orchestrated intensely challenging discussions that enabled me to embrace a vast range of knowledge and to use my newfound skills to reenvision my gifts, strengths, and responsibilities to the world around me.

While in school I studied, attended classes, worked, and cared for my daughter. I gratefully received minimal Aid to Families with Dependent Children (AFDC) "welfare" grants, food stamps, and Medicaid. On a regular basis I sold my plasma at blood banks and engaged in paid medical experiments to pay rent and buy books for classes. And I learned and grew. Little by little the larger social, creative, political, and material world exposed itself to me in ways that were resonant and urgent, inviting me to analyze, negotiate, articulate, and reframe systems, histories, and pathways that had previously seemed inaccessible. The process was invigorating, restorative, and life altering.[2]

My journey, while joyous, was not anomalous. Indeed, in 1987, the year that I entered college, as many as 350,000 welfare recipients around the nation were similarly enrolled in institutions of higher education as a route out of poverty (Wolfe and Gittell 1997, 18). Prior to welfare reform in 1996, countless poor single mothers quietly accessed postsecondary education to become teachers, lawyers, social service providers, business and civic leaders, and medical professionals (Nightengale 2000). While education is important to everyone, my experience and research convince me that it is essential for those who will face the continued obstacles of racism, classism, sexism, and homophobia; to those who have been distanced and disenfranchised from U.S. mainstream culture; and to those who have suffered generations of oppression and marginalization (Adair and Dahlberg 2003; Adair 2005).

Unfortunately, in 1996, Congress enacted the Personal Responsibility and Work Opportunity Reconciliation Act (PRWORA) as a part of welfare reform. This act gravely curtailed the ability of poor women to garner authority and to rewrite their own stories through education in a way that positively altered the trajectories and conditions of their lives. Composed of a broad tangle of legislation, PRWORA "devolved" responsibility for assistance to the poor from the federal to the state level, and through a range of block grants, sanctions, and rewards, encouraged states to reduce their welfare rolls by developing stringent work requirements, imposing strict time limits, discouraging "illegitimacy," and reducing the numbers of applicants eligible for services. Unlike previous provisions in AFDC and JOBS education training programs in existence when I first went to college, Temporary Aid to Needy Families (TANF) restrictions from 1996 do not allow higher education to be counted as work and required a larger proportion of welfare recipients to engage in full-time recognized work activities. This Work-First philosophy emphasized rapid entry into the labor force and penalized states for allowing long-term access to either education or training (Adair 2001; PRWORA 2003; Adair and Dahlberg 2003).

Debates surrounding this crucial legislation in the mid-1990s illustrate the degree to which public imagery reading poor women as pathological drew from the material conditions of our lives and underscored an agenda of increased control and punishment. As Mimi Abramowitz recalls, "In 1996, numerous legislators and witnesses made reference to 'welfare queen' stereotypes, as undeserving women who deliberately avoid both work and marriage; spend their welfare checks on liquor, drugs and fast cars; and produce large broods of children so as to qualify for even a larger government dole" (2000, 2). Throughout the fall of 1996, on the floor of the U.S. Congress, women on welfare were characterized as dirty, oversexed, and dangerous. Senator Mica of Arizona compared welfare mothers to alligators who if allowed would eat their own young, and U.S. congressman Rick Santorum of Pennsylvania referred to recipients as "unfit parents who view their children as nothing more than increases in welfare checks" (Gustafson 2004).

This rhetoric underwrote a logic demanding that welfare recipients be removed from the rolls, made to work, and encouraged—some suggested that they be forced—to marry. Reform was designed to rehabilitate "undeserving" poor single mothers by bringing them squarely under the control of men in the home and in the workplace. This dramatic overhaul of welfare policy forced welfare-recipient students to leave college for low-wage jobs in record numbers. According to the Center on Budget and Policy Priorities, in the first year of welfare reform, tens of thousands of poor women were forced to drop out of school. In states across the nation, the decrease in college enrollments among welfare recipients ranged from 29 to 82 percent (2005, 33).

I was a postdoctoral instructor at the University of Washington, Seattle, in 1996, when I lost three students to welfare reform. Two of the students left the state and the other, Tonya Mitchell, a young African American mother of twin girls, has stayed in contact with me and has since written a chapter in *Reclaiming Class: Women, Poverty and the Promise of Higher Education in the United States* (Adair and Dahlberg 2003, 113–8). Mitchell had wanted to earn a degree that would allow her to work as a nurse, and she was certainly capable and dedicated enough to do so. Nurses in the area make $30–$45 per hour and there is a shortage of, and a great demand for, medical professionals who are people of color and members of the communities they hope to serve (Wages 2005). With a solid A grade average and hours of volunteer work at a low-income community medical clinic, Mitchell's future seemed promising and secure.

However, at the beginning of her junior year, Mitchell was assigned to work full-time in a nursing home. If she refused this Work-First position she would incur sanctions and lose food stamps, childcare assistance, and medical insurance for herself and her twin daughters. On my last trip to Seattle I visited with my student who remains at that nursing home today. After working as an aide for the past ten years Mitchell is making less than $10 per hour. As a result, she and her young daughters are still struggling, living well below the poverty level, and she says she has given up hope.

Mitchell's experience is typical of "welfare leavers" who were forced to abandon school for work as a result of PRWORA policy. A study by the Urban Institute reported that:

> 50 to 75 percent of welfare leavers remain poor two to three years after leaving welfare. Most welfare leavers with incomes above the poverty line still have very low incomes: state-level leaver studies have found that about 90 percent of leavers have income below 185 percent of the poverty level. (Acs and Loprest, 2001)

Pamela Loprest estimated that in 2000 the median hourly wage for "welfare leavers" was $8.06 per hour, and that "about a third of leavers work part-time and [only] a third have employer health insurance" (2001, 18).

As a 2006 study by the Associated Press confirms, welfare reform pushed poor women into work but not toward self-sufficiency. The U.S. Census data reflect that the number of people relying on government services increased from 39 million in 1996 to 44 million in 2003. Although "welfare reform" reduced welfare receipt by as much as 60 percent, ten years after its implementation the overwhelming majority of welfare recipients work but remain poor and dependent upon services including food stamps, housing assistance, and Medicaid (Ohlemacher 2007).

Policy that prevents poor women from entering into and completing college degree programs that could lead to fiscal security and family health and safety is evidence of the material impact of ideology. Such policy begins by reading poor women as unreliable, undeserving, and dangerous and concludes by indelibly marking our bodies and lives. I was able to survive by narrowly escaping the implementation of PRWORA policy. Mitchell and tens of thousands of others have not been so fortunate.

After completing my Ph.D., I was hired as a professor at Hamilton College but continued to be haunted by the memory of Mitchell and so many of my friends, colleagues, and family members on welfare who would never have the opportunity to earn their way out of poverty and into stable and secure employment. And so, within months of arriving at Hamilton I began writing grant proposals and planning a program that would help poor student-parents earn college degrees. Through the funding provided by these grants the ACCESS Project was begun over nine years ago in the winter of 1999 (Adair 2003).[3]

## The ACCESS Project at Hamilton College

The ACCESS Project (Academic Coalition for Full Citizenship through Education and Social Support) at Hamilton College is an educational, social service, and career program that assists profoundly low-income, single parents in central New York in their efforts to move from welfare and low-wage work to fulfilling and secure career employment through the pathway of higher education. Our program supports this increasingly "at risk" population through an intensive introduction to liberal arts education coupled with comprehensive social service, family, and career support. On a daily basis we assist our students with academic supports and address substantial obstacles such as lack of adequate childcare and transportation, domestic violence and battery, homelessness, eviction, utility shut-offs, hunger, and lack of self-esteem. As a result, in the years that our program has been in operation, our students have survived—indeed they have thrived—both at Hamilton College and in their nascent career pathways.[4]

The ACCESS Project adheres to the same rigorous academic standards for which Hamilton College is well known. Students work assiduously to complete coursework successfully and with distinction, and they graduate at unprecedented rates. For example, by the spring of 2006, over 90 percent of our first cohort had graduated with a four-year degree (and a GPA of 82.3 percent), and almost one-third of those students are now enrolled in graduate programs in medicine, law, education, social sciences, humanities, and the arts.[5] All of them are working in their chosen career fields and—unlike 44 million working poor—earning wages above the poverty level (Ohlemacher 2007). Not only were our students earning noteworthy grades, they were additionally providing better care for their children whose well-being, health, and school performances had been recorded and were noted to be substantially enhanced after their parents' exposure to ACCESS. These ACCESS students also gained valuable experience, skills, and networking connections in paid and unpaid work and internships; and they increased their understanding of and commitment to the workings of our communities and the nation (Adair 2003). As a group ACCESS students have overcome enormous obstacles to complete their studies, their work, and to provide care for their children; and they have done so with courage, determination, and with increasing skills and confidence.

In honing sophisticated skill and methodological sets, ACCESS students begin to alter not just the surface skills and knowledge they hold, but they learn to alter the way they think, problem-solve, communicate, work, lead others, and value themselves. They become increasingly able, educated, and engaged thinkers, community leaders, and *citizens* in the fullest sense of the term. Critical and feminist analysis become perfect "operator's manuals" for our students providing them with models that teach them to abandon their former traditional roles in civic engagement which required silence and invisibility. Through our work students come to understand that power and ideology "pulse along cultural isobars that shape and mark our own bodies as well as our thoughts" (Challenger 2005, 31). At a very practical level, they begin to see that knowledge empowers and that different viewpoints can compete, so that in the real material world they can fight back by analyzing, critiquing, and speaking out.

When welfare reform reauthorization came up in 2002, my students and I were studying poverty, representation, and public policy in the United States. In the year leading up to reauthorization we spent days speaking with politicians in Washington, D.C., and testifying before a congressional subcommittee. We made cases that we were sure would convince even reluctant legislators that it was in the nation's best interest to support those poor single-parent students who were able and willing to earn college degrees. We showed politicians and political pundits charts from the U.S. Census Bureau tracing the clear and causal link between educational attainment and higher earnings, illustrating that this was particularly true for women of color, who rank at the bottom of the pay scale in the United States (American 2006). We even shared longitudinal income calculations, demonstrating that many of us had moved from being "tax burdens" to being "tax assets" to the state and federal governments by earning college degrees and moving into a more secure and stable employment stratum (Welfare 2000).[6]

Despite the efforts of so many, key legislation determining the reauthorization of welfare reform in 2002 proved to be even more punitive for low-income women attempting to earn higher education degrees in the United States. The House of Representatives' welfare reauthorization bill put greater limitations on individuals by allowing a maximum of three months of vocational training during a two-year period and counting only "job readiness education"—and not education that would lead to career development and sustainable wages—as work activity. HR 4092 increased both work hours for individual recipients and states' participation requirements. It failed to allocate sufficient childcare funds, and it allowed state superwaivers[7] to take precedence over even minimal federal protections.

For many—certainly for my ACCESS students—the most egregious components of both the House and the Senate reauthorization bills were reductions in allowances for recipients to enter into education programs and in childcare funding. These bills, coupled with the ground-breaking $1.5 billion that was earmarked for federal TANF funds over the next five years, identified a narrow set of rigidly defined "marriage promotion" activities (PRWORA 2003). From the perspective of welfare students, this prohibition against education severely limits their ability to achieve personal fulfillment and independence through education, and for those who are single parents, the reduction in childcare assistance has dangerous implications. Support to needy families to feed and care for their children was denied and welfare mothers were prohibited from entering into educational programs. Instead, these welfare reform bills focused on encouraging and rewarding welfare-recipient parents for their attendance at marriage formation clinics and workshops.

During the last county-sponsored "family formation" seminar that I attended with student recipients—who were required to attend or risk losing medical and food stamp benefits—we were reminded by a very enthusiastic pastor that a good and successful wife yields to both God and her husband, sometimes even against the perceived needs of her own children. When an ACCESS student participant asked a case-manager who was observing our seminar for his thoughts about higher education for the poor, he replied without a trace of irony:

> Oh yes. Education is necessary in order to support and nurture your families. I strongly encourage you to support your husbands in going to school and doing whatever they can to make you and your children healthy and happy. Millions of wives—even my own mother—helped put their husbands through college on the GI bill, and we wouldn't be where we are today if it weren't for that sacrifice.

Obvious questions about heteronormativity arise from these mandates. In addition, participants asked the questions: "Who are poor people to marry?" "How does marrying a poor man and risking more children lift anyone out of poverty?" Such questions have been cleverly addressed by author Barbara Ehrenreich who reminds us:

> Sadly enough, welfare recipients are unlikely to marry CEOs or even the residents of conservative think tanks; they're likely to marry blue collar men—a group whose wages have been declining since the 80s. So, the real question is: How many such men would a woman have to marry to lift herself and her children out of poverty? By my calculations, approximately 2.3, although, strangely enough, the conservative marriage advocates are not offering to abolish the laws against polyandry. (2001, 15)

More fundamentally, legislation that denies poor women the opportunity to earn educational credentials, to be fulfilled as individuals, to be able to stand on their own two feet and care for their own children is born of a logic and rhetoric that suggests that all poor single mothers are bad mothers and that as a nation we can only value "legitimately" married mothers and their children. Such legislation is, or should be, a problem for all feminists.

As a result of reauthorization of PRWORA, the number of students enrolled full-time in programs of higher education further plummeted, from a high of 350,000 in 1992, to a low of 38,000 in 2002, or a reduction of almost 90 percent in ten years (London 2004). Knowing that higher education has the potential to lift poor women out of poverty, engage them in fulfilling and stable employment, give them a voice and authority, and help them raise healthy, happy, and productive children elicits the obvious question: "Why would legislators attempt through this legislation to punish and regulate the poor, sentencing them to lifetimes of poverty?" One answer, of course, is that there is economic pressure to provide employers with a ready-made, nonunion, minimum-wage, compliant—some would argue forced—labor pool. Additionally, poor single mothers have been positioned, framed as it were, as a population that requires regulation, punishment, and containment. Those with power and privilege have told stories of our lack of value, pathology, and danger to others, perpetuating narrative productions from which we have been absent by design.

Wade Horn, the Bush administration's "Fatherhood Czar," insists that we should not encourage education, since recipients have "failed in the past" (Ohlemacher 2007). This is the "they are not smart or motivated enough" argument. Others suggest that these poor single mothers belong in their places as low-wage workers. In Senator Russell Long's now infamous words, "If all poor women get to go to college who is going to iron my shirts?" (Patterson 2000, 188). A third objection suggests that these women don't deserve to go to college, that they have broken the rules by having children, not marrying, and engaging in "bad behavior." This is the persistent theme of Robert Rector of the Heritage Foundation (Adair and Rector 2007). I reject all three propositions as unsubstantiated and insulting. Certainly these beliefs should not provide the foundation upon which to build law and policy (Adair 2007).

## To Tell a Different Story

In the past two decades, public images of the alleged pathology and degradation of poor women and their children have permeated media and political representation in the United States (Hill Collins 2000; Lubiano 1992). As many scholars have noted, these stories rest on and reproduce virulent racist, sexist, heterosexist, and ableist assumptions and understandings of poor women. Further, these often repeated representations underscore and are employed to justify punitive reform policy—as in the case of 1996 reform and reauthorization in 2002. These policy decisions have a real and immediately detrimental impact on our lives. The PRWORA regulations and programs force us to work at low-paying jobs that do not allow us to pay our rent or feed our children properly; they keep us from being able to have our teeth repaired or afford heat; they force us to give up our right to privacy and to labor protections; and they prevent us from earning educational degrees with which we might be able to better our lives and alleviate the pain of material poverty (Adair 2002; Edin and Lein 1997). In a final irony our broken bodies are then read as examples and as proof of our degeneracy, depravity, and the danger we pose to an inviolate society that rests on the articulation and maintenance of scripts of power and authority from which we have been effectively excluded.

By investigating this nexus of representation, ideology, policy, and our own material lives, my ACCESS students and I came to understand that stories have the power to transform our world. As a result, three years ago, we dedicated ourselves to dismantling and then re-telling our own stories, pushing back against those explanatory narratives that have devalued and ultimately harmed us, through our nationally traveling exhibit *The Missing Story of Ourselves: Poverty and the Promise of Higher Education.*[8]

In our fifty-piece installation we represent visual and narrative points of view of contributors who are African American, Afro-Caribbean, Caucasian, Asian American, Latino, Native American, and South East Asian, ranging in age from 18 to 58. Some of us were born in the United States and come from intergenerational poverty; others came to the United States from other countries as poor children. As a group we represent different faiths and sexual orientations; we come from settings that are both rural and urban and from both private and public educational institutions. What binds us is our common experience of being or having been profoundly poor as children or as parents who against all odds successfully entered into programs of higher education as a pathway out of poverty.

Ours are complex, first-person views of what poverty and resistance look like from the inside out. They allow us to delineate and map our own lives and values as well as to offer insights into larger ethical questions of human value and community. We have responded to the challenge of finding our own voices and collective identity through *The Missing Story of Ourselves* by speaking together—personally, creatively, analytically, and theoretically—in an effort to assure a crucial plurality and diversity of perspectives and representations. In telling different stories of our value, and in exposing the processes of ideology through which our value (or lack of) is traditionally determined and disseminated, we hope to interrupt that closed circuit of desire that would otherwise mark and guarantee our place as "other" in cultural, social, and legal matrixes.

The striking diversity of our students and exhibit contributors accurately reflects the demographics of poverty and welfare in the contemporary United States. Poverty is a complex phenomenon tied to but not coterminous with issues of race and gender. In 2006, over 60 percent of the poor in the nation were white, yet poverty disproportionately strikes people of color, women, the rural, children, and the aged (American 2006).[9] Despite a wide range of differences among poor women (as in any group), in public discourse they are most often metonymically reduced to singular images or stereotypes. In *Why Americans Hate Welfare,* Martin Gilens suggests that contrary to the statistical reality of U.S. poverty, the stereotype of the welfare mother is primarily a racial trope. Gilens illustrates that the vast majority of representations of the poor in the popular press over the past 45 years were drawn from and driven by racist images of "blacks as lazy . . . [views] that have prevailed throughout U.S. history" (1999, 27). Don Stewart identifies a broader stereotype of the poor when he notes that the public positions "all women on welfare as just like those cheats we see on the news—fat, lazy, white trash living in a trailer park or a young, single, pregnant uneducated black mother living in a ghetto with five children who is selling her food stamps to buy alcohol" (1999).

Contemporary narrative productions orchestrate the story of poor women as one of moral and intellectual lack and of chaos, pathology, promiscuity, illogic, and sloth, juxtaposed always against the alleged order, progress, and decency of "deserving" citizens. Trying to stabilize and make sense of unpalatably complex issues of poverty and oppression and attempting to obscure hegemonic representation, these narratives reduce and collapse the lives and experiences of poor women to deceptively simplistic dramas, which are then offered for public consumption. The terms of these dramas are palatable because they are presented as simple oppositions of good and bad, right and wrong, independent and dependent, deserving and undeserving.

## "Broodmares and Welfare Queens"

Against these simple, reductive, and pejorative images, in *The Missing Story of Ourselves* we present complex stories that refuse the iconography of the poor woman as law breaker, bad mother, incapable worker, or degenerate citizen. Fransheneka Watson, a young African American woman, tells her own story of being supported by welfare when as a result of her parents' death she moved in with her ill and impoverished grandparents, eventually becoming the sole support of her family at age 16. Despite working full-time, attending the University of Houston-DT, and caring for her younger brother and aged grandparents, Watson is an honor student who hopes to provide counseling to low-income autistic children in the public schools.

Lynn Woolsey, a white woman, relates her life as a frightened, newly divorced mother of two in Silicon Valley, California in her essay. Although she was forced to turn to welfare she was able to go back to school and begin several businesses. With the goal of "serving our nation as an ethical, committed and capable public servant," Woolsey eventually ran for public office. Since 1992 she has been Congresswoman Woolsey, ably representing the people of the Sixth Congressional District (CA) in Washington, D.C. Similarly, Dr. Gita Rajan, originally from India, was thrown into U.S. poverty when after experiencing a devastating divorce she became solely responsible for the support of her young family. After returning to college, while working, using food pantries, and securing school loans, she earned her Ph.D. and is now an award-winning teacher and a gifted scholar and writer. Her latest book, *New Cosmopolitanisms: South Asians in the United States,* was released in 2006 by Stanford University Press to critical acclaim; in the same year her son earned his doctoral degree in neuroengineering.

Shannon Stanfield, a poor, single, white mother from America's "heartland" explains in her story that when she married right out of high school and followed her husband across the county so that he could pursue his career, she was confident she was doing the "honorable and reasonable thing." Yet, fewer than seven years later Stanfield found herself alone with "two small and rather traumatized babies, after being lied to, abused, and eventually abandoned" by the husband she had helped get ahead. Without any savings, with little education or work experience, Stanfield found herself at the mercy of the state. She was assigned to a Work-First position but recalls that her wages "barely covered [her] rent and left nothing for baby diapers, utilities, or transportation." She adds: "Each morning I would leave my children to trudge off to a job that could never support us." Today, Stanfield, a rising university senior with an A grade average, declares that as a result of her entry into college—and for the first time in her life—she has been able to:

> Take my children and climb the stone walls built by hopelessness and helplessness. A new sense of purpose and value has delivered me and my children from a static, uncertain, and violent future. In college I have come to recognize and embrace my own potential as I reshape and stabilize my family's and my own future through knowledge, self respect and fulfillment. (Stanfield 2005, 29)

## "Children Having Children"

The stereotype of the "welfare queen" attached to women needing financial assistance flattens out complexities to produce a trite, unavailing story of poverty. Similarly, the image of the teen mother welfare recipient simplistically underwrites much of the language of welfare reform. While the hot-button topic of "children having children" loomed large in welfare debates the number of unmarried teen mothers actually receiving benefits prior to 1996 was less than 0.5 percent of the total national welfare caseload (Sparks 2003, 20). Nevertheless, as Holloway Sparks points out, "The image of welfare mothers as poor, unwed teenagers who are inept, irresponsible and producing babies for monetary gain is alluring. . . . These stereotypes reduce complexity and channel our fears toward an easy target. Stereotypes of incapable and evil unmarried teen mothers are used to justify social policy" (22).

Against these public and widely proliferated narratives, our colleagues push back with the missing stories of their lives. Claudia Garcia writes of surviving on welfare, leaving her family home, and having a child at age 16. Determined to change her life for the sake of her beloved child, and enduring hunger, exhaustion, and family alienation, Garcia is now a doctor of optometry with her own growing practice and a bright, happy, and well-adjusted, college-bound daughter. Garcia writes: "My daughter has learned that hard work and motivation will help her reach her own fullest potential. Being a mother, a doctor and a business partner can be exhausting. I find the strength that I need when I look at my daughter and see in her better opportunities because of the sacrifices I made for both of us" (2005, 11).

Jamala McFadden was the daughter of a welfare recipient and a single mother herself at age 15 in Chicago. With the aid of welfare and the support of a caring community and college faculty she graduated at the top of her class with a degree in political science from the University of Illinois, attended one of the top ten law schools in the country, clerked for a federal judge, and now practices law at a prestigious law firm in Atlanta. She writes: "My son—now 13 (and already discussing college)—has been with me through it all. For those who believe that welfare is cyclical and repeats throughout generations—for this family, education has broken the cycle" (2005, 35).

Nolita Clark earned her GED at a Native American Academy and in the same year became a single teen mother. In her narrative she recognizes that "the cultural text of my devaluation, as written and read through public policy and welfare reform, suggests that my being a young, unmarried and pregnant woman of color, would mark me as being a problem, as an undeserving human being and mother." She goes on however to counter that: "The truth of my pregnancy was that it changed my life in remarkable and positive ways." She continues:

> Contrary to notions about selfish and unprepared teens giving birth to uncared for babies, with my daughter's birth everything became clearer and better in my life. My daughter looks up to me to provide her with the love and guidance she needs to be successful in life. The life I had growing up was full of hardships and struggle; the fear that my daughter might have to experience the things I did at her age motivates me to get up every morning and continue on the pathway I began a few years ago. In contrast to the stories that we always hear about, becoming an unmarried teenaged mother was a positive, life-enhancing experience. (Clark 2007, 143)

In June of 2006, Clark graduated with a degree in philosophy from Hamilton College. Her beautiful 5-year-old-daughter walked proudly by her side. In the near future Clark will enter law school where she plans to focus on U.S. tribal law, with the goal of serving low-income indigenous populations in New York State.

## "Refusing to Work, Marry, or Follow the Rules"

The Department of Health and Human Services lists the goals of PRWORA as a reduction in "dependency by promoting job preparation, work and marriage; to reduce the percent of out-of-wedlock pregnancies; and to encourage the formation and maintenance of two-parent families" (PRWORA 2003). Underwriting this tripartite mandate is the portrayal of poor single mothers who are "lazy due to years of government programming, illogical . . . out of control" and "crazed trying to meet [their] own selfish needs" (MacDonald, 2002b). These narratives representing poor women as dangerous parasites who have somehow violated the mandates of capitalism and heterosexism, invariably compare "unmarried mothers, misfits and spongers who are idle" to "legitimate and moral members of society who follow the rules, sacrifice and work" (2002c). As a result, policies that connect poor mothers to the public workplace are construed as narratives of rehabilitation that transform "dangerous" poor women's bodies into those of the relatively unmarked classes, safely neutralized under covertures of work and marriage.

Against these reductive and dangerous images we offer Paulette Brown, who by her 40s had served as an enlisted medical assistant in the U.S. Army, a bus driver, a taxi driver, a waitress, and a hotel maid, all while raising her two sons. Then, at the age of 41—without medical insurance, savings, or job security—Brown suffered a heart attack and was forced to rely temporarily on welfare. Afterward, Brown changed her life by enrolling in the ACCESS program, where, she says: "Everyday I learn new skills, am exposed to new knowledge and ways of thinking. Education has complicated my story and provided me with a nuanced understanding of the racist, classist and sexist stories that mark me as 'Other' " (Brown 2007, 140). Today Brown's sons thrive (her youngest entered college in the fall of 2006). She works full-time for Catholic Charities and is completing a college degree in social services at Utica College of Syracuse University. She is a leader, mentor, advocate, and role model for other low-income single mothers and fathers in our community.

We offer another motivational story of a poor, single mother, Stephanie Jones, who has worked full-time since the age of seventeen, attends college, and studies with her sons at the kitchen table each evening. This year both of her children were on their school's honor roll. She writes: "My sons and I have begun to build our education together. Together we learn and grow. Being a worker, single mother, community member and student allows [me] to make a positive and substantial difference in our lives and in our community" (Jones 2005, 19)

Similarly, Rose Perez tells her own cautionary tale of "Welfare to Work" and the long-term benefits of allowing poor single mothers to earn educational degrees as a route out of poverty. Perez begins by describing stories that marked her and her family as living lives of "laziness, selfishness and stupidity," adding: "You all know the story. We have all heard it far too many times."

After the birth of a healthy and beautiful son, Perez turned to the welfare office for assistance, and that story of her family's alleged pathology took "a dramatic turn for the worse." She explains: "To the welfare workers I turned to for help, my baby was 'illegitimate,' the child of worthless and even hopeless people." Lecturing that she must work full-time or risk becoming a "generational freeloader," her caseworker required that Rose become "a better mother, [by] going to work at minimum wage without childcare assistance."

Trying to "squeeze into the state's version of a success story of independence" Perez worked full-time and asked a male acquaintance who was unemployed to babysit in exchange for a place to live. She recalls that:

> One day, annoyed at my child's normal 2-year-old behavior, this man snapped. He beat my child. Trying to cover up the bruises, he put my baby into a bath filled with scalding water. [My son] received third degree burns to his lower legs and feet. He has been permanently scarred since that moment. Each year at the Shriner's hospital in Boston he has to have painful surgeries and skin grafts. The monster that did this to my son will spend the next twenty-five years of his life in jail. Yet the welfare office continued to judge, regulate and punish us. (Perez 2005, 36)

Even though this devastated mother was at work during the time, she was blamed for her son's abuse, accused of making "bad choices," of not providing sufficient care for her baby and of putting her own needs before his. Welfare caseworkers told her that she was "irresponsible for having a child without the protection of a 'legal' father" and Child Protective Services threatened to take her beloved child from her. To date Perez's son has undergone over a dozen painful surgeries to stretch his skin so that his bones can grow. At age 11 he is an intelligent, loving, and responsible young man. As Perez nurtures, guides, and cares for him, she is earning a college degree in criminal justice and working full-time at a shelter for battered women. She concludes by acknowledging that her "story is difficult to tell," but adds that "in pushing back and telling a different story in *The Missing Story of Ourselves*, I want to show those with power that we are human beings with complex lives. If my story can change the mind of one policy maker, law maker or voter or give support to one frightened, hurt and silenced woman (as it has to me) then the effort has been more than worthwhile" (Perez 2007, 137).

## "Welfare Scars Children"

Finally, contemporary rhetoric suggests that welfare itself is bad for the country and dangerous for the children it was designed to help. As a part of the *Republican Contract with America*, then U.S. House majority leader Newt Gingrich proposed that children of welfare mothers be placed in orphanages. His reasoning centered on the idea that out-of-home care would be better than the care—and alleged damage—unmarried welfare mothers would provide, and that cutting the emotional bonds and removing the modeling that poor women inflict upon their young would be good for the nation (Gershaw 1995, 3).

Robert Rector and Patrick Fagan, in "How Welfare Harms Kids," offered a similarly frantic warning, adding that:

> Overall welfare operates as a form of social toxin. The more of this toxin received by a child's family, the less successful the child will be as an adult. If America's children are to be saved [from their own mothers] the current welfare system must be replaced. Higher welfare payments do not help children; they increase dependence and illegitimacy, which have a devastating effect on children's development. (1996)

For these "compassionate conservative reformers" poor women need only be forced to work and marry to save their children and the nation. In Rector's view—articulated in an NPR debate with me and taped for *Morning Edition*—"the idea of poor women going to college is ridiculous. A good mother has a husband and works for her family; she doesn't hide out in school" (Rector 2002).

Against these narratives and in contrast to the rhetoric of welfare reform that suggests that only through work and marriage can poor mothers and their children be redeemed, we present Bich Ha Pham, now an attorney who runs Hunger Action Network in New York City. As a child she recalls coming to this country with her family as a refugee from Viet Nam and needing welfare to secure food, clothing, utilities, school supplies, and books that she would eventually use to gain economic security (Pham 2005). The assistance of welfare and access to higher education allowed Pham to achieve success by engaging in, rather than "hiding out" from, the world and her responsibility to others.

Teresa Willmore applied to college when her love of learning and life had been utterly destroyed by a difficult divorce and years of work that left her "feeling desperate, worthless, disgraced . . . demeaned and demoralized at the end of every day." Teresa, once on welfare, returned to school. She recalls that "some of that weight lifted from my shoulders, and I knew a moment of hope." Enduring "three of the most grueling and rewarding years of [her] life at Hamilton College," Willmore graduated *summa cum laude* in 2003, with a GPA of 94.82 and as a member of Phi Beta Kappa, bound for graduate school. Crucially, Willmore recalls the impact that her own transformative experience of education had on her two young children. She writes:

> I now realize that the world consists of more than the need to fill my children's stomachs. I need to feed their minds as well. Today my son, diagnosed with ADD, after doing homework with me for so many hours, thinks he can succeed without the Ritalin. My daughter is a straight-A student. This happened while I struggled through my classes, and they watched their role model—me. Today I have a rewarding and productive job that in no way leaves me feeling demeaned, and I love, support, nurture, inspire and care for my children on my own. (Willmore 2005, 23)

And, I offer the image and story of my own daughter, Heather, who lay broken in that tiny cot in the shelter next to me 20 years ago. Now an honor student majoring in philosophy at Smith College, she writes of her life as the child of a welfare-mother student and of the long-term impact of higher education on our lives, remembering:

> This is where my life began . . . and my mother's life, too. It is safe to say that without an education, neither of us would exist as we do today. My mother carried home a passion for education that could not help but make an irrevocable impression on my young mind. In me she fostered a reverence for knowledge and education that I clung to in the wake of material want. My mother's determination gave me hope for our future and a belief that we were worth more than what society credited us. Every night I would go to sleep knowing that she was awake, preparing for her classes and working to pull us out of the poverty we had both been born into. (Adair 2005, 8)

Heather concludes that: "Unlike so many people born into poverty, I have been given a renewed vision of life. In addition to the obvious economic, cultural and social benefits of our transformation, I have gained an intense respect for education, civic responsibility and moral engagement that will aid, shape and inspire me throughout my life" (Adair 2005, 7). My own child's understanding of the impact that higher education had in changing our lives materially, emotionally, and intellectually reflects the life-altering transformation of so many of our ACCESS students and their children. They, as we, were once disenfranchised but through access to higher education are now fully able to participate in their own renewed vision of life—a life finally filled with hope and possibility.

## Conclusion

The goal of *The Missing Story of Ourselves* exhibit, initially, was simply to tell our own stories, to replace stories that hurt and marginalized us with more positive, complex, and "authentic" stories. Calling on the early feminist tradition of embracing stories of personal experience that have been eclipsed in canonical productions of knowledge and power, we wanted to tell our stories, that were simultaneously personal and political, as radical alternatives to master narratives and to claims of objectivity. And yet, we were very aware of postmodern critiques pointing out that stories are always structurally essentialist. We also understood the notion that because our own language, narrative, and identities are saturated with ideology, our stories are both suspect and risky. At some level we agreed with the argument that we cannot trust stories to reveal truth or to resist it let alone dismantle the status quo of the power structure. (Scott 1999; Stone-Mediatore 2003).

Yet, in the final analysis we want to retrieve the epistemic value of the images and words of poor women precisely because our stories explore and expose the ways individuals constrained within the social matrix both capitulate to and resist ideology. We believe that stories from the margins, like those in *The Missing Story of Ourselves*, are crucial as they "critically test the prejudices that underwrite narrative norms and that are perpetuated by powerful knowledge producing institutions." As Shari Stone-Mediatore argues: "On-going and serious engagement with such stories is the only way to keep knowledge production accountable to those outside ruling institutions and to sustain democratic communities" (2003, 118).

Creating our visions and sharing our stories and images have allowed all of us to think differently about our identities and relationships to larger ideologies that are designed to control, define, and silence us. In solidarity, in *The Missing Story of Ourselves*, poor, single parent students push back by speaking back. Most of us have struggled, but we use those struggles to focus and increase our resolve to succeed and to understand. In doing so, we analyze and dismantle the stories, policies, and belief systems that would otherwise diminish and demoralize us.

Crucially, telling our own stories reminds us that we are connected and indebted to others who have also been both misread and silenced. We hope that by telling our stories in venues of power and authority we will expose this system of exclusion. We call for a willingness to hear and value the stories of other marginalized men and women who attempt to articulate and theorize their own narratives of identity and experience. We are grateful for the opportunity to speak back, to rewrite our value in the world, to attempt to disrupt the insidious cycle through which we have been marked and then guaranteed as "other," and to begin to tell "the missing story of ourselves."

## Notes

1. Most studies show that women who entered into postsecondary programs while on AFDC benefited from the programs and were able to earn college

degrees successfully. See Joanne Thompson 1993; Thomas Karrier 1998; Erika Kates 1998; and Peggy Kahn and Valerie Polakow 2000.

2. I am indebted to Professors Marilyn Smith, Michael Kischner, Fran Schmitt, Tom Kerns, Barbara Boardman, Karen Stuhldreher, and President Ron La Fayette at North Seattle Community College, and to Professors Joycelyn K. Moody, Sydney J. Kaplan, Donna Gerstenberger, Carolyn Allen, Gail Stygall, George Dillon, and Steve Woodward at the University of Washington, Seattle.

3. We are grateful for the support of the State of New York, New York State Senator Raymond Meier, the Charles A. Frueauff Foundation, the Community Foundation of Herkimer and Oneida Counties, and members of the Hamilton College community.

4. In stark contrast, working poor, single mothers can barely cover their basic expenses, let alone pay for tuition and books. Any reduction in pay or benefits spells disaster as they must then choose between paying all of their rent or part of their heating bill. Additionally, child care assistance that is available to cover a mother's time at work cannot be used while mothers are in classes. Policy thus effectively prohibits poor working mothers from earning degrees and moving toward financial security and independence.

5. For analysis of why students drop out of the ACCESS Project please see *The ACCESS Project at Hamilton College Year End Report 2003*. www.hamilton.edu/college/access.

6. Education enabled me to secure employment that has provided my entire family with stability and dignity. It is true that my education cost my home state more than $30,000 to support me with food stamps, medical coupons, and housing and energy assistance while I earned college degrees. I am grateful for that support. But I also want to point out that within two years of working at Hamilton College I had paid back well over $30,000 in state and federal taxes. Today I pay double that amount. If I am able to work for an additional 20 years, I will have paid more than $600,000 in federal and state taxes that I would not have paid had I not earned those degrees. Supporting poor single parents as they move from being tax liabilities to tax assets makes fiscal as well as moral sense.

7. Superwaivers allow states to create employment programs for welfare recipients without adhering to state and federal labor protections.

8. *The Missing Story of Ourselves*. Please see: www.hamilton.edu/college/access.

9. There are approximately 299,398,484 individuals living in the United States 80.2% of those individuals are white, 12.8% are black; and 14.4% are of Hispanic origin. In 2006, over 37,764,789 individuals lived below the poverty line: About 60% (22,657,417) of those individuals were white; yet, individuals

are more than twice as likely to be born poor if they are black or Latino than if they are white. In 2006, 10.5% (22,657,417 out of 216,049,704) of white individuals were poor; 25.3% (8,968,940 out of 35,425,212) of black individuals were poor; and 21.8% (9,293,416 out of 43,306,059) of individuals of Hispanic origin lived below the poverty line. Similarly, although over 80% of the U.S. population live in urban centers, urban poverty is about 11.2% of the urban population while rural poverty rates are higher at 14.2%. (U.S. Census, American Community Survey, 2006. Retrieved August 2006: http://fastfacts.census.gov/servlet/CWSSTable?_bm=y&-geo_id=01000US&-qr_name=ACS_2006_EST_G00_S1701&-ds_name=ACS_2006_EST_G00_)

## References

Abramowitz, Mimi. 2000. *Under Attack, Fighting Back: Women and Welfare in the United States.* New York: Monthly Review Press.

Acs, Gregory, and Pamela Loprest. 2001. *Initial Synthesis Report of the Findings from ASPE's "Leavers" Grants.* The Urban Institute. Retrieved 2 October 2000, from: http://newfederalism.urban.org/html/series_b/anf_b1.html.

Adair, Heather. 2005. *The Missing Story of Ourselves: Poverty and the Promise of Higher Education, Gallery Guide.* The ACCESS Project at Hamilton College. Rome, N.Y.: Canterbury Press, 6–7.

Adair, Vivyan C. 2000. *From Good Ma to Welfare Queen; A Genealogy of the Poor Woman in American Literature, Photography, and Culture.* New York: Garland Publishing, .

———. 2001. "Poverty and the Broken Promise of Higher Education." *Harvard Educational Review* 71(2): 217–39.

———. 2002. "Branded with Infamy: Inscriptions of Poverty and Class in the United States." *Signs: Journal of Women in Culture and Society* 27(2): 451–72.

———. 2003. *The ACCESS Project at Hamilton College: Year End Report.* Rome, N.Y.: Canterbury Press.

———. 2005. "Class Absences: Cutting Class in Feminist Studies." *Feminist Studies* 31(3): 575–603.

———. 2005. "The Missing Story of Ourselves: Poverty and the Promise of Higher Education, Gallery Guide." The ACCESS Project at Hamilton College. Rome, N.Y.: Canterbury Press.

Adair, Vivyan C., and Sandra Dahlberg. 2003. *Reclaiming Class: Women, Poverty and the Promise of Education in America.* Philadelphia: Temple University Press.

Adair, Vivyan C., and Robert Rector. 2007. "Welfare Reform and Social Service Dependency." *News and Notes.* National Public Radio, March 5, 2007.

"American Community Population Survey 2006." 2006. *United States Bureau of the Census.* Washington, D.C.: U.S. Government Printing Office. Retrieved August 2006, from: http://fastfacts.census.gov/servlet/CWSSTable?_bm=y&-geo_id=01000US&-qr_name=ACS_2006_EST_G00_S1701&-ds_name=ACS_2006_EST_G00

Brown, Paulette. 2005. *The Missing Story of Ourselves: Poverty and the Promise of Higher Education.* The ACCESS Project at Hamilton College. www.hamilton.edu/college/access.

———. With 2007. Nolita Clark, Rose Perez, Shannon Stanfield, and Vivyan Adair. "Poverty and Storytelling in Higher Education." *Storytelling, Self, Society: An Interdisciplinary Journal of Storytelling Studies.* 3(2): 135–55.

Center on Budget and Policy Priorities. 2005. "Funding Issues in TANF Reauthorization." *Policy Brief.* Retrieved 10 May 2005 from http://www.cbpp.org/

Challenger, Don. 2005. "Telling a Different Story: Vivyan Adair, New York's CASE Carnegie Professor of the Year, on the Transformative Power of Education." *Hamilton Alumni Review* 70(1): 24–31.

Clark, Nolita. 2005. *The Missing Story of Ourselves: Poverty and the Promise of Higher Education, Gallery Guide.* The ACCESS Project at Hamilton College. Rome, N.Y.: Canterbury Press. 26–27.

———. With Paulette Brown, Rose Perez, Shannon Stanfield and Vivyan Adair. 2007. "Poverty and Storytelling in Higher Education." *Storytelling, Self, Society: An Interdisciplinary Journal of Storytelling Studies.* 3(2): 135–55.

Edin, Kathryn, and Laura Lein. 1997. *Making Ends Meet: How Single Mothers Survive Welfare and Low-Wage Work.* New York: Russell Sage Foundation.

Ehrenreich, Barbara. 2001. "Prodding the Poor to the Altar." *The Progressive* 65(8): 14–5.

Garcia, Claudia. 2005. *The Missing Story of Ourselves: Poverty and the Promise of Higher Education, Gallery Guide.* The ACCESS Project at Hamilton College. Rome, N.Y.: Canterbury Press, 10–11.

Gershaw, David. 1995. "From *Boys Town* to *Oliver Twist*: Separating Fact from Fiction in Welfare Reform and Out-of-Home Placement of Children and Youth." *American Psychologist* August: 565–80.

Gilens, Martin. 1999. *Why Americans Hate Welfare: Race, Media and the Politics of Anti-Poverty Policy.* Chicago: University of Chicago Press.

Gittell, Marilyn, Margaret Schehl, and Camille Fareri. 1990. *From Welfare to Independence: The College Option.* New York: Ford Foundation.

Gustafson, Kaaryn. 2005. "To Punish the Poor: Criminalizing Trends in the Welfare System." *Women of Color Resource Center Working Paper* No. 3.

Hill Collins, Patricia. 2000. *Black Feminist Thought: Knowledge, Consciousness and the Politics of Empowerment.* New York: Routledge.

Jackson, Laura Riding. 1973. "The Telling." *Collected Works of Laura Riding Jackson.* Tallahassee: University of Florida Press, 11–2.

Jones, Stephanie. 2005. *The Missing Story of Ourselves: Poverty and the Promise of Higher Education, Gallery Guide.* The ACCESS Project at Hamilton College. Rome, N.Y.: Canterbury Press, 18–19.

Kahn, Peggy, and Valerie Polakow. 2000. *Struggling to Stay in School: Obstacles to Post-Secondary Education under the Welfare-to-Work Restrictions in Michigan.* Ann Arbor: University of Michigan, Center for the Education of Women. Retrieved 1 February 2003, from: http://www.umich.edu/~cew/pubs/polakowkahn2000.pdf.

Karrier, Thomas. 1998. "Welfare Graduates: College and Financial Independence." *Public Policy Notes 1.* The Levy Economics Institute of Bard College. Retrieved 7 July 2006, from: www.levy.org/.

Kates, Erika. 1998. "College Can Help Women In Poverty." In *For Crying Out Loud: Women's Poverty in the United States,* ed. Diane Dujon and Ann Withorn, 341–8. Boston: South End Press.

London, Rebecca. 2004. "Welfare Recipients' College Attendance and Consequences for Time-Limited Aid." *Center for Justice, Tolerance, and Community. Poverty and Income Security.* Paper. Retrieved 5 February 2006, from: http://repositories.cdlib.org/cjtc/pis/cjtc_RL_2004_01.

Loprest, Pamela. 1999. *How Families That Left Welfare Are Doing: A National Picture.* The Urban Institute. Retrieved 2 October 2000, from: http://newfederalism.urban.org/html/series_b/anf_b1.html.

———. 2001. *How Are Families That Left Welfare Doing? A Comparison of Early and Recent Welfare Leavers.* Vol. Series B. The Urban Institute. Retrieved 5 November 2002, from: http://newfederalism.urban.org/html/series_b/anf_b1.html.

Lubiano, Wahneema. 1992. "Black Ladies, Welfare Queens and State Minstrels: Ideological War by Narrative Means" *Racing Justice, Engendering Power,* ed. Toni Morrison, 323–63. New York: Pantheon Books.

MacDonald, Heather. 2002a. "Work=Slavery?" *Daily News: The Manhattan Institute for Policy Research.* Retrieved 11 November 2005, from: http://www.manhattaninstitute.org/html/_nypost-work.htm.

———. 2002b. "Welfare Frauds Return?" *Daily News: The Manhattan Institute for Policy Research.* Retrieved 11 November 2005, from: http://www.manhattaninstitute.org/html/_nypost-work.htm.

———. 2002c. "Love, Honor and Get Off Dole." *Daily News: The Manhattan Institute for Policy Research.* Retrieved 11 November 2005, from: http://www.manhattan-institute.org/html/_nypost-work.htm.

McFadden, Jamala. 2005. *The Missing Story of Ourselves: Poverty and the Promise of Higher Education, Gallery Guide.* The ACCESS Project at Hamilton College. Rome, N.Y.: Canterbury Press, 34–5.

Mitchell, Tonya. 2003. "If I Survive It Will be Despite Welfare Reform." *Reclaiming Class: Women, Poverty and the Promise of Higher Education in America,* ed. Vivyan C. Adair and Sandra Dahlberg, 113–8. Philadelphia: Temple University Press.

Nightengale, Demetra Smith. 2000. "The Welfare-to-Work Grants Program: Evaluation Design and Preliminary Evidence." Lecture presented at the UMBC Honors University Lecture Series, 25 April, University of Maryland, Silver Spring, Maryland.

Ohlemacher, Stephen. 2007. "Welfare Rolls Keep Growing Despite Years of Overhauls." February 26. Associated Press. San Diego Union Tribune.com

Paterson, James T. 2000. America's Struggles against Poverty in the Twentieth Century. Cambridge, Mass.: Harvard University Press.

Perez, Rose. 2005. *The Missing Story of Ourselves: Poverty and the Promise of Higher Education, Gallery Guide.* The ACCESS Project at Hamilton College. Rome, N.Y.: Canterbury Press, 36–7.

———. Clark, Nolita, Paulette Brown, Shannon Stanfield and Vivyan Adair. 2007. "Poverty and Storytelling in Higher Education." *Storytelling, Self, Society: An Interdisciplinary Journal of Storytelling Studies*. 3(2): 135–55.

Pham, Bich Ha. 2005. *The Missing Story of Ourselves: Poverty and the Promise of Higher Education*. The ACCESS Project at Hamilton College. www.hamilton .edu/college/access.

"PRWORA Regulations." 1996. *United States Department of Health and Human Services*: Regulation brief. Retrieved 9 Oct. 2005, from: www.acf.hhs .gov/programs/cse/fct/irspam.htm.

Rajan, Gita, and Shailja Sharma. 2005. *The Missing Story of Ourselves: Poverty and the Promise of Higher Education*. The ACCESS Project at Hamilton College: www.hamilton.edu/college/access.

———. 2006. *New Cosmopolitanisms: South Asians in the U.S.* Palo Alto: Stanford University Press.

Rector, Robert, with Vivyan Adair. 2002. "Welfare and Higher Education, Debate." *Morning Edition with Claudio Sanchez*. National Public Radio: www .npr.org/templates/archives/php.

———, and Patrick Fagan. 1996. "How Welfare Harms Kids. Backgrounder #1084. *The Heritage Foundation*." Retrieved 25 Sept. 2005, from: http:// www.heritage.org/Research/Welfare/index.cfm.

Scott, Joan. 1999. *Gender and the Politics of History*. New York: Columbia University Press.

Sparks, Holloway. 2003. "Reform Debate Tainted by Racism, Sexism." *Penn State News*. Retrieved 22 Sept. 2005, from: //pus.edu/ur/2003/welfarequeens.html.

Stanfield, Shannon. 2005. *The Missing Story of Ourselves: Poverty and the Promise of Higher Education*. The ACCESS Project at Hamilton College. Rome, New York: Canterbury Press: 28–9.

———. Clark, Nolita, Paulette Brown, Rose Perez and Vivyan Adair. 2007. "Poverty and Storytelling in Higher Education." *Storytelling, Self, Society: An Interdisciplinary Journal of Storytelling Studies*. 3(2): 135–55.

Stewart, Don. 1999. "Usual stereotypes don't apply to every welfare recipient." *The Digital Collegian; Pennsylvania State*. Retrieved 10 Oct. 2000, from: www.collegian.psu.edu/archive/1999.

Stone-Mediatore, Shari. 2003. *Reading across Borders: Storytelling and Knowledges of Resistance*. New York: Palgrave Macmillan.

Thompson, Joanne. 1993. "Women, Welfare and College: The Impact of Higher Education on Economic Well Being." *Affilia* 8(4): 425–41.

"Wages and Compensation for Nursing Professionals in the Northwest." 2005. *Nursing jobs.com*. Retrieved 5 Sept. 2005, from: nursing-jobs.com/email_form.html.

Watson, Fransheneka. 2005. *The Missing Story of Ourselves: Poverty and the Promise of Higher Education, Gallery Guide*. The ACCESS Project at Hamilton College. Rome, New York: Canterbury Press: 14–5.

"Welfare Made a Difference." 2000. *National Welfare Campaign*. c/o Community Food Resource Center, New York City.

Willmore, Teresa. 2005. *The Missing Story of Ourselves: Poverty and the Promise of Higher Education, Gallery Guide*. The ACCESS Project at Hamilton College. Rome, New York: Canterbury Press, 22–3.

Wolfe, Leslie, and Marilyn Gittell. 1997. *College Education Is a Route out of Poverty for Women on Welfare.* Washington, D.C.: Center for Women's Policy Studies.

Woolsey, Lynn. 2005. *The Missing Story of Ourselves: Poverty and the Promise of Higher Education.* The ACCESS Project at Hamilton College. www.hamilton.edu/college/access.

CHAPTER NINE

# Fashion Photography and Women's Modernity in Weimar Germany: The Case of Yva

MILA GANEVA

> The most striking proof of photography's extraordinary validity today is the increase in the number of *illustrated newspapers*. In them one finds assembled everything from the film diva to whatever is within reach of the camera and the audience. . . . The new fashions also must be disseminated, or else in the summer the beautiful girls will not know who they are.
>
> —Siegfried Kracauer ([1927]1995, 57)

> Photography is a wonderful, interesting and, at the same time, difficult profession for women. . . . In reality, photography is a large, all-encompassing field offering a variety of opportunities.
>
> —Lotte König (1931, 292)[1]

As the above quotations testify, many of the present debates about women and their role in modernity have their origins in the early twentieth century. After lagging for decades behind developments in England and France, post–World War I Germany entered a period of unprecedented social, economic, and cultural modernization, a period that coincided with the rise and fall of the Weimar Republic (1919–1933). Dazzling changes took place in all spheres of everyday life, and the emergence of the "New Woman"—both as a mass-produced image and as a sociological phenomenon—constituted one of the most visible, and thus, most debated trends among the new realities. In his famous 1927 essay "Photography," Siegfried Kracauer discusses with apparent irony the ubiquitous presence of women's images in the mass press and hints at the manipulative power of photography, especially of fashion photography, to attract female consumers and cultivate their tastes. Unlike Kracauer, Lotte König, herself an "enthusiastic photographer," focuses on women in photography not as objects of representation but as active agents in modern life. In her essay, "Die Frau als Photographin" ("The Woman as a Photographer"), König describes in very practical terms the institutional conditions that allowed women in Weimar Germany to become professional photographers and also highlights the actual achievements of individual freelance female photographers.

---

Originally published in the Fall 2003 issue of the *NWSA Journal*.

Both König and Kracauer reveal some important connections between women, fashion, and photography in Weimar mass culture. Fashion photography as well as advertisement photography bear testimony to a rather paradoxical cultural reality in which sociological, technological, and aesthetic aspects are hard to detach from one another. As has been pointed out in many critical studies including Kracauer's, photography was the visual medium that contributed most to the construction and proliferation of images of "modern women," and these images also were employed effectively in the competition among illustrated magazines. Beginning in the 1920s, many mass publications started to place photographs of beautiful women on their covers in order to stimulate sales. This trend was made possible, in part, by the rapid development of photographic and printing technologies and their widespread application in all spheres of public life—from science and medicine to industry and business. Taking pictures and producing photographs in mass periodicals was no longer a costly and complicated adventure. Moreover, cameras such as Ermanox and Leica became affordable and consumer-friendly items that were marketed to women, and women obviously took full advantage of this.[2] Numerous advertisements for cameras from the late 1920s, for example, showed a female hand holding the camera or a woman's face behind it.[3]

On the other hand, however, the press's depiction of women on a mass scale reflected the indisputable fact that more women actually took part in public life than ever before. Photography offered women, to an extent that did not exist before the 1920s, a venue for both artistic self-expression and professional realization. As König observed in the article quoted above, a record number of women in Germany were trained and worked as professional photographers in various genres (fashion, industrial, and journalistic photography) as well as in x-ray laboratories. In partnership with two other women, König herself founded a studio in 1931; it was one of over 100 studios in Berlin owned and managed by women (Bojunga and Leipold 1995).

The biographies of female photographers are emblematic of widespread social changes for a whole generation of Weimar women. As Ute Eskildsen (1995) has observed, it was predominantly young middle-class women who became professional photographers and freelance photojournalists. Most belonged to the generation born in the period around 1890 and many came from conventional, bourgeois Jewish families. Lured by economic freedom, artistic challenge, mobility, and public exposure of the profession, Weimar women photographers turned photography into an "instrument for individual flexibility and personal exploration of their environment" (62–3).[4] Thus, it is in the work of these photographers that we can find astute interpretations of various themes in women's modernity—beauty, technology, de-individualization, and sexuality—from a female point of view.

This paper examines the relevance of fashion photography as a source for the study of women's modernity in Germany of the 1920s and 1930s. Traditionally, the uneasy alliance between women and modernity in the sphere of visual arts has been explored somewhat one-dimensionally from a sociological angle, without engaging the formal and aesthetic dimensions of their avant-garde work. Despite all laudable endeavors to rescue the opus of Weimar female photographers from historical oblivion, there has been little scholarly analysis of their individual achievements.[5] In this paper, therefore, I attempt to combine all three levels of explanation—the formal, the sociological, and the technological—as I focus on the work of a fascinating and prolific professional photographer in Berlin of the late 1920s and early 1930s: Else Neuländer Simon, known by her artistic name Yva.

Yva has made herself a name primarily as a fashion photographer. Here is how critic Van Deren Coke introduces her to today's public:

> Else Simon, who used the professional name YVA, was an imaginative Berlin photographer of the 1930s who specialized in nudes, portraits of dancers, and pictures of new fashions. Her achievements again emphasize the number of outstanding women photographers at this time. The most distinctive pictures she made were those in which she wove together the new contemporary design concepts—that is image patterns and subtle theatrical lighting—to convey the sense of mystery and glamour. The work of Yva confirms that assignments for commercial work, such as pictures of accessories for a fashionable wardrobe, did not necessarily subordinate the creativity of a truly resourceful spirit. We know this was the case with Edward Steichen in America and the German- and Russian-born photographers Horst Horst and George Hoyningen-Huene, who began their professional careers in Paris and then became very innovative fashion photographers in America. Yva found fashion photography not a bit constricting. She used an oblique approach to photography in which she hinted at the glamour a woman accrued while wearing this or that attire or adornment. Her lenses were as exacting as Renger-Patsch's, but her vision, feminine and sensuous, conferred a quality that is missing from almost all other German photography of the 1930s. (1982, 69)[6]

Yva was respected by her contemporaries no less than other contemporary female photographers such as Marianne Breslauer, Lucia Moholy, Florence Henri, Anneliese Kretschmer, Lotte Jacobi, Grete Stern, and Ellen Auerbacher.[7] Her works were included in almost every exhibition of German photography from the mid-1920s on, and her photographs were widely published in the trade press and in mainstream fashion, women's, and illustrated magazines. Nevertheless, until recently, Yva's highly challenging opus has not been given careful critical attention.[8] In the field of fashion photography, creative and revolutionary development of that media in the 1920s and 1930s has always been credited to men such as Man Ray, Edward Steichen, George Hoyningen-Huene, Umbo, and Martin Munkacsi.

And in the history of the photographic avant-garde the critical acclaim often went to either Bauhaus photographers such as Walter Peterhans, László Moholy-Nagy, and Lucia Moholy, or to masters of the commercial genre of product advertising such as Albert Renger-Patzsch, Hans Gorny, and Hans Finsler. Thus, in the eyes of historians, Yva stands in the shadow either of *Neue Sachlichkeit*, experimental photographers, or the Bauhaus.

One explanation for scholars and art historians' long neglect could be found in exactly those qualities of her work that were praised by Van Deren Coke: Yva's opus was uncomfortably positioned at the intersection of several sets of borderlines—between commercial and purely artistic production, between avant-garde experiments and conventional portrait aesthetics, between fashion photography and product advertising. The modernist vocabulary of her images was heavily commercialized, and vice versa: the commercial photography that she produced featured strong experimental and modernist tendencies. These circumstances made a definite and clear categorization of her contribution to photography very difficult. In addition, she worked independently at her own studio and was not personally or institutionally associated with the Bauhaus and its prominent photographers. Thus, she did not benefit from the venues of publicity and self-promotion accessible to the Bauhaus artists. And last but not least, the relatively late discovery of Yva—in the mid-1990s—is due to the fact that her entire photographic archive of negatives was destroyed during the bombing of Hamburg in 1943 and very few vintage pictures survived.[9] Now they are scattered in several personal and museum collections in Germany and the United States.

Before analyzing in more detail Yva's participation in, and contribution to, photographic modernism, a review of what little is known about her life and career may be useful.

## 1. Who Was Yva?

Yva is the artistic name of Else Neuländer Simon, born in 1900 in Berlin to a Jewish middle-class family. According to her friend Elisabeth Röttgers, a fellow photographer and close collaborator, Yva graduated from the Lette School, Berlin's famous arts and crafts school for women; she also completed a short internship at a Berlin movie studio, where she learned lighting.[10] Her career as a photographer started in 1925 at the studio of Heinz Hajek-Halke, an experimental avant-garde photographer based in Berlin. Their brief cooperation ended abruptly in 1926 after the publication of a photograph entitled *Futuristisches Selbstbildnis der Photographin Yva* (*Futuristic Self-Portrait of the Photographer Yva*) in *Das Magazin*. Hajek-Halke claimed that it was *his* "futuristic touch" that was superimposed over Yva's photographic self-portrait and requested an honorarium from the magazine (Buran 1992, 7). The honorarium was denied with the assertion that this was primarily Yva's work; Hajek-Halke sued and not only lost the legal dispute but was also forced to pay the costs of the court case.

The dispute with Hajek-Halke, as well as the entire body of her experimental photography, is never mentioned in the short paragraphs on Yva included in most photographic retrospectives of the 1920s and 1930s. Moreover, some scholars even claim that Yva was formed as a photographic artist under the influence of Hajek-Halke. This misrepresentation is highly symptomatic of the entire reception history of Yva's work. Since her huge photographic opus covers a wide thematic and stylistic spectrum—from fashion photography to advertisement to daring act photos and avant-garde images—she has been very difficult to classify. Critics have found it easier to label her a "successful fashion photographer" or to mention her name alongside Hajek-Halke rather than study the conscious, complex, and often playful mixture of approaches and visual idioms that she was using.

Yva's subsequent professional accomplishments testify to the originality of her talent and to her unique participation in Weimar's modernity. In 1926, Yva opened her own studio in Berlin with about ten employees. With the help of her brother, Ernst Neuländer, a co-owner of the famous Berlin fashion salon Kuhnen, she established herself as one of the city's most interesting fashion photographers. Her big breakthrough came in 1927 with ten photographs in *Die Dame* and from then on she was constantly present on the pages of that top-circulation women's magazine. From 1929 on, Yva's *Fotoserien* (photographic stories) appeared in the pages of another of the publisher Ullstein's magazines, *Der Uhu* (Beckers and Moortgat 1994, 239). Her works were included in landmark exhibitions of the period such as the 1929 Film and Foto in Stuttgart and the 1930 Das Lichtbild in Munich.

In the course of the late 1920s and the early 1930s, Yva's work was featured regularly in virtually all important publications of the fashion press—*Die Dame, Elegante Welt, neue linie, Blatt der Hausfrau, Konfektionär*—as well as in respected photographic trade magazines such as *Gebrauchsphotographie, Photographik, Gebrauchsgraphik, Der Photofreund, Das deutsche Lichtbild Jahrbuch,* and *Der deutsche Kamera-Almanach.* Her name became well known also to the sensation-hungry readers of the illustrated *Berliner Illustrierte Zeitung* (where she published over 150 photographs) as well as to the distinguished intellectual public of *Der Querschnitt.*

Surprisingly, Yva's professional activities were little affected in the first few years of the Nazi regime. Although her name was included in a blacklist of "Jewish and foreign photographers for the press" that was published in *Deutsche Nachrichten* from August 1933 (quoted in Kerbs, Uka, and Walz-Richter 1983, 65), she continued to work and publish relatively undisturbed by the changes in the political climate. Scholar Ira Buran attributes this to the fact that her Jewish origin was not immediately evident from the artistic name Yva—very few people knew her by her real name. Also, the studio appeared "aryanized" since in 1936 Yva's long-time friend Charlotte Weidler, an art historian and co-author in some of the *Fotoserien* in *Der Uhu*, took over and officially held the position of principal photographer. In reality, however, it was still Yva who ran the business and produced the photographs. From 1936 until 1938, she even took on an intern—young Helmut Newton (later to become famous as a fashion photographer for *Vogue* magazine)—who quickly became a valuable assistant and has on many occasions paid tribute to his first teacher in the art and trade of fashion photography.

By the end of the 1930s, the clouds over Yva's career and life thickened. Most of Yva's photo models—divas from the film and theater world like Ellen Estelle and Sybille Schmitz—discontinued all business contacts with the Jewish-owned studio. Yva's work became unacceptable for publication in the illustrated press. The last photographs attributed to the studio appeared in the August issues of *Die Dame* and *BIZ* in 1936. In 1940, *Die Koralle* reprinted a photograph by Yva that had been previously published in *Der Uhu*, but this time the copyrights were attributed to Deutscher Verlag (the Nazi successor of the publishing house Ullstein) and not to Yva's studio. In the few years before she and her husband were detained in the concentration camp in Majdanek/Sobibor on 1 June 1942, Yva is known to have worked as an x-ray technician at a Jewish hospital in Berlin. The exact date and place of her tragic death are not known; most probably Yva died in Lublin, Poland, in 1944.

## 2. Yva's Early Experimentation

In 1926, only a year after she started her career as a professional and experimental photographer, Yva's work was noticed by an influential critic. In an article published in *Photofreund*, Hans Böhm praised "the young German woman photographer who in the era of photographic experimentation and *Neue Sachlichkeit*" is following "her own, rather original pathways" (1926, 430).[11] The three photographs published along with the review article testify indeed to the emerging uniqueness of Yva's style. The artist demonstrated that she was completely at ease with the rather complex avant-garde "sandwich technique" in photography (called by Moholy-Nagy *Fotoplastik*), while at the same time developing her own distinctive signature.

Before moving on to the analysis of her style, let us clarify the nature and status of this technique. A *Fotoplastik* is a composition of two or more separate camera images, usually produced by mounting several successive exposures onto one negative (that is, a photograph of a photomontage). Although *Fotoplastik* resembles photomontages that were widely used in dadaist art, Moholy insisted that there was a difference. *Fotoplastik,* he contended, minimizes the visibility of the montage process, eliminates the discrepancies within the material used, and creates a new "seamless," synthetic image with "an independent meaning" (quoted in Hight 1995, 148). Böhm did acknowledge that there was, indeed, a "fantastic" and "visionary" element in Yva's usage of this technique and draws parallels between her work and the work of Moholy-Nagy and Man Ray. However, what he considered the most flattering comparison is the closeness of Yva's technique to that of the master cameraman Guido Seeber. Yva's photographs, Böhm argued, produced an effect that is similar to the images of metropolitan chaos that Seeber had created in his film *Man spielt nicht mit der Liebe* (*Don't Fool Around with Love*): "Yva has revolutionized the field of photography in a way that is comparable to the masterful achievements of Guido Seeber in cinema" (1926, 431).

In the following years, Yva's photographic experiments continued to attract critical attention and were discussed as examples of "productive photography" created by the *entfesselte Kamera* (camera set free) (Warstat 1929, 45). Her works, mostly photograms, alongside Moholy-Nagy's and Hugo Erfurt's, were featured in comprehensive review articles on modern photography and on the art of photographic advertisement by the prominent critic of photography, Willi Warstat. As he analyzed in detail Yva's still-life *Linsen* (*Lenses*) and her synoptic picture *Schachspieler* (*Chess Player*), Warstat equated the method of these *Lichtphantasien* (fantasies of light) to the artist's attempt to transcend the temporal and spatial limitations of traditional photography and to characterize a personality or a phenomenon from a variety of vantage points and in different moments of time. What had continuously distinguished Yva from the other experimenting artists, according to Warstat, was her effort to retain even in the most complex "spatial synthesis" of *Fotoplastik* a sense for the "material objects that are palpable and clearly recognizable" (52).

Let us return, however, to Yva's work featured in Böhm's 1926 article in *Photofreund*. There we find compelling evidence that despite some similarities to other leading modernists of her time, especially her use of experimental techniques, Yva's early photographs foreshadow the artist's continuous preference for, and her distinct treatment of, the representation of women themes—artists, performers, or fashion models. One of the photographs, titled *Sisters G.* (fig. 9.1) (reproduced later as an advertising

9.1 *Sisters G.*, 1926. Black and white photograph. © Marion Beckers and Elisabeth Moortgat, *Yva—Photographien 1925–1938/Yva—Photographs 1925–1938*, Hg. Das Verborgene Museum. Wasmuth Verlag Berlin/Tübingen, 2001.

poster for a revue), offers glimpses into the work of three sisters who are cabaret dancers;[12] another one is of the female cellist Margit Werlé; and the third one is a self-portrait of Yva. So what is the effect produced by the use of the avant-garde technique of *Fotoplastik* in combination with a specific theme?

The first picture characterized by the author as a *synoptisches Bild* (synoptic image) is a composition blending five negatives: the upper right corner shows the three dancers in full size as they perform in a chorus-line (fig. 1). Emphasized is the symmetric silhouette of the three dancers and their synchronous movement; very little can be seen of their faces. Diagonally, from the top-left corner to the lower-right corner, follow three close-ups of the faces of the three dancers. Each one is viewed from a different angle and is wearing a different hat—an approach used by Yva to underscore the unmistakable difference of individuality and personality. And in the lower left is the fifth image—three legs shown from the knees down in the middle of the dance, severed from the rest of the bodies, poised almost vertically in the air.

In the second photograph, three images are imposed upon each other: the face of the female cello player serves as the background onto which two smaller images are blended: one of the instrument held by the left hand and another one of the bow held by the right hand of the musician. The iconography of both this and the previous photograph seems to suggest that the modern woman, especially when she appears in the spotlight of the public gaze, is always perceived in a fragmented fashion—her head—that is, her value as individuality, mind, and character—is recognized separately from the body. The body itself disintegrates into parts—hands, thighs, lower legs—some of which are highly valued as sexual symbols or as instruments of artistic perfection.

The most interesting of all three *Fotoplastiken* is the third one—Yva's self-portrait with a futuristic touch (cover image). This is one of the rare instances in her vast opus in which the artist demonstrates intense self-reflection, and, as a result, this photograph can serve as a general statement of Yva's credo as a female photographer. The central image is of a female head, looking straight into the camera, expressing no visible emotions, and wearing no jewelry or accessories such as a scarf, a veil, or a hat. The hair is straight, short, barely reaching the line of the ears, and smoothly combed away from the face so that it almost blends with the background. Thus, the face of the artist assumes cold, androgynous features. Obviously, Yva is embracing the promised modernist antidote to sexualization and overfeminization of women in art by emphasizing the ungendered image.[13] The modernist soberness of the self-portrait is further accentuated by the symmetrical positioning of the head along the distinctly marked vertical axis of the *Fotoplastik*—a line passes exactly through the middle of the nose, mouth, chin—and the pure geometric lines of the V-neck of the artist's dress. In addition to the head, the portrait includes the artist's hands positioned, again perfectly symmetrically, across her breast. As in the photograph of the female cellist Margit Werlé, the hands seem to be detached from the rest of the body and are presented in the picture as symbolic elements, as parts of the productive apparatus of the artist rather than parts of an organic whole, that is, the female body. This is, in fact, a photomontage of two images of the same hand: once it is turned with its back to the viewer and once it is turned with its palm to the viewer, which produces an unsettling, surrealist effect.

It is obvious that Yva's self-perception is marked by her determination to view herself in a very unromantic and clearly sober light. It seems that she is consumed by an effort to conceal distinct features of femininity such as her lush and long hair, the use of adornments, and makeup. If we compare her appearance here to the self-portrait of d'Ora (Dora Kallmus), another famous female fashion photographer of the Weimar period, the differences become quite obvious. Both d'Ora's and Yva's self-portraits contain similar elements: a face looking straight into the camera and a pair of hands. D'Ora, however, demonstrates certain narcissistic pleasure in ostentatiously staging her femininity and playful seductiveness in front of the camera: There are more details visible about the woman's hairstyle than about her face, and her hands are coquettishly placed around a black cat. In contrast, Yva is presenting a colder, more analytical, even a dissecting view of her artistic personality stripped of any embellishments. That is not to say that Yva's self-portrait is lacking any femininity. Femininity is, however, as the photographer defines it, not something emanating organically from the female face or body; rather, it is perceived as an abstract quality of the artist's work.

Yva's image in her self-portrait (fig. 9.2) is softened by the combination of intertwined circular and wavy lines that are superimposed onto the face. As these lines cross, they form segments of various shadings and, as a result, the face appears as a mosaic of differently colored elements. The lines draw both precise geometric forms (concentric circles and triangles formed by the axes that radiate from an invisible center of the circles located somewhere in the middle of the face) and unpredictable, free, softly curved waves that disturb the perfect symmetry. Therefore, as a whole, this unusual self-portrait conveys a sense that the artist we see cannot be captured in a single, flat image—she is a complex personality consisting of various shades, moods, facets—and is the center of her own creative world. The formal means of getting this message across are unambiguously modernist, influenced by New Photography's love for experiments with geometric forms, lines, and abstract images, but the content of the message is unique and personal for the female photographer.

9.2 *Futuristic Self-Portrait of the Photographer Yva,* originally published in the German periodical *Das Magazin,* 1926. © Marion Beckers and Elisabeth Moortgat, *Yva—Photographien 1925–1938 / Yva—Photographs 1925–1938,* Hg. Das Verborgene Museum. Wasmuth Verlag Berlin / Tübingen, 2001.

## 3. Yva's Modern Woman: Between Advertisement and Fashion Photography

Elements of her early work remain prominent in Yva's later, mostly commercial photographs for the illustrated press and the fashion trade press. Her photography continued to combine bold, experimental, avant-garde techniques with subject matters such as fashion, clothes, jewelry, and cosmetics in order to achieve wide commercial acceptance. The difference from her early work was that by 1929 the accomplishments of the studio YVA were known not to just a few fans of photographic experimentation but to numerous nonexpert and mostly female audiences. It is safe to say that by the late 1920s, Yva's distinctive use of avant-garde techniques in product advertisement and fashion photography became part of the masses' experience of modernism. Modernism was reaching the public through the various venues of popular entertainment in everyday life: illustrated magazines, movies, and photographic exhibitions.

Yva's work—as heterogeneous as it appeared in its position between serious experimentation and strong commercial commitment—shared the spirit of the modern movement of photography that itself was informed by similar duality. German photography of the 1920s and early 1930s associated itself often with film as the paramount form of popular culture. Renger-Patzsch pointed out repeatedly that photography exerts an enormous influence on the masses through film and illustrated magazines (1928, 19). Photography and film in that period shared a lower rank in cultural hierarchy (film versus literature and photography versus painting) while seeking legitimacy and artistic autonomy (Honnef 1997, 13). At the same time, film and photography in Germany gained enormous popularity. German photographic and multimedia exhibitions from the mid-1920s until the early 1930s were unique in Europe and turned into unprecedented occasions for the mass experience of technological and artistic advances.[14]

Photography sought out another powerful venue for mass acceptance and that was modern advertisement (Schmalriede 1989, 17). As many scholars of Weimar visual arts have pointed out, advertising became one of the main forces behind innovation in photography and one of its chief sponsors. Photography started displacing other graphic arts from the realm of visual ads and there were hardly any Weimar artists who had not worked for advertising (Moldering 1988, 27). In theoretical writings and photographic practices, the art of *Werbekunst* (advertisement) was often praised as "truly social, collective, a genuine mass art, the only one that still exists" (Hartlaub 1928, 173). These were the words of a prominent art critic of the 1920s, G. H. Hartlaub, who wrote on advertisement and often published advertising photography and posters in the otherwise highbrow art journal *Das Kunstblatt*:

> The art of advertisement today, along with pragmatic architecture, is the single truly public art. It alone—as graphic art and print—speaks the aesthetic language that reaches the anonymous masses of the cities whose enthusiasm is sparked not by religion and politics, but by sports and fashions. It can reach those compact majorities at the soccer stadiums, at the boxing rings and six-day races, . . . in other words that large and wide "public" that feels at home everywhere but in the galleries, exhibitions and theaters. It is today's art of advertisement that shapes the collective visual habits of the anonymous public. (1928, 131)

Lázsló Moholy-Nagy was another strong proponent of the use of experimental photography in advertisement. Surprisingly, he was not as suspicious of the manipulative function of advertisement as much as he was enthusiastic about the possibility of linking the creative powers of the photograph with the vast media of advertisement. He was convinced that the combination of avant-garde photographic art with advertising would prevent the terrible consequences that might occur if business were run by businessmen or unimaginative photographers, or as he called them "*die Kulturlosen*" (1925, 258). The successful alliance between photography and advertisement, according to Moholy-Nagy, would be a possible realization of the main task he saw for modern photography—to reshape the optical perception of the world, to teach a new type of vision, or as he put it "*Photographie als optische Gestaltung*" ("photography as an optical shaping") (1927, 260).

During the peak of her career, between 1926 and 1933, Yva completed numerous projects for product advertisements, and in this sphere of professional realization she demonstrated again a clear preference for products related to women's beauty and used in women's everyday life: cosmetics, stockings, shoes, jewelry, and accessories like gloves, belts, umbrellas, and scarves. At the same time, even when it was produced for a commercial application, her photography preserved particular elements of the style and spirit of her early experimentation and of her distinct concept of women's modernity.

For *Die Dame*, Yva created a large number of photographs of mass-produced objects common in the everyday life of the woman, such as coffee cups and saucers, umbrellas, scarves, and gloves, where she applied many of the principles typical for the photography of *Neue Sachlichkeit*.[15] She arranged the objects in clean geometrical lines, shot them from odd perspectives, mostly from an extreme close-up, and avoided any decorative elements in the background in an effort to underscore more the mass consumer value rather than any aesthetic uniqueness of the product. Like other photographers who took pictures of products for mass consumption (Renger-Patzsch, for example), Yva displayed an emphatic matter-of-fact interest in the texture and surface of the material. Her particular power and her unique style in advertisement photography were best demonstrated, however, when the products were displayed on a live female model. It was in those photographs that Yva showed undisputed mastery and originality. If we can speak of her "own genre," it can be located on the cryptic borderline between still-life, fashion photography, and female portrait, a "genre" that marked critical intervention within the system's idealization and fetishization of the woman's image prevalent in Weimar advertising.

Here is a closer look at several of these mixed-genre photographs. Most publicized were her few photographs of female legs wearing synthetic silk stockings. One of them, *Beine* (*Legs*) (fig. 9.3), was one of Yva's five photographs included in the landmark 1929 Film und Foto exhibition, and subsequently included in the San Francisco exhibit Avant-Garde Photography in Germany. It is worth noting that in the exhibit this picture was displayed in the section featuring typical *Neue Sachlichkeit* photography. Yva's *Beine* was surrounded by still-lifes—Aenne Biermann's *Ashtray*, Hans Finsler's *Light-Bulb* and *Cuffs*, Paul Outerbridge's *Collar*, and different photographs of drinking glasses by Renger-Patzsch, Walter Peterhans, and Ewald Hoinkis. All of these works reproduced, with clean exactitude and emphatic soberness, products of the modern industrial world used in everyday life. In that context, the two female legs in fashionable transparent stockings appear as mere objects and the photograph could be considered a still life, a view designated for mass consumption by the male observer. The impression of still life is reinforced by the fact that the upper frame of the photograph ends about an inch above the knees, and the legs seemingly have no connection to a living female body.

At the same time, inherent in Yva's photograph, is the intention to undermine or at least to subdue this appearance of the female legs as a typical sexual symbol. In comparison with other contemporary photographs of female legs in stockings (see Friedrich Seidenstücker's photographs), the melodramatic lighting and heavy retouching is missing, and the legs in this image are not staged against the seductive background typical in such pictures—the intimate interior of a private room. Also, no other parts of the female body (such as hands touching the legs) are shown. Instead, the legs are positioned in perfect symmetry to an invisible central vertical line, with knees firmly pressed together, and the camera is focused on the material covering the legs—the stockings. The viewer's attention is powerfully directed to the exact pattern of the weave and the fine texture of the stocking.

But who was the viewer of these photographs? Given the context within which Yva's numerous photographs appeared—namely women's magazines and fashion publications such as *Die Dame* and *Elegante Welt*—the targeted consumer of Yva's images was the female gaze. The critical writing on fashion photography identifies the female spectator of such images as a consumer exposed to the manipulative seduction of advertising. It is widely argued that the female spectator is engaged primarily in a process of passive, "one-way prescriptive identification" (Kolbowski 1999, 156). As some theorists suggest, however, the female gaze at the photographic image of feminine perfection could be taking on a number of other forms that are not passive: the gaze of the critical observer aware of the schism between subject and object, the gaze aligned with that of the photographer, and the gaze positioned behind the photographer. Thus, the viewer's pleasure, Kolbowski argues, resides not only in a masochistic alignment with the image of idealized femininity, but also in the playful "slippages of positions" and in the "misalignments." On a formal level, especially in her still-life representations of body fragments instead of organic wholeness, Yva seems to invite female spectatorship to reflect critically upon a prevalent fetishization or to direct the attention of the female gaze to the texture of a mass-produced material (the stocking) as opposed to the form of nature's given—the legs. In that respect, it is important to note again the context in which these photographs appeared in the 1920s and 1930s press. A women's magazine, such as *Die Dame*, was full of practical advice for middle-class and middle-aged women in matters of fashion, particularly on ways in which they should adjust the extremities of high fashion to the realities of their own financial situations and bodies. Thus, we may argue that Yva's strategy of focusing on the texture of the stockings can be interpreted as geared definitely toward women's specific concerns and interests as consumers of the product.

A more playful and erotic variation of the idea behind the photograph *Beine* was realized in a number of photo-advertisements for stockings that Yva created for the fashion press (figs. 9.3 and 9.4). This time the photographs give a full view of the knees and even of a portion of the legs above the knees, while the legs are positioned in a more seductive pose—diagonally across the picture. In these instances, the photographer uses the diagonal—as many modernists did—as an eye-catcher. Still, it remained Yva's trademark to show the female legs severed from the body and isolated against a very neutral, mostly dark background, with the main focus fixed on the texture and geometric patterns of the material covering the skin.

Another example of the mixed genre of fashion/still-life/portrait photographs for which Yva had a clear preference is her 1928 work called *Schmuck* (*Jewelry*) that was also included in the 1929 Fifo and in the 1982

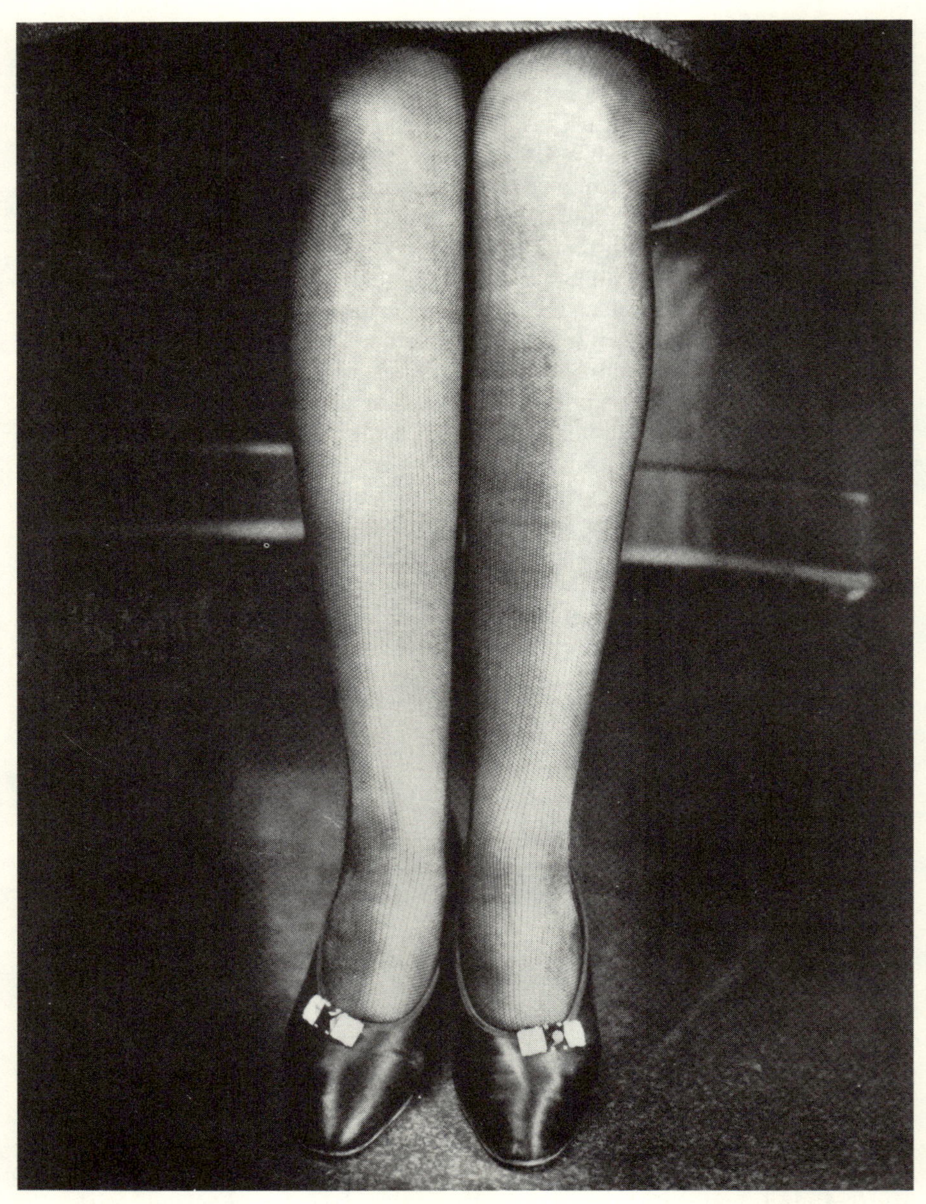

9.3 *Beine* (*Legs*), 1929. © Marion Beckers and Elisabeth Moortgat, *Yva—Photographien 1925–1938/Yva—Photographs 1925–1938*, Hg. Das Verborgene Museum. Wasmuth Verlag Berlin/Tübingen, 2001.

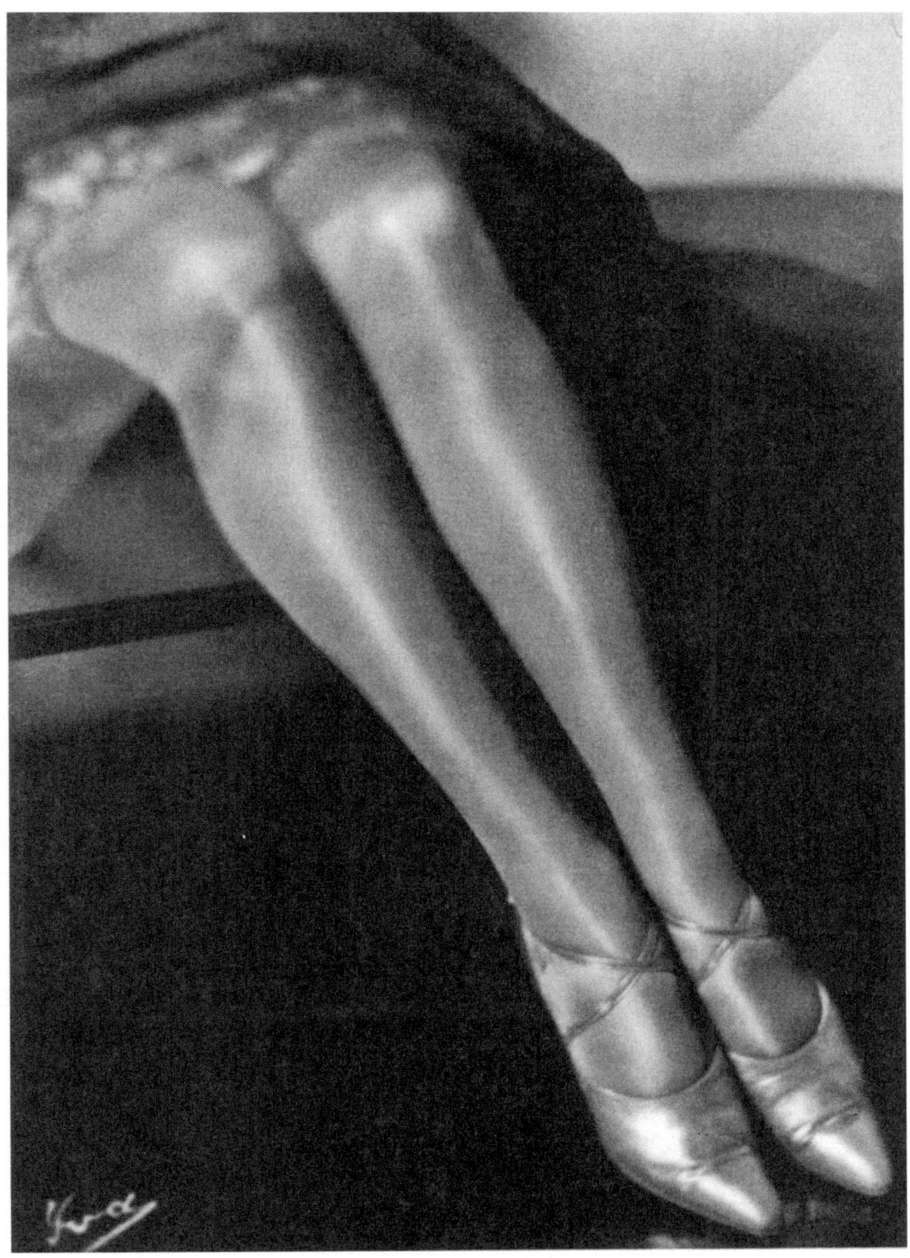


9.4 *Beine* (*Legs*), 1927–28. © Marion Beckers and Elisabeth Moortgat, *Yva—Photographien 1925–1938 / Yva—Photographs 1925–1938,* Hg. Das Verborgene Museum. Wasmuth Verlag Berlin / Tübingen, 2001.

Avant-Garde in Germany exhibitions (fig. 9.5). Again, as in the photograph of legs, a part of the female body appears to bear no clear connection to the rest of the body. This time there are two hands—visible only from the elbow down—that display two bracelets and a ring. In this photograph there is an elaborate staging that is very unusual, hard to decipher, and contributes to the viewer's sense of surrealist disorientation. Against the background of a female body dressed in black (with an ambiguous positioning of the body), the lower arms cross to form an obtuse angle with one hand pointing vertically toward the bottom-left corner and the other reaching the upper-right edge of the photograph. A glittery material that resembles a ruffled water surface forms the background for the body dressed in black. As in the photographs of legs and stockings, this one too was presumably created to advertise a certain fashionable product and to present an isolated view of just that part of the female body that is wearing the product. Thus, *Schmuck* too can be considered as a fashion still-life photograph. At the same time, however, these photographs serve as portraits and offer an interpretation of the actual woman or model displaying the product on her body. It is, paradoxically, the very absence of a female face that allows us to consider them portraits. The strongest characteristic of the portrayed women—their desire for self-determination and preservation of their individuality in a society of conspicuous consumption of products and images—is expressed in their symbolic refusal to have distinctive renderings of their faces and bodies shown to the mass viewer. Such an approach, in addition to the extreme focus on details and the material nature of the product itself, as mentioned earlier, practically eliminates the male viewer by targeting just the expert woman's eye.

A similar impression—the impression of deliberate detachment of the modern woman from the product that she is displaying in front of the camera—is created by Yva's fashion photographs of dresses and other fashionable objects in which the display of the model's face could not be avoided. The products, of course, are visible to the last detail, while the woman remains an enigma, and she is not easily accessible to the eye. Therefore, whether Yva displays the woman in full size or her face only, the model is staged in such a way that her glance is emphatically diverted from the viewer. In some cases—as in the 1929 photograph *Der Brilliantenschmuck* (*Diamond Jewelry*) (fig. 9.6) published in *Deutscher Kamera Almanach*—the face of the woman is covered down to the chin by a non-transparent black lace veil, which makes visible just her hand wearing a bracelet and a ring and her neck with a necklace. In other instances—as in the 1933 close-up photograph *Frau mit Hut* (*Woman Wearing a Hat*)—the head and the glance of the model are demonstratively turned away from the viewer. The choice of such a position serves a double function—to allow for a better view of the hat from various sides and, at the same time, to underscore the cold detachment of the

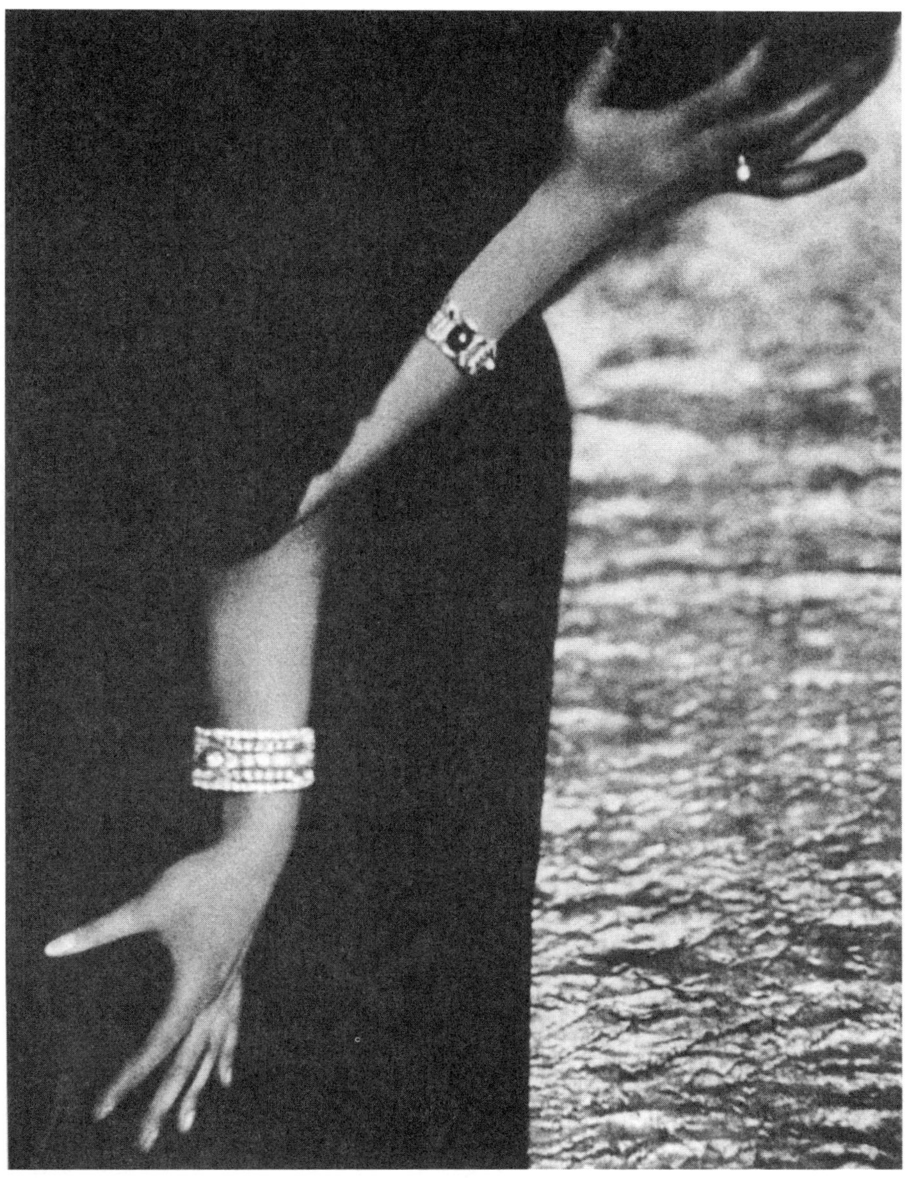

9.5 *Schmuck* (*Jewelry*), n.d. © Marion Beckers and Elisabeth Moortgat, *Yva—Photographien 1925–1938 / Yva—Photographs 1925–1938*, Hg. Das Verborgene Museum. Wasmuth Verlag Berlin / Tübingen, 2001.

9.6 *Der Brilliantenschmuck* (*Diamond Jewelry*), 1929. © Marion Beckers and Elisabeth Moortgat, *Yva—Photographien 1925–1938/Yva—Photographs 1925–1938,* Hg. Das Verborgene Museum. Wasmuth Verlag Berlin/Tübingen, 2001.

woman from the observer. In a more radical move, one of Yva's 1933 untitled fashion photographs portrayed the famous film star Asta Nielsen with her back turned to the camera while another displayed a rear view of two seated women granting the viewer of the photograph only a scant glimpse of their profile from a distance (fig. 9.7). In the latter photograph both women are facing the smooth, reflective surface of a lake—an emphatic gesture of narcissistic self-observation that is common to a great number of Yva's fashion and advertising photographs in which the models

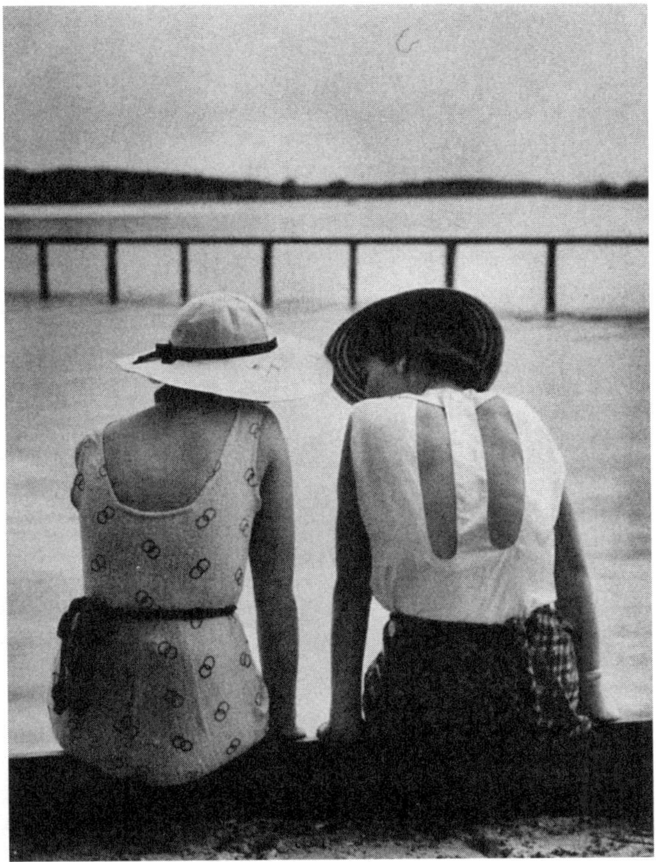

9.7 *Zwei Frauen am Strand* (*Two Women at the Beach*), 1936. © Marion Beckers and Elisabeth Moortgat, *Yva—Photographien 1925–1938/Yva—Photographs 1925–1938*, Hg. Das Verborgene Museum. Wasmuth Verlag Berlin/Tübingen, 2001.

glancing away from the viewer are looking either at the water's surface or at a mirror.

Finally, I would like to take a look at two photographs that use overtly modernist techniques to achieve this effect of "detachment" and self-preserving alienation. The first is a *Modefoto* (fashion photograph) showing a woman who is dressed in a long evening gown and reclining on a couch (fig. 9.8). This image demonstrates masterfully the convergence of realistic and unrealistic elements inherent in fashion photography in particular, and in the fashion industry as a whole. On the one hand, the camera is capturing with crisp clarity every detail of the dress and every fold of the garment. Of course, this is exactly what the sober photography of *Neue Sachlichkeit* would like to do—it sees its task as revealing something about the material nature of objects by way of representing their external shape, form, appearance, and surface. On the other hand, however, the unusual horizontal position of the model, her head, right arm, and upper body leaning almost over the edge of the sofa, contributes to an undoubtedly surrealist atmosphere. The woman in this photograph

9.8 *Untitled* (Modefoto or a fashion photograph), 1929. © Marion Beckers and Elisabeth Moortgat, *Yva—Photographien 1925–1938 / Yva—Photographs 1925–1938,* Hg. Das Verborgene Museum. Wasmuth Verlag Berlin / Tübingen, 2001.

creates the impression that she may at any moment fall off the couch; thus, the photograph as a whole leaves the viewer more disturbed than seduced by the glamorous appearance of the fashion model.

The other photograph is relatively less known and entitled *Junge Frau steht hinter einem Zaun* (*A Young Woman Standing behind a Fence*). It is one of the rare instances in Yva's work when the woman portrayed in a photograph directly faces the viewer. Yet the viewer's access to the emotional world of the young woman, or her mood at the moment, remains blocked. One obstacle between the viewer and the photographed woman is her stern facial expression that will not grant the viewer even the slightest seductive smile; the other quite visible obstacle is the fence raised between the woman and the camera. Traditionally the fence would be associated with some kind of imprisonment, a restriction of personal freedom. Here, however, the symbolic meaning of the fence in the context of the appearance and position of the woman—with a calm, resolute face and her arms stretching upwards, easily reaching the upper rim of the fence—suggests more a state of uninhibited freedom than a sense of limitation. The photograph contains many of the elements of constructivist photography—clear geometric forms (squares in this case) superimposed with absolute symmetry upon the human body.

This series of photographs located on the borderline between genres—fashion photography, advertising, and portrait—outlines Yva's unique critical rejoinder to the conventions of the visual representation of women's images for women's audiences in the 1920s and 1930s. What theorist Mary Ann Doane has written about film and about the female spectator's problematic identification with an idealized female star as a fetish object applies also to the visual codes of photography (1982). Doane suggests that masquerade is a way to avoid the negative choice between narcissistic identification and destructively masochistic identification with the image. The mask imposed on the feminine image provides the female gaze with distance from, and control over, the observed image. By prohibiting direct access of the viewer's gaze to the staged body in the fashion photograph, by raising a fence between the woman and the camera, by looking at the models from oblique angles or disorienting perspectives, Yva endowed her images of women with an invisible mask of coolness and artificiality. Her emphasis on the artifice then could be read as exercising control over any impulses of uncritical identification with the fashion model.

It appears that Yva's greatest achievement was, as Van Deren Coke has hinted earlier, that she found a respectable compromise between effective commercial advertising and photographic experimentation. She discovered her own unique and attractive visual language somewhere between the commercial clichés and the modernist idioms of her time. But the historic significance of her work goes beyond that. As a successful professional female photographer, Yva continuously searched for an image of the woman in fashion and advertisement photography of the 1920s and 1930s that was not degrading for the woman. In an era when images of the woman as a sexual symbol were dominating the mass media and were proven to attract customers, Yva tried to position her photographed female model in a way that did not reduce her to a mere eye-catcher for the male spectator.

## Notes

1. This and all other translations from German are mine unless otherwise noted.

2. On the transformation of the print media by new photographic technologies see Lohse (1980) and Güssow (1980).

3. Many of the magazine photographs, especially those used in advertisements, were produced with a female viewer and consumer in mind. As Maud Lavin argues, the woman was not only presented as a commodity—an ideal, desirable, perfectly pampered and groomed object—but also addressed as an "empowered" consumer of those products—cosmetics, underwear, jewelry, and clothes—that would enable her to turn into the perfect commodity (2001). On photography, idealization, and fetishization, also see Burgin (1982, 190).

4. A similar point about women photographers at the Bauhaus is made by Suzanne Pastor. She writes: "Women were, in general, much more active in camera work than men" (1985, 21). On the relationship between biographical circumstances and professional development of female photographers, see Philipp (1992), Bruns (1987), and Baumhoff (1992).

5. Female photographers of that period have been vaguely and somewhat condescendingly characterized as "the avant-garde with charm" (Schreiber 1970, 3). Schreiber limits herself to stressing the courage of photographers such as Lotte Jacobi, Aenne Biermann, Ruth Hallersleben, and Erna Lendvai-Dircksen who founded and sustained their own photographic studios, some, such as Lendvai-Dircksen, as early as 1916. Another example of an attempt to restore interest in the names and work of "successful women photographers of the twenties and thirties [who] are often absent from the history of the period" is the exhibit organized by the J. Paul Getty Museum in 1993 (Keller and Ware 1993, n.p.). The catalogue contains biographical data on, and some photographs by, Trude Fleischmann (1895–1990), Lucia Moholy (1894–1989), Florence Henri (1893–1982), Ellen Auerbach (1906), Grete Stern (1904), Else Thalemann (1901–1984), and Erna Lendvai-Dircksen (1883–1962).

6. Coke organized the 1979 landmark exhibit, German Avant-Garde Photography, in San Francisco.

7. Many of those women photographers were also virtually unknown until the late 1980s or early 1990s. Ute Eskildsen's pioneering research and organizational work led to the recent "discovery" of these photographers and a careful analysis of their work (1995, 1980).

8. The first comprehensive exhibit of Yva's work, YVA-Photographien 1925–1938, was staged by Marion Beckers and Elisabeth Moortgat in 2001 and toured in Berlin, Munich, Aachen, and Bremen.

9. Her works were packed in big trunks in the Hamburg harbor, preparing to be shipped abroad. I owe this information to conversations I had in the Galerie Bodo Niemann in 1996. This private gallery in Berlin organized the first Yva exhibition in 1995, YVA—Eine Berliner Photographin der dreißiger Jahre.

10. Elisabeth Röttgers (1908–1999) worked as a contact to the press for Yva's studio, 1932–1936. Her own photographic work includes advertisement photography and numerous portraits, among them one of Yva, and was featured in several exhibitions of women's photography and advertisement photography. I refer to Röttgers's interview with Ira Buran. Most of the biographic details I found in Buran's study (1992).

11. Experimental photography (New Vision) and *Neue Sachlichkeit* were the two main directions that German photography took in the 1920s and early 1930s. Moholy-Nagy was the chief theoretician and practitioner of the photographic avant-garde and New Vision. He believed that while photography had been primarily used to *reproduce* objects from nature, now photography should be employed in the *production* of radically new images. In order to accomplish this goal, one was to experiment with the photographic process itself and with its main agent, light. Moholy-Nagy argued that the medium should be explored in terms of its inherent characteristics *Eigengesetzlichkeiten*, that is, the reaction of light-sensitive materials to the manipulation of a light source (1925, 8). Thus, the photograms or the "cameraless photographs" became the staple of his experimental work in the 1920s. Moholy-Nagy produced collage photograms of abstract, overlapping circular and rectangular forms (very much in the style of Zurich dadaists) as well as photograms of distinct, recognizable objects of daily life in unlikely and unsettling combinations (close to the surrealist style of Man Ray and his "rayographs"). Moholy-Nagy was the chief theoretician and practitioner of the photographic avant-garde and of the New Vision. Renger-Patzsch, the other towering figure in German photography, became the main promulgator of the movement known as *Neue Sachlichkeit* and associated with "restraint, sobriety, and objectivity in conformity with the purpose of the object" that photography represented (Hight 1995, 100). The *object*, the object in nature, or the various products of flourishing industrial and technological development in the interwar years became the main preoccupation of photographers like Renger-Patzsch. His photography emphasized the formal aspects of "material things"—plants, architecture, machines, and objects of mass consumption—by reproducing with extreme precision forms,

textures, and structures of objects. He was convinced that the true superiority of the photographic medium is in its ability "to capture the magic of material things" through exact "mechanical reproduction of form" ([1927] 1989, 104) and to "create a permanent record of the transient beauty of flowers or to reproduce the dynamism of modern technology" ([1929] 1989, 142).

12. This photograph was reprinted in the 1928 issue of the prestigious art journal *Das Kunstblatt* as an example of the modern connection between photography and advertisement.

13. Modernism of the 1920s and 1930s identified with the invention of new identities for women (in opposition to tradition) and seemed to offer a space for women to reinvent themselves as "New Women." On the limitations and paradoxes of this approach see Pollock (1996).

14. A culmination point in photography's new status was the 1929 Film und Foto exhibition (nicknamed Fifo) that constituted the most comprehensive expression of the new media's standing within art, science, and mass communication. Other important exhibitions that demonstrated the conceived closeness of film and photography as media were the 1925 Kino-und Photoausstellung in Berlin (nicknamed Kipho), the 1928 exhibit Neue Wege in der Photographie in Jena, and the 1929 exhibit Fotografie der Gegenwart at the Folkwang Museum in Essen. Ute Eskildsen discusses in detail the public effect of these exhibitions (1980, 35–46).

15. Margit von Plato has reviewed Yva's work in advertising and presented a sample of her still lifes (1931, 30–7).

## References

Baumhoff, Anja. 1992. "Frauen und Foto am Bauhaus: Ein modernes Medium im Spannungsfeld von Geschlecht, Kunst und Technik." *Frauen Kunst Wissenschaft* 14:36–42.

Beckers, Marion, and Elisabeth Moortgat. 1994. "Ihr Garten Eden ist das Magazin: zu den Bildgeschichten von Yva im UHU 1930–1933." In *Fotografieren hieß teilnehmen: Fotografinnen der Weimarer Republik*, ed. Ute Eskildsen, 239–49. Düsseldorf, Germany: Richter.

Böhm, Hans. 1926. "Der Expressionismus in der Photographie." *Photofreund* 6(23):429–31.

Bojunga Heike, and Ilona Leipold. 1995. "Die Lust am Experiment—Fotografinnen in den zwanziger Jahren." In *Neue Frauen zwischen den Zeiten: ein studentisches Projekt an der Freien Universität Berlin*, ed. Petra Bock and Katja Koblitz, 150–65. Berlin: Hentrich.

Bruns, Brigitte. 1987. "Die 'Fesselung' des Blicks: Fotografinnen zwischen Weimarer Republik und Drittem Reich." *Kairos. Mitteilungen des Österreichischen Fotoarchivs* 5/6:70–82.

Buran, Ira. 1992. "Else Neuländer-Simon ('YVA'): Eine Berliner Fotografin der zwanziger und dreißiger Jahre-Leben und Werk." Unpublished manuscript in the Art Library in Berlin.

Burgin, Victor. 1982. "Photography, Fantasy, Function." In *Thinking Photography,* ed. Victor Burgin, 177–216. London: Macmillan.

Coke, Van Deren. 1982. *Avant-Garde Photography in Germany 1919–1939.* San Francisco: Museum of Modern Art.

Doane, Mary Ann. 1982. "Film and Masquerade: Theorizing the Female Spectator." *Screen* 23(3–4):74–87.

Eskildsen, Ute. 1995. "A Chance to Participate: A Transitional Time for Women Photographers." In *Visions of the "Neue Frau": Women and the Visual Arts in Weimar Germany,* ed. Marsha Meskimmon and Shearer West, 62–76. Aldershot, U.K.: Scolar Press.

———. 1980. "Exhibits." In *Avant-Garde Photography in Germany 1919–1939,* 35–46. San Francisco: Museum of Modern Art.

Güssow, Ingeborg. 1980. "Die neusachliche Photographie." In *Kunst und Technik der 20er Jahre: Neue Sachlichkeit und gegenständlicher Konstruktivismus,* ed. Ingeborg Güssow, 94–107. Munich: Staatliche Galerie im Lenbachhaus.

Hartlaub, G. H. 1928. "Kunst als Werbung." *Das Kunstblatt* 12:173–7.

Hight, Eleanor. 1995. *Picturing Modernism: Moholy-Nagy and Photography in Weimar Germany.* Cambridge, Mass.: MIT Press.

Honnef, Klaus. 1997. "German Photography—Mirror of the German Mindset?" In *German Photography 1870–1970: Power of a Medium,* ed. Klaus Honnef, Rolf Sachsse, and Karin Thomas, 13–9. Cologne, Germany: DuMont.

Keller, Judith, and Katherine Ware, eds. 1993. *Women on the Edge: Twenty Photographers in Europe, 1919–1939.* Malibu, Calif.: J. Paul Getty Museum.

Kerbs, Diethart, Walter Uka, and Brigitte Walz-Richter, eds. 1983. *Zur Geschichte der Pressefotografie 1930–1936. Die Gleichschaltung der Bilder.* Berlin: Frölich & Kaufmann.

Kolbowski, Silvia. 1999. "Playing with Dolls." In *Over Exposed: Essays on Contemporary Photography,* ed. Carol Squiers, 153–68. New York: New Press.

König, Lotte. 1931. "Die Frau als Photographin." In *Die Kultur der Frau. Eine Lebenssymphonie der Frau des XX. Jahrhunderts,* ed. Ada Schmidt-Beil, 292–5. Berlin: Verlag für Kultur und Wissenschaft.

Kracauer, Siegfried. (1927) 1995. "Photography." In *The Mass Ornament: Weimar Essays.* Trans. and ed. Thomas Y. Levin, 47–63. Cambridge, Mass.: Harvard University Press.

Lavin, Maud. 2001. *Clean New World: Culture, Politics and Graphic Design.* Cambridge, Mass.: MIT Press.

Lohse, Bernd. 1980. "Cameras." In *Avant-Garde Photography in Germany 1919–1930,* ed. Van Deren Coke, 47–9. San Francisco: Museum of Modern Art.

Moholy-Nagy, Lázsló. 1925. *Malerei, Photographie, Film.* Munich: Langen.

———. 1927. "Die Photographie in der Reklame." *Photographische Korrespondenz* 63(9):257–60.

Moldering, Herbert. 1988. *Fotografie in der Weimarer Republik.* Berlin: Nishen.

Pastor, Suzanne E. 1985. "Photography and the Bauhaus." *The Archive: Center for Creative Photography Research Series* 21(March):1–44.

Philipp, Claudia Gabrielle. 1992. "Fotografin—Beruf und Berufung." In *Frauen Kunst Wissenschaft* 14:28–35.

Plato, Margit von. 1931. "YVA Fotos." *Gebrauchsgraphik* 11:30–7.

Pollock, Giselda. 1996. "Inscriptions of the Feminine." In *Inside the Visible: An Elliptical Traverse of 20th Century Art in, of and from the Feminine,* ed. M Catherine de Zegher, 67–88. Cambridge, Mass.: MIT Press.

Renger-Patzsch, Albert. (1927) 1989. "Aims." In *Photography of the Modern Era: European Documents and Critical Writings, 1913–1940,* ed. Christopher Phillips, 104–5. New York: Metropolitan Museum of Art.

———. 1928. "Die Freude am Gegenstand." *Das Kunstblatt* 12:19–20.

———. (1929) 1989. "Photography and Art." In *Photography of the Modern Era: European Documents and Critical Writings, 1913–1940,* ed. Christopher Phillips, 142–4. New York: Metropolitan Museum of Art.

Schmalriede, Manfred. 1989. "Fotografie und Werbung von 1924 bis 1988." In *Werbefotografie in Deutschland seit den Zwanziger Jahren,* ed. Ute Eskildsen, 7–27. Essen, Germany: Museum Folkwang Essen.

Schreiber, Helene. 1970. "Einführung." In *Fotografinnen: Beispiele aus der Arbeit von Fotografinnen in Deutschland seit 1925,* ed. Otto Steinert, 2–3. Essen, Germany: Museum Folkwang.

Warstat, Willi. 1929. "Die 'entfesselte Kamera' und die 'produktive Photographie': Zu den Ideen Professor Moholy-Nagys." *Deutscher Kamera-Almanach* 19:43–60.

# PART III Iconographies of Communal Identity

CHAPTER TEN

# Iconographies of Gender, Poverty, and Power in Contemporary South African Visual Culture

KIM MILLER

> Storytelling is an urgent project for black women in post-apartheid South Africa where so much forgetfulness is willed upon people.
>
> —Mamphela Ramphele, *Across Boundaries* (1995, xi)

> I made this design to show where I come from. I wanted to show everyone what is happening here.
>
> —Nontsikelelo (Ntsiki) Stuurman, Philani artist (1998)

There are two primary ways impoverished women are represented within the well-established iconography of poverty. One romanticizes the conditions of female poverty, trivializing the harsh and often very desperate realities of daily life (Adair 2000, 2008 [chapter 8 in this volume]; Ellis 1998; Godby 1999; Platt 2004). The other presents poor women as deviant victims devoid of agency or power and deserving of their circumstances (Adair 2000, 2008; Ellis 1998; Godby 1999; hooks 1995; Platt 2004).[1] By depicting poor women in this insulting and one-dimensional fashion, this iconography contributes to the deep inequalities that underlie and perpetuate the conditions of female poverty. For theorist Vivyan Adair, predominant representations of the poor "obscure hegemonic stakes in representation . . . [that] collapse the lives and experiences of poor women into deceptively simplistic dramas, which are then offered up for public consumption" (2000, xi). The very visibility of poor women within this iconography is dependent on their silence; poor women rarely have a say in if, or how, they are depicted or in how their images are received.[2] This combination of inequality with silence has consequences for impoverished women that extend well beyond the realm of representation. There is a fundamental relationship between images of poor women and the injurious public policy decisions that negatively affect their lives and welfare. As Jacqueline Ellis has noted, images of poor women consistently "appropriate the perspective of the economically deprived subject for a political purpose that serve the interest of the viewer" (Ellis 1998, 6). Adair offers many compelling examples of "the circuit of power" that

Originally published in the Spring 2007 issue of the *NWSA Journal*.

is the relationship between the spuriousness of representation and the reality of public policy (2000; 2008).

I have been inspired by Adair's and Ellis's assertions to explore the complicated relationship between women's poverty, representation, and power. Specifically, in this essay, I am concerned with the empowerment possibilities that visual culture can offer impoverished women: Can women be concurrently poor and empowered? Can visual culture be activated to address the realities of women's economic deprivation while also celebrating their ability to survive them? What are the most effective and honorable ways to represent the conditions of life faced by poor women, and who should do the representing? And, perhaps most important for the purposes of this paper, how can impoverished women express themselves creatively, or access art-making, as a mode of self-realization, agency, and activism in order to represent themselves within the wider cultural discourse?

Some of these questions can be productively addressed, I believe, through an examination of the work of the Philani Project, a women's art-making cooperative located in the impoverished township of Crossroads, South Africa. In many ways, the Philani Project is an ideal site from both practical and theoretical perspectives for the exploration of the activism-inflected, self-representation of female poverty. Economic status is what unites the Philani artists because it is the basis for their inclusion in the art-making project. The project was initiated as part of a nationwide anti-poverty project in South Africa, with the long-term goal of battling child malnutrition and raising families out of poverty by training unemployed mothers to be commercial artists. The project provides three-month-long skills-training classes in textile design, painting, and printing, as well as printing facilties to unemployed mothers with children under the age of five. The women who become artists through the project produce bold and vivid designs, often autobiographical, which are silkscreened and hand-painted onto variously sized cotton wall hangings and pillow covers, as well as t-shirts and aprons, and sold locally and internationally.

Building on a long history of women's activism in Crossroads, Philani artists engage in activist art, using art-making as a vehicle to address and confront social and gender inequalities (Cole 1987; Miller 2003a; Miller 2003b). The cooperative is unique in that the women are equally concerned with economic survival and with self-representation, and both efforts equally engage the women in creative, theoretical, and political action. As Adair has rightly argued, "When poor women are allowed to read, write, and claim their own experiences, a new story emerges" (2000, xviii). The Philani Project is an ideal space to examine the emergence of such stories, as the artists demonstrate the varied ways in which poor women can take a central position in shaping the manner in which their futures will be accounted for politically through creative acts.

Against the background of the above-mentioned predominant and negative iconographies of female poverty, this article considers Philani artists as antipoverty art activists who have deployed striking imagery that celebrates their success at addressing, if not completely overcoming, their impoverished circumstances. Of key importance is, of course, the connection of the Philani Project to the overall context of women's art and activism in South Africa and how the project clearly illustrates the connection between African feminism, feminist theory, and visual culture.

## Mountains, Meanings, Metaphors

> Much remains to be done to ensure equal access by women to economic opportunities.
>
> —Commission on Gender Equality, South Africa (1999, 12)

> The most devastating impact of apartheid on poor black South Africans has been the destruction of people's faith in themselves as agents of history.
>
> —Mamphela Ramphele, *Across Boundaries* (1995, 212)

Nigerian feminist theorist Molara Ogundipe-Leslie's influential essay "African Women, Culture, and Another Development" offers a theoretical framework for considering the situation of poor women in Africa (1993). Ogundipe-Leslie reframes the idea of multiple oppressions—a common thread linking much black feminist theory and practice in the United States to that in Africa and elsewhere—as "six mountains" African women carry on their backs. Each mountain represents a different form of oppression. Two of the "mountains" are particularly relevant in considering how art has been deployed by the women of the Philani Project.

One of the mountains that Ogundipe-Leslie identifies as burdening the great majority of African women is economic disadvantage, particularly the dearth of employment for women because "employment guarantees economic independence which leads to other forms of social and spiritual independence" (1993, 115). Widespread poverty among African women, traceable to the difficulty of earning a living, is the primary impediment to women's ability to "mobilize political, economic, educational, human, social, and cultural resources" (Steady 2006, 18).[3] For women in Africa, relief from poverty is essential for personal agency, and economic independence can be the basis for other forms of feminist empowerment. For Ogundipe-Leslie and other African feminists, "The liberation of women in society is . . . about the larger problem of the redistribution of privilege, power, and property between the rich and the poor, encompassing the smaller problem of the redistribution of power, property, and privilege between men and women" (1993, 114).

Another "mountain" on a woman's back, identified by Ogundipe-Leslie as "the most important" one for women to combat, is "herself." She explains:

> Women are shackled by their own negative self image, by centuries of the interiorization of the ideologies of patriarchy and gender hierarchy. Their own reactions to objective problems therefore are often self defeating and self crippling. Woman reacts with fear, a dependency complex and attitudes to please and cajole where more self assertive actions are needed. (1993, 114)

In her call for raising women's consciousness about the need to assert personal power, Ogundipe-Leslie is not blaming women for the perpetuation of patriarchy or the conditions of oppression that burden them; rather, she encourages women to take a hard look at the role they must play in eradicating these conditions by taking control over the ways in which they are represented and understood. Calling for women to take control of their own representation and engage in consciousness-raising as a form of activism, Ogundipe-Leslie urges women to "throw" this mountain off their backs (1993, 114).

Two related works created at the Philani Project, *Crossroads to Cape Town* (fig. 10.1) and *Welcome to Cape Town* (fig 10.2) can serve as useful examples of how poor African women have used art to throw both of the "mountains" identified by Ogundipe-Leslie off their backs. Ironically, both include the image of Cape Town's magnificent Table Mountain. In each image, Table Mountain draws attention to the Philani artists' dislocation and marginalization from the center of wealth, while demonstrating the agency that comes from making this dislocation visible.

10.1 The Philani Project, *Crossroads to Cape Town,* 1998. Acrylic paint on cotton. Photograph by Kim Miller.

Table Mountain is celebrated for its beautiful, commanding presence in the center of the city and is predominant in local visual culture, from postcards and tourist brochures to popular and fine art. Access to the mountain, its beauty, and its richness has long been restricted to Cape Town's privileged white population; their opulent homes, private schools, swimming pools, and exclusive shopping malls encircle the base of the mountain and line its long stretches of beach. For impoverished Crossroads residents, the presence of the mountain stands as a constant reminder of the divisions created by apartheid's system of racial classification—divisions that supported white privilege and helped sustain the conditions in which Crossroads residents continue to live. To many residents of Crossroads, the mountain is a constant reminder of what life *could* be like, if only one had been born and classified as "white" under apartheid rule. Even in post-apartheid South Africa, this race/class division persists.

In *Crossroads to Cape Town,* Philani artists exploit the symbolic value of Table Mountain and all of its associated meanings in order to draw attention not to the splendor of the mountain but to the poverty that remains unacknowledged in most of its representations. This is a politically significant act given the near absence of meaningful attention to the artists' lives, particularly in the realm of visual culture. In this black and white image, reminiscent of documentary photography, Table Mountain stands as the background while the artists' own living conditions are the focus. Tens of thousands of small handmade shacks crowd together on a narrow stretch of barren land.[4] This image presents us with two rows of these homes, recognizable by their box-like structure and flat, corrugated iron roofs. Often referred to as "informal" housing because they are composed primarily of discarded and easily perishable materials, the homes do not have electricity or plumbing, and most are too small to accommodate local families. Insecure in both construction

10.2 The Philani Project, *Welcome to Cape Town,* 1998. Acrylic paint on cotton. Photograph by Kim Miller.

and security, the homes often lack doors or entire walls, offering limited privacy and making safety a constant concern. These and other issues related to housing are of particular concern for Crossroads women, who have long struggled for access to space, shelter, and safety in this area (Cole 1987). As 62-year-old Ncediswa Mantlana describes, "Crossroads is just made by shacks. There is no water, no toilets, no playgrounds for children, and a lot of crime in this place" (Mantlana 1999).

Although *Crossroads to Cape Town* is visually uncomplicated—it lacks color, depth, narrative, or detail—it succeeds in making visible the extreme differences in economic strata that is characteristic of not just Cape Town but most of South Africa. In its emphasis on division and separateness, *Crossroads to Cape Town* brilliantly expresses the barriers that allow those living privileged lives to maintain distance from abject poverty and perpetuate denial that keeps uncomfortable economic realities at bay. In *Crossroads to Cape Town,* the Philani artists bring these divisions into very sharp focus, making it quite clear that the opportunities and privileges available to residents of the rich enclaves in the mountain's shadow are completely out of reach to the inhabitants of Crossroads. In *Crossroads to Cape Town* the sense of Crossroads residents' isolation from both Cape Town residents and international tourists—and the potential resources that these groups represent—is unmistakable.

The imposing airplane, hovering above this landscape, provides information on another important aspect of Crossroads' location. The township sits just off the side of a major highway near Cape Town's busy international airport. Crossroads is one of the first sights to greet air travelers as they move toward the city; it is quite impossible not to see the tens of thousands of handmade homes crowded against each other and lining the highway, an unavoidable and overwhelming vision of poverty that is both the first and last thing tourists see as they arrive and depart. The image makes a powerful and disquieting statement about the invisibility of the poor in relation to the eyes of the privileged, despite their very physical and visual presence.

The Philani artists' studios are located in a large warehouse set in the center of Crossroads. From the Philani studio's long series of windows, the city of Cape Town and the majestic profile of Table Mountain in the distance are clearly visible. Thus, the image of the mountain in *Crossroads to Cape Town* is quite naturally emphasized, as it is forever in their line of vision as they work. In *Crossroads to Cape Town,* the artists are deliberately showing what they want us to see from *their* point of view: the visual experience of being surrounded by poverty while working to transform the very experiences that they depict. Shown from "the inside out," these artists visualize the priorities of African feminists and answer the activist art theorist Carol Becker's call to help others "think about representing poverty and other social concerns" (Becker 2004, 11).

In *Welcome to Cape Town,* Table Mountain conveys something very different. In this image, Philani artists complicate their relationship to Table Mountain. In this brightly colored work, township residents are shown traveling on foot, in buses, and in taxis in order to sell food, artwork, and other items to the people residing in the city. As they move between the two spaces, the geographical division between them visually collapses; township shacks, local food stands, and *spaza* shops[5] are no longer isolated in the desolate township but are pressed up against the base of a lush, green Table Mountain, which is now surrounded with people of diverse racial backgrounds.

The Philani artists are acutely aware that the beauty of this mountain, and the oceans that surround it, help to draw hundreds of thousands of tourists to Cape Town every year, and that the continued existence of the cooperative depends in large part on the income generated by these visitors. As artist Noluvuyo Guza explains, "My favorite design is *Welcome to Cape Town* because it is a design that is showing tourists and it shows Table Mountain which attracts visitors" (2001). For Guza and the other Philani artists, a sense of personal agency and the real possibility of economic empowerment through involvement in the Philani project is intimately tied to the tourist industry, especially those visitors who seek out "socially conscious" tourist experiences. In *Welcome to Cape Town,* there is a sense of optimism about the artists' attempt to negotiate the tourist industry and its relationship to the extremely polarized conditions depicted in *Crossroads to Cape Town.*

Although the lives of Crossroads women form the basis for the content of Philani work, the artwork is not intended for sale to Crossroads residents because the cost of the work, which must be priced high enough to allow the artists to earn a reasonable profit, renders Philani artwork virtually unaffordable for township residents, most of whom continue to struggle to afford basic needs for their families. Instead, the textiles are created for consumers—including tourists—who live outside of Crossroads. In creating images such as this, and making them available for sale, Philani artists express confidence that what is important to them will become important to the more privileged purchasers and that what they depict will help prevent the privileged from remaining "distanced" from the realities of the poor.

Groups of tourists and other visitors are always welcome where the artists work. The artists manage a small shop adjacent to their studio, in which a wide range of Philani products are kept on display and are available for sale. *Welcome to Cape Town* hangs on the door of their shop in recognition of the meaningful and profitable relationships the artists maintain with local gallery owners and tourist companies. The importance of these relationships cannot be overstated given that abject poverty, geographic isolation, and limited access to transportation and modern forms of communication restrict their ability to participate in the public sphere as artists or activists. They must therefore rely entirely on the interest and efforts of local gallery owners who periodically display and sell their work, along with local tourist companies who bring groups of people into Crossroads to visit the artists' studios and shop.

South African scholars recognize the important role that tourism can play in promoting the empowerment of marginalized peoples and in transforming the unjust conditions referred to in *Crossroads to Cape Town*. In their recent book, *Tourism in the New South Africa: Social Responsibility and the Tourist Experience*, Garth Allen and Frank Brennan write:

> The role of the tourist industry and tourist development in promoting economic regeneration, political confidence and stability and a new social and moral order . . . is wrapped up inside the warmth of a high-profile blanket commitment by all the main tourist organizations to empowerment as the main political procedure for realizing significant social change. (Allen and Brennan 2004, 207)

The possibility of such change is brilliantly illustrated by *Welcome to Cape Town*. Philani artists visually connect Crossroads and Cape Town by focusing on the exchange of bodies, goods, and money between the two areas that is made possible by tourism but is initiated and negotiated by the residents of Crossroads themselves, offering the artists a unique and powerful way to enter their voices into the public sphere.

Philani artists actively seek to transform their lives by initiating and sustaining their connection to Cape Town and the people who visit there. Clearly illustrating the very empowerment that Allen and Brennan speak of, visual emphasis in *Welcome to Cape Town* is placed on the energy and agency of township residents, who are central to the work, shown acting on their own behalf to transform the economic conditions that determine their quality of life. Philani artist Nombongo Noboza favors this design for this very reason. As she explains, "*Welcome to Cape Town* shows how our people depend on selling fruits and meats to the people in town" (Noboza 2001). Philani artist Ntsiki Stuurman agrees, "I made this design to show where I come from. I wanted to show everyone what is happening here" (2001). Like Garth and Brennan, Philani artists recognize that the tourist industry is essential to their survival and to the telling of their stories, and the artists do all that they can to nurture this mutually beneficial relationship.

Though political motivation may not be immediately clear when first viewing these two works, it is there, especially when the Philani artists' imagery is considered in the context of women's art and activism in South Africa and in the broader context of African feminist theory and visual culture studies. Philani artists operate within an African feminist tradition of participation in women's associations. In her book *Women and Collective Action in Africa,* Filomina Chioma Steady argues that work carried out through these collectives is an important form of feminist activism, as seemingly subtle acts can have significant impact on larger social and political movements. She explains:

> [African] women's associations operate on a more pragmatic level . . . their impact is discreet and incremental. The cumulative nature of their activities . . . can have cascading effects, similar to large social movements . . . they can also be regarded as the real "experts" in articulating and defining women's needs, concerns, and aspirations. They seek to advance social goals through their efforts and a brand of feminism. (Steady 2006, 18)

In articulating their needs, concerns, and aspirations in the pursuit of economic justice, Philani artists use visual culture as the vehicle to tell their stories, and through them, to demonstrate the need for change.

In *Crossroads to Cape Town* and *Welcome to Cape Town*, Philani artists are directly involved in the creation of visual depictions that counter the prevalence of demeaning representations of poor women—images that affect the perceptions of economically disadvantaged women not just in Crossroads, not just in South Africa, but throughout the world. As Adair has argued about the prevailing negative iconography of poverty, "In the shadow of this frenzied and profitable proliferation of representation exists a profound crisis in the lives of poor women and children whose bodies continue to be the site and operation of ideology, as they are read as dangerous and then erased and rendered mute in venues of authority and power" (2000, xi). Refusing to be "rendered mute," Philani artists harness the political potential of art through both subject matter and style. The artists have developed a celebratory aesthetic that expresses their consciousness, agency, and ingenuity, characterized by brilliant color, active figures, bold designs, and narrative repetition. The works display a certain unrefined quality that make them compelling; the works' rejection of Western visual conventions such as one-point perspective and the creative distortions of the body contribute to the visual appeal of the designs. In addition, these visual choices suggest a sense of hope and optimism on the part of the artists, despite the often disturbing and dismal themes they depict. The power of the imagery derives from the ambivalent combination of this celebratory aesthetic with difficult subject matter that often includes depictions of violence, malnutrition, exploitation, and death—direct corollaries of the poverty experienced by Crossroads inhabitants.

*Crossroads to Cape Town* and *Welcome to Cape Town* are also representative of Philani artists' creation of an inventive strategy of resistance—a strategy that bell hooks has called "liberatory imagination." For hooks, using one's imagination to create art objects that are at once meaningful and visually beautiful is an important strategy of resistance for people living in oppressive situations. According to hooks, this strategy has been particularly useful for economically disadvantaged women of color: "Even during the most dire circumstances of oppression and exploitation, [women] could find ways to express their creativity—to display artistry. They dared to use their imagination in ways that were liberatory" (1995, 150). This liberatory imagination expresses a worldview that does not visually mimic reality but instead thinks beyond it to create beautiful visions that celebrate the artists' survival: "Learning to see and appreciate the presence of beauty is an act of resistance in a culture of domination that recognizes the production of a pervasive feeling of lack, both material and spiritual, as a useful colonizing strategy" (hooks 1995, 124). For Philani artists, their aesthetic strategy visualizes a new kind of reality that is both active and empowered, an inventive strategy of resistance through which they articulate their experiences and transform them into sellable objects that help them address their economic problems. hooks's "liberatory imagination" intersects with Ogundipe-Leslie's vision of African feminism, as a determined act of throwing off one's back the "mountains" of oppression.

## On Bread and Bodies

> Before, because I was not working I was suffering. Now I can buy and cook for the kids. It is better than to stay at home.
>
> —Nomfundo Bawuti, Philani artist (2001)

> I can say yes, it is a good job even if it is not enough [money] because I can buy bread for the kids.
>
> —Mavis Makinana, Philani artist (2001)

In *From Good Ma to Welfare Queen: A Genealogy of the Poor Woman in American Literature, Photography, and Culture,* Vivyan Adair argues that poor women's bodies are ascribed negative meaning as "the embodiment of decay and disease" and as dangerous and chaotic. These meanings are "juxtaposed always against the innocence, order, and logic of the privileged . . . narratives [that] reduce and collapse the lives and experiences of poor women to deceptively simplistic dramas, which are then offered up for public consumption" (Adair 2000, xi–v). Although Adair was not speaking in this quotation directly about impoverished women in South Africa, her words are meaningful in this context, where an estimated 75 percent of black women under the age of 30 are still unemployed and where poor women have been similarly imaged, perceived, and ignored.

In the work *Mielies* (fig. 10.3), Philani artists directly counter these prevailing stereotypes by presenting the poor woman's body as empowered and dignified, through a focus on women's ability to care for, sustain,

10.3 The Philani Project, *Mielies,* 2000. Acrylic paint on cotton. Photograph by Kim Miller.

and nourish their families. The woman depicted in this work is shown in the active process of preparing mielie meal, an affordable and staple food for many of South Africa's peoples. As she cooks, various items essential to her work surround her: ripe cornstalks, decorated bowls, a mortar and pestle for grinding. The woman's arms are outstretched and her strong hands are spread wide as they actively reach forward toward the large, round bowl full of mielies that sits before her. The fullness of the bowl is important, for it acknowledges women's work and talents not only as cooks but also indirectly as cultivators of this important food in Africa. The act of food preparation is a routine form of domestic labor in which women worldwide engage on a daily basis, with a wide range of cultural, and gendered, meanings and messages. In this particular context, food preparation is very clearly linked to survival, as mielie meal is an important part of the daily diet because it is both nutritious and filling, critical factors when a surplus of food is not available, as is frequently the case in South Africa (Wylie 2001, 207).

One of the most striking features of this work is the physical presentation of the woman's body, which stresses her dignity. Dressed in clothing and jewelry particularly fancy given the routine task in which she is engaged, she works while kneeling on the ground, her folded legs revealed beneath her colorful attire. Through body adornment, the artists responsible for this image indicate admiration and respect for the woman pictured and the importance of her task. Around her body is wrapped an *umbhaco,* an ankle-length, wraparound skirt that is typically made from a blanket or cotton sheet, encircled with rows of woven black stripes and worn by Xhosa women. The number of black stripes denotes the status of the woman in her household and society at large (Costello 1990, 59). A number of *iiwatsha*, brass bracelets that are worn by married women, grace the length of her forearm, from wrist to elbow, their bright color also conveying important information. As Costello reports, the color yellow may be used to signify fertility and life (1990, 13). In this context, fertility relates to the abundance of the mielie crop and the life that is sustained by it. Finally, this working woman wears an ornate *icanci*, a Xhosa beaded collar, which is worn around the neck. Through this body adornment, the artists indicate their respect and admiration for this woman, the importance of her task, and the centrality of this particular food not just for health and survival but as central to group identity (Wylie 2001, 23). In the figure of this engaged and proud woman, the Philani artists directly counter more prevalent images of poor black women as disempowered, idle, or abject (Adair 2000, xv).

The formal presentation of the woman's body in *Mielies* also can be read as visualizing physical strength and the contributions that women make to individual and community survival. The artist has placed visual emphasis on the subject's arms and hands, which are disproportionately long and large in comparison to the rest of her body. They are very clearly, and on first sight perhaps oddly, a focal point of the piece. This "distorted" presentation is not an indication of lack of skill but rather a deliberate stylistic move. Art historian Henry Drewal describes intentional distortion in African art as "conceptual proportion." A purposeful and meaningful technique found in many genres of African art and practiced by artists throughout Africa in widely different contexts, conceptual proportion places visual emphasis on those parts of the human body that are *conceptually* important to the meaning of the work. Drewal argues that this aesthetic approach is essential to conveying the intellectual content of African art and the localized ideas and beliefs behind specific works. Drewal explains, "Africans think with art. It is fundamentally *conceptual* not perceptual. It presents philosophical ideas about the world rather than simply re-presenting the world as we perceive it through our senses" (1988, 3).[6] In *Mielies*, the enlarged hands and arms show the important role that women play as nurturers and nourishers of the family and how central women are to survival in difficult circumstances with very limited resources.

In the case of *Mielies*, the woman's arms and hands communicate that she is a productive and valued part of the community and that she has both physical strength and creative capabilities. Not only are her arms and hands emphasized by their elongation, but also the fancy jewelry adorning them draws our eye firmly to them. In discussing this work, Philani artists emphasize that the hands of women, as wives, mothers, daughters, and friends, are also used in other tasks that ensure the physical and emotional survival of family and community: holding, touching, and loving. These seemingly simple acts can be framed as acts of empowerment for black South African women who have, until recently, had to fight for their right to remain with their families and work in their own homes. The woman in this piece recognizes this, for as she works, she simultaneously presents herself to us. Displaying herself honorably, her arms stretched toward the bowl of mielies as her upper body twists in the opposite direction, we are permitted to see her in full frontal view. Staring directly at the viewer, she smiles, acknowledging and understanding the significance of her task. The strength of the woman's arms engaged in work is directly connected to the survival of her family and community. The women working at Philani celebrate this fact through the creation of this image.

Priscilla Mantlana and Nontsikelelo Stuurman, two of the primary artists of this work, recognize the many ways in which working with one's hands can be a source of pride for women. They speak to this in discussing their creative work as artists and wage earners at the Philani Project. Mantlana says:

> I came here because I was unemployed. At first I didn't realise that the course was to do things with your hands. I then had that interest to do things I'd never thought I would be able to do as well as having a skill that I would benefit from by earning money at the end of the day, to be able to feed my children and enlighten the skills to other mothers. I am proud now because I have skills. (1999)[7]

Stuurman echoes Mantlana's views, "Before the 14th of April 1997 I was staying at home without a job. But now I'm working with my own hands doing my own job" (1999). In the creation of *Mielies*, these artists echo Ifi Amadiume's assertion that women's individual and collective power can be derived "not from their affiliation to men but from women's own economic roles and contributions to the development of their society" (Steady 2006, 7). Philani artists demonstrate this sense of power by imaging a body like their own, empowered through the act of work, helping to counter a prevailing visual climate of erasure in regard to respectful images of poor women in Crossroads.

A visual text that speaks on many levels, *Mielies* also is important because it acknowledges that the economic challenges faced by women frequently differ from those faced by men, connecting the Philani artists to local South African women's rights activists of the past and global women's rights activists in the present. By focusing in this image on food preparation as an empowering act rather than a restrictive one, the artists draw on a long history of South African women's activism around "breadline" problems, which encompass a range of issues essential to basic survival, including demands for "access to a healthy diet, to child care, and to money raised from the sale of crops or handmade clothing" (Higgs 2004, 122).

Furthermore, in the context of South Africa, breadline problems have historically affected black women to a much greater extent than their white counterparts, leading noted trade unionist Emma Mashinini to identify them as a key black feminist issue: "white mothers . . . do not have to suffer anxiety over what we call breadline problems" (Mashinini, cited in Higgs 2004, 122). Indeed, as a primary issue of concern for black women who faced mounting poverty as racial segregation took hold in South Africa, breadline problems prompted many South African women to organize and agitate in the early twentieth century by joining Zenzele ("help-yourself") clubs (Higgs 2004, 122). Popularly known as "self-improvement associations," Zenzele clubs were a primary way by which women sought both to empower themselves and influence the political sphere by restoring "a degree of economic independence to African women, especially in rural areas" (Higgs 2004, 130). Zenzele clubs were, and continue to be, critical spaces for women's mobilization and collective action and were particularly important during apartheid years when black women's political activities were severely restricted through formal exclusion from the political sphere, as well as within most black resistance organizations including the African National Congress (ANC) (Walker 1990). In South Africa, where struggles for racial justice took precedence over gender issues, these clubs can be seen as early examples of feminist action around issues that were specific to women and which have since become central to theorizing about South African feminism. The Philani Project is solidly situated within the woman-specific anti-poverty activism of the Zenzele club tradition and within a much wider movement in African feminist activism, a movement that Steady terms a "gender revolution . . . in Africa" that has adopted the eradication of poverty as its central feminist issue. She writes:

> This revolution has more to do with the economic challenges of underdevelopment and poverty . . . it is a revolution against the economic injustice of the global economy that is wreaking havoc on African countries and on the social fabric and well-being of African peoples. . . . This calls for an international feminist agenda that gives priority to promoting economic justice at the global level. (Steady 2006, 178)

Through images like *Mielies,* artists at the Philani Project contribute to this revolution by drawing attention to women's poverty on levels that are both personal and political. The first step the Philani artists take through their art is in affirming the bodies and experiences of poor women, making their stories visible. Second, by offering their works for display in the public arena, and for sale, Philani artists not only are raising awareness about the economic deprivation of women but also are working in a direct way to change this situation by earning income from their art. Philani artists enhance their potential for political and economic empowerment by promulgating self-empowering alternative visions of themselves as productive and capable citizens, and by extension portraying the critical role women play in creating and sustaining African societies.

## Active Women, Activating Art

> The new South African feminism . . . has given a voice to the concerns of many formerly unheard women.
>
> —Kemp, Madlala, Moodley, and Salo, "The Dawn of a New Day: Redefining South African Feminism" (1995, 159)

> Yes, Lady. Philani has helped women to be strong.
>
> —Tonono Nomqo, Philani artist (2001)

The works discussed in this article are but a few examples of the many Philani works that enhance the possibilities for gender justice by depicting the unique experiences of impoverished women in postapartheid South Africa. African feminist theory offers a useful paradigm for considering Philani artwork as a feminist activist art. Indeed, the very existence of the Philani Project stands as an important reminder that poverty and creative agency are not mutually exclusive and that it *is* possible for women to move themselves away from impoverishment, represent their own experiences, and lead dignified lives despite the many obstacles that stand in their way. Their work demonstrates that there are ways to visualize poverty in ways that do not romanticize or victimize the poor. Philani artists have refused to see, or to depict, themselves as victims. And in a situation where, as South African feminist activist Mamphela Ramphele notes, the victim image is "ultimately disempowering . . . because it denies human agency in history which is inherent in the very essence of our humanity" (cited in James and Busia 1993), the very act of representing oneself as dignified and empowered is a necessary and politically significant act.

Joining the many South African resistance artists who came before them, Philani artists continue the tradition of using the power of visual culture in a difficult political struggle, a struggle against the many mountains of oppression that presently burden Africa's women. The Philani Printing Project is about women creating and embracing economic viability and the ability of visual culture to celebrate, resist, instruct, and empower. As art activists, the women of the project not only identify in their work the problems that poor black women continue to face in postapartheid South Africa, but also they reach out to individuals at local, national, and international levels who see in art a powerful approach to creating change.[8] As Steady remarks, such efforts have become "an integral part of . . . an African feminist agenda" (2006, 178).

## Acknowledgments

Because Philani is organized as a collective, the majority of the works are created through a collaborative process and are therefore unsigned by individual artists. So that the artists do not go unnamed in this essay, I would like to take this opportunity to acknowledge each of them, concurrently offering my sincere thanks for the time that they all graciously gave to me and allowing me to interview them and observe their work. As of June 2001, the women working at the Philani Printing Project were Jane Solomon, Lungiswa Pikoko, Nontsikelelo (Ntsiki) Stuurman, Priscilla Mantlana, Ncediswa Mantlana, Nomaledi Nkinqa, Nomfundo Dyantyi, Neliswa Fanteni, Lilian Bambiso, Fundiswa Gam, Xoliswa Nyakiso, Nolwando Fani, Nosipho Mququ, Wendy Mdleleni, Nowthando Mtosele, Tonono Nomqolo, Zandile Mayekiso, Nombongo Noboza, Noluvuyo Guza, Nonceba Gobizembe, Nomfanelo Ntumase, Consance Ndzishe, Nomakhaa Katsi, Nothembentoni Nqfiyi, Nomfundo Bawuti, Nothozamile Mfundisi, Mavis Makinana, and Nothembentoni Nqayi.

## Notes

1. Most theories of visual representations of poverty center on social documentary photography as the primary form of representation. Although this essay will examine painted and printed works, and not photography, the established theoretical discussion offers an important framework for thinking about larger questions about the visual representation of poverty. And, as Ron Platt has persuasively said, "the tradition of documentary photography . . . continues to inform visual representations of poverty to this day" (Platt 2004, 19).

2. A few important exceptions are worthy of mention. In his essay, "The Evolution of Documentary Photography in South Africa as Shown in a Comparison between the Carnegie Inquiries into Poverty (1932 and 1948)," Michael Godby tells that during the second Carnegie Inquiry (1948), many efforts were made to "find ways for poor people to represent themselves directly to the public on the occasion of the Report" (1999, 36). The Report culminated in the publication of the book *South Africa: The Cordoned Heart*. Although the images included in the final publication "Celebrate the Humanity of Those Who Endure the Most Extreme Forms of Deprivation" (Godby 1999, 37), they do not in fact include self-representations of the poor. A second example can be found in Ron Platt's essay accompanying the poverty-themed exhibition *Borne of Necessity*. Platt outlines three main ap-

proaches to artistic engagement with poverty (2004, 20). Self-representation, and a concentrated focus on gender issues, is absent here as well. A more recent photographic exhibit, entitled "The Missing Story of Ourselves: Poverty and the Promise of Higher Education," offers a unique example of visual self-representation by poor women. Organized by Vivyan Adair at Hamilton College, New York, the exhibit includes more than fifty color photographs of individual women coupled with first person narratives about their lives as impoverished women working toward transformation.

3. For other African feminists who speak to this issue, see Ake 1996; Amadiume 1997; Oyewumi 1997; Nnaemeka 2003; Steady 1981, 2006; Tarrow 1998.

4. Government-sponsored homes made from the more durable materials of brick and concrete also are present in Crossroads, appearing in increasing numbers as democratic rule has become a reality in South Africa. The presence of these homes is both welcome and problematic, for although they help fulfill a desperate need for permanent, stable shelter, they simultaneously maintain apartheid segregation by transforming a postapartheid Crossroads into a "permanent" black settlement. In another painting, Philani artist Ncediswa Mantlana addresses the local violence that has erupted over disputes related to government housing. In her work, she visualizes the contrast between the old and new homes, emphasizing differences in material and color while calling attention to the similarities in size and location. For a reproduction and discussion of this image, please see Kim Miller's "T shirts, Testimony and Truth: Memories of Violence Made Visible" (2005).

5. Spaza shops are informal businesses set up by township residents as one strategy to combat widespread unemployment and poverty, especially among women. Typically, they are small retail outlets attached to a residence so that women can concurrently sell wares and tend to their children.

6. Drewal speaks specifically about Yoruba artistic traditions but makes the point that the practice of conceptual proportion is found in other artistic traditions throughout the continent of Africa (1988).

7. As an artist, Priscilla Mantlana was particularly proud of the work that her own hands did in creating this particular design. A brochure printed by the Philani Project shows her standing in front of *Mielies*, her favorite work, wearing a t-shirt with the same image. Taken on her graduation day, when she advanced from the status of trainee to fully employed artist at the project, the photograph, as well as *Mielies*, mark an important transition in Mantlana's life and liberation. Like the woman making mielies, Mantlana looks directly at us with a satisfied smile. Sadly, the end of Mantlana's story is not a happy one. Shortly after this photograph was taken, Mantlana suffered an asthma attack from which she did not survive. Her death is one of Philani's most tragic stories, and one of the many examples of how the conditions of poverty exacerbate ill health. Mantlana's illness

was treatable and would have certainly been considered a minor condition in other locations, yet even the most basic medical resources were not available to her.

8. For examples of images that are more overtly didactic, see Miller 2003a; 2003b; 2005.

## References

Adair, Vivyan. 2000. *From Good Ma to Welfare Queen: A Genealogy of the Poor Woman in American Literature, Photography, and Culture.* New York: Garland Publishing.

——— 2008. "The Missing Story of Ourselves: Poor Women, Power, and the Politics of Feminist Representation." Forthcoming. *NWSA Journal.*

Ake, Claude. 1996. *Democracy and Development in Africa.* Washington, D.C.: Brookings Institute.

Allen, Garth, and Frank Brennan. 2004. *Tourism in the New South Africa: Social Responsibility and the Tourist Experience.* New York: I. B. Tauris.

Amadiume, Ifi. 1997. *Male Daughters, Female Husbands: Gender and Sex in an African Society.* London: Zed Books.

Bawuti, Nomfundo. 2001. Personal interview. Crossroads, South Africa. June.

Becker, Carol. 2004. "Making Things Visible." In *Borne of Necessity,* ed. Ron Platt, 11–8. Greensboro, N.C.: Weatherspoon Art Museum.

Cole, Josette. 1987. *Crossroads: The Politics of Reform and Repression 1976–1986.* Johannesburg: Ravan Press.

Commission on Gender Equality. 1999. *Annual Report of the Commission on Gender Equality, April 1998-March 1999.* Johannesburg.

Costello, Dawn. 1990. *Not Only for Its Beauty: Beadwork and Its Cultural Significance among the Xhosa-Speaking Peoples.* Pretoria: University of South Africa.

Drewal, Henry. 1988. *Shapes of the Mind: African Art from Long Island Collections.* New York: Hofstra University.

Ellis, Jacqueline. 1998. *Silent Witnesses: Representations of Working-Class Women in the United States.* Bowling Green: Bowling Green State University Popular Press.

Godby, Michael. 1999. "The Evolution of Documentary Photography in South Africa as Shown in a Comparison between the Carnegie Inquiries into Poverty (1932 and 1948)."*Democracy's Images: Photography and Visual Art after Apartheid,* ed. Rory Bester, Jan-Erik Lundstrom, and Katarina Pierre, 34–7. Umea BildMuseet.

Guza, Noluvuyo. 2001. Personal interview. Crossroads, South Africa. June.

Higgs, Catherine. 2004. "Zenzele: African Women's Self-Help Organizations in South Africa, 1927–1998." *African Studies Review* 47(3):119–41.

hooks, bell. 1995. *Art on My Mind: Visual Politics.* New York: New Press.

James, Stanlie M., and Abena P. A. Busia. 1993. *Theorizing Black Feminisms: The Visionary Pragmatism of Black Women.* New York: Routledge.

Kemp, Amanda, Nozizwe Madlala, Asha Moodley, and Elaine Salo. 1995. "The Dawn of a New Day: Redefining South African Feminism." In *The Challenge of Local Feminisms: Women's Movements in Global Perspective*, ed. Amrita Basu, 131–62. Boulder: Westview Press.

Makinana, Mavis. 2001. Personal interview. Crossroads, South Africa. June.

Mantlana, Priscilla. 1999. Personal interview. Crossroads, South Africa. February.

Miller, Kimberly. 2005. "T shirts, Testimony and Truth: Memories of Violence Made Visible." *Textile: The Journal of Cloth and Culture* 3(3):246–71.

———. 2003a. "The Philani Printing Project: Women's Art and Activism in Crossroads, South Africa." *Feminist Studies* 29(3):618–38.

———. 2003b. *The Philani Printing Project: Women's Art and Activism in Crossroads, South Africa.* Dissertation, University of Wisconsin-Madison.

Nnaemeka, Obioma. 2003. "Negro-Feminism: Theorizing, Practicing, and Pruning Africa's Way." *Signs* 29(2):357–85.

Noboza, Nombongo. 2001. Personal interview. Crossroads, South Africa. June.

Nomqo, Tonono. 2001. Personal interview. Crossroads, South Africa. June.

Ogundipe-Leslie, Molara. 1993. "African Women, Culture, and Another Development." In *Theorizing Black Feminisms: The Visionary Pragmatism of Black Women*, ed. Stanlie M. James and Abena P. A. Busia, 102–27. New York: Routledge.

Oyewumi, Oyeronke. 1997. *The Invention of Women: Making an African Sense of Western Gender Discourses.* Minneapolis: University of Minnesota Press.

Platt, Ron. 2004. *Borne of Necessity.* Greensboro, N.C.: Weatherspoon Art Museum.

Ramphele, Mamphela. 1995. *Across Boundaries: The Journey of a South African Woman Leader.* New York: Feminist Press.

Steady, Filomina Chioma. 2006. *Women and Collective Action in Africa.* New York: Palgrave.

Stuurman, Nontsikelelo (Ntsiki). 1998. Personal interview. Crossroads, South Africa. December.

———. 1999. Personal interview. Crossroads, South Africa. February.

———. 2001. Personal interview. Crossroads, South Africa. June.

———, ed. 1981. *The Black Woman Cross-Culturally.* Cambridge: Schenkman Publishing.

Tarrow, Sidney George. 1998. *Power in Movement: Social Movements, Collective Action and Politics.* New York: Cambridge University Press.

Walker, Cheryl. 1990. "The Women's Suffrage Movement: The Politics of Gender, Race and Class." In *Women and Gender in Southern Africa to 1945*, ed. Cheryl Walker, 313–45. Cape Town: David Phillip.

Wylie, Diana. 2001. *Starving on a Full Stomach: Hunger and the Triumph of Cultural Racism in Modern South Africa.* Charlottesville: University Press of Virginia.

CHAPTER ELEVEN

# Cultural Trauma, Memory, and Gendered Collective Action: The Case of Women of the Storm Following Hurricane Katrina

EMMANUEL DAVID

## Introduction

On December 11, 2005, the *New York Times* printed an editorial titled "The Death of an American City," which projected a dire outlook for post-Katrina New Orleans: "We are about to lose New Orleans. Whether it is a conscious plan to let the city rot until no one is willing to move back or honest paralysis over difficult questions, the moment is upon us when a major American city will die, leaving nothing but a few shells for tourists to visit like a museum." Warning against the city's death by attrition, the editors continued, "Lawmakers need to understand that for New Orleans the words 'pending in Congress' are a death warrant requiring no signature."

The invocation of the museum metaphor to caution against the abandonment and continued decay of a vibrant city following disaster taps into the broader debate over the importance of memory in recovering from extreme and traumatic events. As Judith Herman (1997) has pointed out, public remembering is an integral process that helps victims voice their suffering. But public remembering is not only concerned with the past, as embodied in public memorials, museums, or anniversaries; it also encompasses how memory work functions to confront urgent needs in the present and to influence conditions in the future. To demonstrate the complex intersection of these goals, I focus on the relationship between remembrance work, cultural trauma, and social change by examining the collective actions of one group, Women of the Storm, which formed in Hurricane Katrina's wake. I contend that remembrance practices, and more specifically *gendered forms of cultural memory,* were uniquely activated by Women of the Storm to address what has become the cultural trauma of Katrina.

My analysis draws upon the work of feminist scholars who have begun to explore how gender affects a group's cultural memory of events layered with trauma, violence, and terror (Baumel 1998; Baumel and Cohen 2003; Hirsch and Smith 2002; Jacobs 2004, 2008; Lentin 1997; Ringelheim 1998).

---

Originally published in the Fall 2008 issue of the *NWSA Journal.*

Feminist scholarship has engaged with questions of cultural memory through writings on sexual abuse and violence against women, and more recently has turned to mass trauma such as slavery or the Holocaust and explored the intersections of gender, sexuality, race, nation, and class (Hirsch and Smith 2002). In part, this article's investigation of Women of the Storm serves as a modest corrective to what Hirsch and Smith (2002, 4) call the "'uneven developments' of feminist studies and memory studies" and adds to the recent literature on the gendered dimensions of cultural memory.

In what follows, I use the notion of cultural memory to examine the performative and change-driven collective actions of Women of the Storm. The interdisciplinary field of memory studies has begun to explore transmissions of memories related to violent and traumatic cultural events through the lens of group interaction, performance, commemoration, representation, and memorialization (Schwartz 1982; Sturken 1997; Taylor 2003; for a detailed discussion of the origins of memory discourse, see Klein 2000). Just as trauma discourse has extended from the psychological realm to that of cultures and collectivities, theoretical moves that decenter the psychological and historical dimensions of memory result in an emphasis on how memories reside within, and are transferred through, social group interactions and political cultures (Connerton 1989; Fentress and Wickham 1992; Halbwachs 1992; Olick 1999). The recent expansion of memory studies to include group analysis allows for broader understandings of collective traumas and extreme events such as the Holocaust, genocide, mass rapes and killings, war and postwar cultures (Lembcke 1998; Sturken 1997), transformations of the nation-state (Neal 1998; Taylor 2003; Vinitzky-Seroussi 2001, 2002), natural and technological disasters (Erikson 1976, 1995), and more recently, 9/11 and other terrorist attacks (Haskins and DeRose 2003; Smelser 2004; Weissman 2005; see also the section on gender and September 11 in Hirsch and Smith 2002). The social frameworks of memory are critical in that individual memory is acquired and activated through membership in particular social groups (Halbwachs 1992). In a similar approach to understanding memory as situated within social relations, Connerton (1989) emphasizes the ways in which group memories are conveyed and sustained through social practices, particularly commemorative ceremonies and bodily practices, and argues that these "images of the past and recollected knowledge of the past are conveyed and sustained by (more or less ritual) performances" (40). Following the analytical shift toward the spatialization of memory (Nora 1989; see also Bosco 2004; Crang and Travlou 2001; Rice 2003; Roach 1996), I explore these performances staged within spaces of congressional decision making and also at various *lieux de mémoire* (Nora 1989)—sites of memory—in post-Katrina New Orleans.

It is also important to understand the Katrina catastrophe as cultural trauma (Alexander 2004) rather than solely an individual, psychological, or physical trauma. According to cultural sociologist Jeffrey Alexander, a "cultural trauma occurs when members of a collectivity feel they have been subjected to a horrendous event that leaves indelible marks upon their group consciousness, marking their memories forever and changing their future identity in fundamental and irrevocable ways" (2004, 1). It would be difficult to argue that Hurricane Katrina and the near death of New Orleans did not create the conditions for a crisis and reconstruction of collective identity. Alexander further claims that "however tortuous the trauma process, it allows collectivities to define new forms of moral responsibility and to redirect the course of political action" (2004, 27).

## Women of the Storm

On January 10, 2006, an emergent group of women conversed at kitchen tables in Uptown New Orleans and began a grassroots endeavor to bring the members of Congress to the city to witness the storm and flood damage firsthand. They began by calling women throughout the city, seeking to create a diverse group of women to travel to Washington, D.C., to extend hand-delivered invitations to lawmakers. By late January 2006, they had taken the name "Women of the Storm" and become a formal social movement organization, extending a long tradition of women-centered advocacy, volunteerism, and reform in New Orleans (Tyler 1996). Aware that the survival, rebirth, and cultural memory of an American city were at stake, the women mobilized around the goal of inviting every member of Congress to tour Katrina's devastation.

On January 30, 2006, Women of the Storm assembled 130 Louisiana women, some of whom had lost their homes in the flood, and took a chartered flight to Washington. The plane was filled with women from diverse class and race backgrounds and life experiences—ranging from philanthropists to florists, from attorneys and small-business owners to former debutantes and Mardi Gras royalty, from housewives and mothers to bankers, writers, and two Catholic nuns. The women recognized the urgent need to bring decision makers to the city and claimed that "nothing is more powerful than witnessing the devastation first-hand and experiencing the hardship and triumph that accompany recovery and rebirth of the state" (Women of the Storm 2006a). At a press conference that morning, they unfurled in unison bright blue umbrellas, symbolically representing the same shade of blue tarp that covered thousands of homes across the region. Afterwards, the women split into pairs intended to represent the racial diversity of New Orleans and set out two-by-two to extend hand-delivered, formal invitations to every member of Congress to tour the destruction.[1]

At the time of Women of the Storm's January 2006 trip, while lights remained out across the desolate and depopulated city, in neighborhoods such as Lakeview, Gentilly, Mid-City, the Upper Ninth Ward, and the Lower Ninth Ward, only 55 U.S. representatives and 30 U.S. senators had visited post-Katrina New Orleans (Alpert 2006a). As Women of the Storm founder Anne Milling put it, "It was a storm that was felt around the world. . . . Yet, who would dream that 87 percent of the House of Representatives and 70 percent of the Senate haven't found time to visit the site of the largest catastrophe in the history of America?" (Alpert 2006a; for a discussion of the differences between emergencies, disasters, and catastrophes, see Quarantelli 2006). Seemingly, the region had been forgotten by national lawmakers as thousands of (still displaced) residents tried to rebuild their lives. The women mobilized behind Milling's persuasive call to action: "Our elected officials need to see for themselves—block by block, mile by mile—the immense devastation and the pressing challenges faced by so many people in this region" (Women of the Storm 2006b).

Armed with personal, hand-delivered invitations, the group offered lawmakers an all-expense paid, 36-hour trip to New Orleans with an itinerary that included meetings with civic and business leaders, land tours of the abandoned neighborhoods, visits to the major levee breaches, and flyovers of the storm-damaged region and eroding coastal wetlands in Blackhawk helicopters, assisted by Brigadier General Hunt Downer of the Louisiana National Guard (Williams 2006). In addition to the invitations, the women presented lawmakers with the book *America's Wetlands* on the erosion of Louisiana's coast, and shared haunting photographs of the flooded homes of some of their members. Perhaps most importantly, the women communicated personal and collective stories of loss, trauma, and resilience. One Women of the Storm participant in her early 50s explained:

> People brought whatever they wanted to, but what we really brought were stories. The stories of [long pause] . . . my two [adult] children lost everything. And when I say everything, I literally mean everything. And to a congressional person, looking at someone probably like myself, they don't understand how anybody like me could lose everything. Well my children did and now they live with me. Until they find . . . they'll be fine, they both have good jobs, you know. But, so we really brought stories to the people in Congress and their aides.

In addition to providing organized tours for congressional leaders who accepted the women's invitation, the group partnered with an environmental protection organization, America's Wetlands, to encourage federal support for a sustainable revenue source drawn from offshore oil and gas royalties to help protect and restore Louisiana's coastal wetlands. In March 2006, lawmakers began visiting New Orleans, including a bipartisan visit by a 32-member congressional delegation led by Speaker of the

House Dennis Hastert and House Minority Leader Nancy Pelosi (Alpert 2006b). Shortly thereafter, Women of the Storm partnered with four national women's groups—the Association of Junior Leagues International; the National Women's Leadership Council, United Way of America; the Links Incorporated; and the National Council of Jewish Women—thereby extending its base outside of Louisiana (Women of the Storm 2006c). In September 2006, Women of the Storm made a second trip to Washington, continuing to invite members of Congress and link the Katrina catastrophe to broader environmental concerns. The group has kept an ongoing count of congressional visits to post-Katrina New Orleans (specifying name, state, and political party affiliation) on the Women of the Storm Web site (http://womenofthestorm.net), and more recently, expanded its efforts to other spheres of U.S. politics through the (ultimately unsuccessful) bid to the Commission on Presidential Debates site selection committee to hold the 2008 presidential debates in New Orleans, which was endorsed by seven presidential candidates.[2]

## Don't Forget Us: Remembrance Work as Postdisaster Activism

I first became interested in Women of the Storm while conducting fieldwork in post-Katrina New Orleans. Given that elite groups are often inaccessible to social science researchers (Marcus 1983), the opportunity to study an elite women-organized social movement has relevance beyond a particular historic event; "studying up" has democratic significance for understanding relations of power and inequality (Nader 1972). While Women of the Storm represents itself (on its Web site, in press releases, and in organized political actions) as a diverse organization, with participants from different cultural, racial, and class backgrounds, between the major collective actions, the core organizers who maintained the group are arguably part of the city's social and economic elite. Continuity and survival of women's movements over time has often depended upon the stewardship of elite women, as demonstrated by Taylor (1994) in her work on the twentieth-century women's movements.

The focus of this research is on the methods used by Women of the Storm, particularly remembrance practices and cultural memory, to activate a political response to the many crises plaguing New Orleans in the aftermath of Katrina. Ethnographic research provides the tools to study the dynamics and processes of memory (Prus 2007; see also special issue of *Symbolic Interaction* [Fine and Beim 2007] on interactionist approaches to collective memory). Accordingly, I conducted ethnographic field research in New Orleans between October 2005 and September 2006, conducting in-depth interviews with women activists in the New Orleans area, attending weekly meetings, observing collective actions, and collecting documents.

Women of the Storm, made up of women from New Orleans and south Louisiana, played a pivotal role in the region's ongoing recovery following Hurricane Katrina.[3] In this article, I propose that the group accomplished this largely through performative actions, some of which were patterned after traditional gender norms, remembrance practices, and place-based rituals. These actions were designed to pressure Congress to pass federal legislation related to Hurricane Katrina recovery efforts. While the group did not frame its actions as political and in fact explicitly describes itself as nonpolitical, this research indicates that the actions of the group politicize remembrance and forgetting through their claims and requests for material and symbolic resources.

On Women of the Storm's first trip to Washington, the group collectively unfurled what would become its signature symbol: blue-tarp umbrellas. Created by Women of the Storm specifically for this debut, the umbrellas unfurled at the morning press conference were the same distinctive shade of blue as the tarps that covered thousands of tattered homes across the region. This reference to a particular blue pointed to the fact that the hue had entered the region's postdisaster cultural syntax through the FEMA (Federal Emergency Management Agency) relief effort. In the hands of Women of the Storm, the umbrellas were strategically and symbolically used in gendered performance, remembrance practices, and collective actions. Absorbed into the visual nomenclature of postdisaster New Orleans, Women of the Storm's collective raising of blue-tarp umbrellas synthesized symbols associated with protection from storms and widespread government failures.

This symbolism took on particular significance for the women participants. Overflowing with excitement during our in-depth interview, a woman in her mid-50s explained to me the symbolic power of the reference to blue tarps:

> It was blue tarp. I mean it's [the color of] a blue roof. But it was very . . . three buses of women and we all opened our umbrellas as soon as we got off of the bus. It was very visual because you see these, we walked for about a block and a half I guess, and I was on the third bus, and you see these blue umbrellas going up and then you see them coming up the Hill. And I think it was very impressive . . . and I know one person told me that she thought that Senator Landrieu, when she turned around and saw that, people including her mom, Verna was on the plane, that the cavalry had come. You know, it was like she had been holding the fort virtually alone, she and the delegation, but here is the support, here is the cavalry, in this visible way, heading up the Hill. (5 February 2006)

Another interviewee, a woman in her early 60s, suggested that the blue-tarp umbrellas not only referenced the actual tarps that covered homes, but also symbolized the human dimensions of the Katrina catastrophe:

> It was unbelievable, those umbrellas, the impact. Just simply because it's blue tarps. That's what it represents, the people that are still struggling to get their lives together and their houses, everything. (14 March 2006)

The double reference speaks to the materiality of patching damaged homes as well as of those who suffered direct loss. Describing how the blue tarps affected her emotionally, a woman in her early 60s spoke about how the symbols invoked a "stinging" sense of loss:

> It's still stinging when you go into an area where there's an unusual number of blue roofs. It just—I'm in an area where I don't see a lot of it, but then I go into other areas, and it's a stinging feeling, because you realize that we are three months from hurricane season, and we still have so many houses that are not up and running. (16 March 2006)

As her narrative suggests, the symbols did not just reference the past; these were also poignant reminders about disaster vulnerabilities in the near future. At the same time, they came to symbolize women's solidarity, as she went on to note:

> I think that the experience that was most warming and satisfying and exciting to me was marching up the Hill. We got off the buses at the bottom of the Hill, and all of the women were together and we opened our umbrellas, and marching up the Hill, I was near the front, and when I looked back down the Hill to see all those little umbrellas, I thought, "God, this is just so incredible, that we are women of—we're not young women, and we are together, marching up the Hill, marching on the Hill." The thing about—one of the things I think is so significant about the Women of the Storm is that, first of all, our blue umbrellas say to people that we're gentle. We're not here to hurt you or hurt your feelings or anything like that. We're just trying to represent New Orleans in the best possible way. (16 March 2006)

The actions of Women of the Storm were performative, and they were gendered. Accordingly, the use of the umbrellas invoked a gentle, nonthreatening symbol of collective action, instead of, for example, accusatory statements on placards or oppositional activities that shut down organizational or institutional operations.

While these narratives speak to how the use of umbrellas garnered attention through performance and invocations of emphasized femininity (Connell 1987), some participants also recognized how this particular symbol might not have been understood by intended audiences and the general public outside of New Orleans and the Gulf Coast. Another woman in her early 60s spoke of the performative dimensions of the collective deployment of the storm symbol in just this way:

> They were blue, so they had the "blue tarps," although I'm not sure a lot of them in Washington understood that part. But it was very effective, because immediately we were spotted. We got off the buses and popped those umbrellas. People driving by asked, "What is this?" One of the cops in front of the Rayburn Building stopped and said, "What is this?" and [a Women of the Storm partner] talked to him and said, "I've lost my home and I'm up here because I want things changed." So the cop was even—he took notice of us. (21 March 2006)

In this regard, gaining attention through performance does not always involve comprehension of symbolic codes. While umbrellas are a powerful, place-based symbol tied to New Orleans culture, it is understandable that the icon may not be immediately legible to lawmakers in Washington or to readers of this essay.[4]

The currency of Women of the Storm's performances derives from the broader sociocultural context of memory traditions in New Orleans. The use of symbolism in rituals surrounding death and rebirth is a visible aspect of the culture of New Orleans, where the umbrella, among other objects, has served as an important prop in mourning and remembrance practices. For instance, ritual spectacles involving umbrellas are part of a long tradition of jazz funerals in New Orleans, which themselves have origins in West African ritual traditions. The traditional jazz funeral often includes a solemn procession from the church service to the cemetery, which is followed by a moment referred to as "cutting the body loose" whereby "the deceased parts company with the procession in his honor" (Roach 1996, 278) and the mourners turn back as uplifting music, joyous shouts, and laughter fill the air. This transitional moment in the mourning ritual gives rise to what is known in local vernacular as the "second line," a type of parading that consists of celebratory elements like brass bands, upbeat music, unfurled umbrellas that are popped and twirled, improvised dancing, and gendered ritual performance and attire, including, for some women, baby doll outfits (Coclanis and Coclanis 2005; Roach 1996, 2001). This highly stylized, place-specific script for mourning and celebration is rooted in the history of the city's working-class African American community. After the Civil War, such symbolic rituals became more visible throughout the region as they were appropriated by the tourism industry and other segments of society, including the city's elites (Regis 1999, 2001).

In this cultural context, the women drew upon the religious symbol of mourning and celebration unique to the city and transformed these rituals tied to death and rebirth into secular and aesthetic rituals. Through the performative unfurling of the blue-tarp umbrellas, this reconfigured place-based ritual is itself a form of rebirth in Katrina's wake. To be sure, the use of acts of remembrance could point in a troubling way to racial and class-based disparities in people's ability to return to the city, as well as to the cultural appropriation of memorial practices. In this regard, displaced residents who could not return to New Orleans used the second line tradition, in consideration of their relationship to New Orleans as home (Breunlin and Regis 2006).

It could be argued that the group's modification of cultural practices tied historically to communities of color is less about the cultural appropriation of ritual remembrance practices by elite women than an attempt to establish a coherent narrative of collective mourning grounded in the politics of place and the preservation of the city's cultural memory. Thus, in addition to the struggle over material resources, Women of the Storm was also engaged in a larger symbolic struggle over the meaning of a place, the moral challenges and contradictions of speaking on behalf of the displaced, and the gendered responsibility of repairing a sense of home and community.

In focusing on the redirected course of political action and attempts to define new forms of moral responsibility by Women of the Storm, my intent is to call attention to the ways in which the cultural trauma of Katrina was constructed. My aim is not to depoliticize the catastrophe, which some may argue occurs when drawing on and deploying psychological discourses that might suggest that trauma inevitably and uniformly results from extreme events themselves. As Alexander (2004) points out, this would be a naturalistic fallacy that erases the political complexity of processes that produce cultural trauma. Instead, I want to direct attention to some of the ways in which the cultural trauma of Katrina was constructed and made visible, especially through the concerted efforts of a group of women guided by a sense of collective and moral responsibility. In this regard, the women displayed agency, innovation, and resiliency in times of extreme uncertainty. My approach to cultural trauma, informed by social constructionist research on the topic, helps move our understandings of suffering, violence, and loss out of the recesses of the individual psyche and into the body politic.

The transformation of cultural symbols and the practice of representing the displaced were ultimately a struggle over being remembered, as one member in her mid-40s reflected:

> It was a phenomenal day for me, one that I will never forget as long as I live. Just the fact that we felt like the American process was in action. We had the ability to go to Washington, meet with our Congressmen, voice our concerns, meet with the White House, that this is part of being an American. In that respect, I think it was very worthwhile and fulfilling for us. We were actually

> doing something, we were working with the government to open up some communication lines and begin the process of the federal government assisting our state. Because I think we all felt that there was a strong possibility that things would just move on and we would be forgotten. (7 April 2006)

A woman in her mid-50s spoke in a similar way about reminding the nation not to forget New Orleans:

> The rest of the nation can't close their eyes and forget it. We have to constantly remind them. This is day-to-day stuff. (20 March 2006)

For many Women of the Storm participants, memory work as political activism was characterized by its repetition and persistence. A woman in her mid-30s described how persistence over time defines the group's efforts:

> So you just have to keep at it. But I am not naïve . . . to think "oh that is fine, they are all going to come down and they are going to sign off on two hundred and forty billion dollars to New Orleans and it is all going to be saved." And I think pretty much everybody else feels the same way, that we did our part but it is a long, long, long road that won't have been solved by one, one-day trip to Washington. So, [I feel] both. Excitement, but also realization cracking in a little bit. That it is so much bigger than you are. (4 February 2006)

This work was also saturated with elements of gendered cultural practices. After returning from Washington, Women of the Storm sent handwritten thank you notes to elected officials reminding them of the group's invitation to visit. The invitations served to keep the memory of post-Katrina New Orleans alive while simultaneously pressuring elected officials on the point that local and regional disaster recovery necessitated federal support through congressional appropriations. These handwritten correspondences were a gendered form of communication connected to what many view as women's traditional role of building and maintaining familial relationships and other social ties (di Leonardo 1987), and they correspond to notions of refined, polished, and cultured femininities. One interviewee, a woman in her early 50s, explained the gendered cultural practice in this way:

> Southern women write thank you notes, that's what we do. That is part of our makeup. We have to get our thank you notes out to every single person that we saw. Whether it be an aide or a congressman or whatever. And we have to do it now. So all of them are due today. (3 February 2006)

Despite uncertainty about the outcomes, the women's performances were publicly validated through widespread media attention.[5] The collective performance demanded that the public and the state pay attention to issues the group defined as important, which included responding to

Katrina as a serious issue in need of immediate attention. Describing the first trip to Washington, another woman in her early 50s stated:

> So we all put on our pins and we all had an umbrella. And um, the only props that we had, and we wanted to make sure that no one thought that this was not a serious trip. This wasn't Mardi Gras. This wasn't Bourbon Street. This wasn't second lining in Washington DC. This was women saying "pay attention to us." (3 February 2006)

While the blue-tarp umbrellas undoubtedly conjure imagery of the traditional jazz funerals, the interviewee's words make clear that the women's actions should not be mistaken for the moment of "cutting the body loose," which would emblematically signal a transition to the second line celebration of New Orleans' own passing. Instead, the symbolic crossover to celebration had yet to occur, and the mournful tone extended onwards, reflecting the urgency and despair of a nearly forgotten city. In these ways, Women of the Storm, on its first trip to Washington, used performance "in the transmission of traumatic memory, drawing from transforming a shared archive and repertoire of cultural images" (Taylor 2003, 187). That is, the women highlighted cultural traditions and the symbolic meaning of a particular shade of blue, which continues to conjure memories of "the storm." The widespread recognition by elected officials and media agencies in turn encouraged social cohesion among the Louisiana women, a recharging of group sentiments that set the stage for collective actions over the subsequent months in multiple, place-based locations of loss and suffering.

## Storm Warnings and Mapping Landmarks in Time: Performance, Ritual, and the Cultural Appropriation of Disaster Symbols

Following the January 30, 2006, trip to Washington, the group brought the performances back home and engaged in actions within spaces of loss in New Orleans. Here, I offer a detailed description of one of its interactive performances that was part of a sustained effort to convince members of Congress to visit the area. The women continued to request federal funds for the Gulf Coast recovery and began a more concerted attempt to highlight the importance of restoring Louisiana's coastal wetlands to mitigate future disaster losses.[6]

The event, titled Storm Warnings II, was staged at the Tad Gormley Stadium in New Orleans' City Park on June 1, 2006, more than nine months after levee breaches inundated the city with floodwaters.[7] Women of the Storm, along with the nonprofit environmental group America's

Wetlands, mapped congressional visits and absences on a football field–sized map of the United States. The group chose a football field, because it spatially represented the rapid loss of coastal Louisiana, washing away at a rate of 100 yards (an area the size of a football field) every 30 to 38 minutes (Committee on the Future of Coastal Louisiana 2002; Louisiana Coastal Wetlands Conservation and Restoration Task Force and the Wetlands Conservation and Restoration Authority 1998). This point is significant because coastal wetlands help minimize hurricane storm surge and protect levees, which in turn protect the built environment and reduce the area's vulnerability to floods (Kousky and Zeckhauser 2006; Van Heerden 2007).

In addition to highlighting environmental loss and increased vulnerability, the women publicly thanked members of Congress who accepted their invitation to visit post-Katrina New Orleans and encouraged members of Congress who had not visited following the storm to make the trip. The group's founder stated, "While we thank the members of Congress who have visited and gained an understanding of our plight, we remain shocked that 400 U.S. senators and representatives have not found the time to visit the site of the worst natural disaster ever to strike our nation" (Women of the Storm 2006d). At the time of the event, nine months after Katrina's landfall, "seven states [had] yet to send a single member of their Congressional delegations to the devastated region, while 21 states [had] not sent a senator and 19 states [had] not sent a member of the House of Representatives" (Women of the Storm 2006d).

The map of the United States became a stage on which the women would dramatize the number of members of Congress who had visited post-Katrina New Orleans. Anne Milling, the group's founder, read a roll call of the states in alphabetical order over a loudspeaker, and reported for each state the number of senators and representatives who had visited, and the number yet to come. Like chanting during religious rituals and memorial naming of those killed in political violence, or perhaps like piacular rites, those ritual ceremonies "that are conducted under conditions of uncertainty or sadness" (Durkheim 1912 [1995], 393), the performative reading of the roll call drew upon rhythmic repetition and stylized speech patterns. As each state's name echoed throughout the nearly empty stadium, several women walked to the state, opened their blue-tarp umbrella, and stood silently before a small crowd and cameras. At one point, the women dispersed to cover each state during a helicopter flyover, thus symbolically tying themselves, and Louisiana, to the nation. A local marching band played and the women began raising the umbrellas up-and-down as the notes filled the air. As the band continued and the helicopter swooped overhead, the women collectively raised the blue-tarp umbrellas to the sky.

In addition to the rhetoric of performance, the event drew upon visual discourses that had cut deeply into the city's body politic. On each state, a tarp was marked with an "X." Part of the new post-Katrina New Orleans visual syntax, such marks cover homes across the region and serve as reminders of the systematic search-and-rescue operations immediately after the storm. The markings reflect an improvised effort to account for human life following the Katrina catastrophe and contain information on the date of the search (top quadrant), the search and rescue team (left quadrant), the number of living people found upon entry (right quadrant), and the number of bodies found (if any) at that location (bottom quadrant). It is important to note the weight of these symbols at the time of the June 1 event; decaying bodies were still being found, and even two months after this event, remains of what was believed to be yet another Katrina victim were discovered under piles of debris (see DeBerry 2006; Filosa 2006; and the *Times-Picayune*, June 18, 2006, and August 1, 2006). Undeniably, these haunting search and rescue marks on properties throughout the region have entered the broader cultural memory of the Katrina catastrophe and were invoked strategically as a powerful and symbolic resource.

In the immediate aftermath of Hurricane Katrina, a rapid absorption and transformation of disaster symbols occurred throughout the city as the signs circulated within broader public and cultural discourses. In this context, Women of the Storm transformed the search and rescue marks, as well as the tarps used to cover storm-damaged homes, to communicate visually the number of congressional visits to the city. On states that had at least one elected official visit, the tarps were blue, and states that had no members visit since the storm were highlighted with silver tarps. The top quadrant of the X indicated the state's abbreviation. The number on the left communicated the number of members of the Senate that had visited, on the right, the number of House members, and on the bottom quadrant, the total number from each state yet to visit. In this way, disaster symbols were drawn from the regional context and transformed through the production of highly performative political actions. In my field journal, I jotted down an initial reaction to the women's use of disaster symbolism:

> The Xs on the states were brilliant, a haunting reminder of the human tragedy, transformed and imposed on members of the United States government, those in control of the federal funding that is requested for the rebuilding of the city. It was transformed and imposed on those unaffected, forced on them through the eyes of the media as implicated in each and every one of the homes searched. The X is absorbed into the performance culture, a fascinating recirculation of signs of trauma, from the systematic and bureaucratic to the political and symbolic. They took the haunting signs of the state apparatus and transformed them symbolically to implicate the

state in its failures to respond to the ongoing crisis in New Orleans and along the Gulf Coast. (1 June 2006; personal field journal)

Through reconfigured storm symbols, cartographic communications, and performative actions, the group engaged in acts of transferring cultural and traumatic memory. First systematically inscribed on homes across the region, storm symbolism was reinscribed in the cultural memory through repetitive displays during the performance.

Storm Warnings II, which also included remarks by then governor Kathleen Babineaux Blanco and U.S. Senator Mary Landrieu, coincided with the first day of the 2006 Atlantic hurricane season—a day that evoked visceral reactions, fear, and anxiety for many residents who survived the destruction of the previous storm season. The event became a "landmark in time," which "not only serve[s] to divide up the passage of time," but also "nourish[es] our thought, like the technical, moral, or religious notions which our thought does not localize in the past but rather in the present" (Halbwachs 1992, 175). The event marked a beginning within an annual cycle of storm seasons, one that was set against ongoing uncertainty surrounding the fragile state of the city's infrastructure in the months following the previous (2005) storm season.

In addition to strengthening group sentiments, the collective performance of women's bodies, en masse, also bears the symbolic weight of the storm through the use of blue-tarp umbrellas and gendered movements. Through the choreography and display of collective representations, the women formed cohesive patterns with their bodies during the performance, and in this way, Women of the Storm, as a collective of women, imbued the stadium space (implicitly masculine by virtue of its association with organized sports) with alternative gendered actions geared toward social change and remembrance.

## Les Lieux de Mémoire: "Grounding" Performance in Sites of Memory

Further illustrating how repetition of performative acts is crucial for the transmission of cultural memory and pursuit of change following Katrina, members of Women of the Storm also raised their umbrellas in unison during several key events held at levee failures throughout New Orleans. For example, Women of the Storm organized a press conference at the 17th Street Canal levee breach in the Lakeview neighborhood of New Orleans to mark visits by Senators John McCain and Lindsey Graham in March 2006. At this press conference turned performative action, Women of the Storm stood among the ruins of homes with umbrellas unfurled as the motorcade transporting the senators approached the breach. Within a block of the levee breach, the women stood on grounds scattered with debris—once personal possessions within now-destroyed homes—and the mud-soaked residue left when the floodwaters receded. All around the women were houses still inscribed with crosshatched search and rescue marks, and visible traces of the flood lines, some as high as the roof tops. As engineers briefed the senators on the levee failures, the women, in an improvised action, ascended the levees and encircled the elected officials. The senators stood between the exposed pilings of the once-breached levee and a crescent formed by women with blue-tarp umbrellas unfurled.

In the midst of ongoing uncertainty related to flood protection and national support for the recovery, this collective action at one of the many hastily patched breaches in the city's levee protection system allowed the group to interact physically with the site of violence and loss, as well as with influential government representatives who came to see the damage firsthand. These levee breaches throughout the city became *lieux de mémoire*, a phrase coined by Pierre Nora to describe "the embodiment of memory in certain sites where a sense of historical continuity persists" (1989, 7). The women's actions forced an expansion of meaning through memory work, as opposed to a commemoration of the past that would serve to fix boundaries around meanings of past events and locations of loss. In this way, *lieux de mémoire* are always open to multiple interpretations that blur divisions of time and space through the active process of memory work.

On at least two more occasions, Women of the Storm visited *lieux de mémoire* during official state-sponsored events at the invitation of then Louisiana governor Kathleen Babineaux Blanco. For instance, on August 26, 2006, three days before the first anniversary of Katrina, Women of the Storm was invited by Governor Blanco to the London Avenue canal to attend a press briefing on the status of levee repairs. The event at the canal, which suffered two breaches during Katrina, included a briefing by representatives of the U.S. Army Corps of Engineers, as well as a demonstration of how the new floodgates would close.

About a month later, on September 27, 2006, Governor Blanco invited Women of the Storm to attend a press conference at the 17th Street Canal breach, where she endorsed a series of constitutional amendments, some of which related to Women of the Storm's goals, especially legislation that would establish a fund that would allocate federal dollars for coastal restoration and protection projects. When the announcement went out to members of Women of the Storm requesting their presence at the press conference, the core organizers encouraged the women to carry their blue-tarp umbrellas. Recognized by state officials, especially the governor, as an influential emergent group, Women of the Storm and its ritual raising of the blue-tarp umbrellas stood in for, and at the same time excluded, the many families displaced by Hurricane Katrina and the subsequent levee failures.

## Representation and Responsibility

Women of the Storm, composed of many of the city's elite white women and elite women of color, became a public face of those affected by the catastrophic events, producing new meanings that challenged narratives suggesting that progressive change had taken place. Through the construction of cultural traumas, members of social groups, in this case Women of the Storm, assume moral responsibility and "define their solidarity relationships in ways that, in principle, allow them to share the sufferings of others . . . expand(ing) the circle of the we" (Alexander 2004, 1).

In discussions of gendered solidarity, I do not wish to overlook issues of power or difference, as these dynamics are crucial for understanding post-Katrina suffering. Indeed, at stake here is the issue of representation, and more specifically the problems related to speaking on behalf of others (the less privileged, the displaced, the dead) and engaging in social action motivated by the women's sense of moral responsibility. Alexander (2004) claims that when trauma is experienced at the level of culture, even social actors relatively removed from traumatic experience can potentially share in the suffering of others and "take on board" some significant responsibility for it. For many Women of the Storm participants, the recovery efforts in New Orleans in general, and the women's individual actions in particular, were tied to attempts to define new forms of moral responsibility. For example, moral discourses tied to recovery efforts were evident when New Orleans was rejected as a host site for the 2008 presidential debates, as made clear in a November 2007 statement by Anne Milling: "New Orleans is the clear moral choice for a 2008 presidential debate. Unfortunately, it appears that politics has trumped in the site selection process carried out by the Commission on Presidential Debates."

Discourses of moral responsibility are also present in the actions of smaller groups and individuals. One interviewee, a woman in her mid-60s, stated that Women of the Storm was "working in the moral center, not—they're not doing it for their own gain. They're not doing it for their husbands' gain. They're doing it because they think it's the right thing to do" (14 March 2006). Later, she continued to speak about moral action and helping behaviors in paradoxical ways, which suggests the helpers in post-Katrina New Orleans are also in need of assistance as well:

> I think they're real right-minded people. But basically, I think that they're very moral, right-minded, and they wouldn't want to save the city for, let's say, white people. They want to save the city for the people. And that's the appeal that the group has for me. Because anybody that would do it for their own gain wouldn't be interested in having me as a volunteer anyway.
>
> (You don't think so?)
>
> I wouldn't work for them. I'm just—I'm not oriented that way. I'd much rather help people that can't help themselves. I mean, the people that can help themselves are gonna help themselves, right? But I think that some of the things, even for those of us that can help ourselves, the wetlands—we can't do that. The levees—we can't build the levees. (14 March 2006)

As this narrative suggests, there is more at stake in Women of the Storm's actions than representing the displaced. Wetlands restoration, levee reconstruction, and enhanced flood protection will help even those who can help themselves. In addition to helping others, the women are also responding to threats to the very foundations of power relations in the city that have enabled their volunteerism in the first place. As such, these elite women had investments in New Orleans as a place to call home. In other words, if New Orleans disappears from the map, washes away like the coastal wetlands, so too does power and privilege of the members of Women of the Storm. This leaves even the most privileged contending with the possibility of future displacement; the chance is enough for anyone with resources to take action. In this way, Women of the Storm draws on moral responsibility both to represent others and themselves.

At the same time, this claim requires an examination of how those individuals and groups with material, political, and symbolic resources have unevenly taken action and shaped cultural memories of the Katrina catastrophe. Enabled by "a politics of mobility and access" (Massey 1994, 150), Women of the Storm strategically mobilized social, economic, and cultural capital to move across geographic scales. The members extended their spheres of influence during the disaster recovery period when many displaced New Orleanians could not return home to visit family or friends or retrieve personal belongings, let alone move back to gut their flood-damaged homes, contend with insurance companies, or rebuild their abandoned neighborhoods.

Thus, we arrive at a sobering challenge in understanding post-Katrina struggles for social change and survival. Through efforts to bring about social change through gendered collective actions, those efforts to "expand the circle of the we" through gendered solidarity, the group simultaneously reinscribed a politics of power surrounding the uneven social practices of remembrance work in the context of disaster recovery. Put differently, cultural memory is transferred within the parameters of existing power relations, and given the contested politics of the Gulf Coast recovery, we must not forget that "control of a society's memory largely conditions the hierarchy of power" (Connerton 1989, 1).

## Conclusions: The Persistence of Memory

In the months immediately following Hurricane Katrina, during which many across the nation believed that New Orleans and its residents had already recovered from the storm, Women of the Storm constructed and delivered a cultural memory to the nation's elected officials and global media audiences. Drawing on social and cultural capital that facilitated access to power structures, Women of the Storm highlighted the persistence of memory and remembrance through performative deployments of symbolic systems to advance its requests for disaster-related assistance and significant policy commitments from the state.

In this essay, I have focused on the ways in which Women of the Storm's collective actions contributed to the construction of cultural memory and cultural trauma through symbolic performance and actions derived from collective appeals to moral responsibility. These symbolic and political actions are grounded in historical practices and rituals linked to place-based acts of public, collective mourning, and "circum-Atlantic memory" (Roach 1996). Rooted in historical and cultural traditions of New Orleans such as jazz funerals and second line parades, Women of the Storm's creative use of umbrellas in highly visible performative actions draws upon and creatively adapts rituals related to death, rebirth, and collective mourning. The group also appropriated signs of the state (search and rescue marks) in a powerful effort to keep the urgent needs of New Orleans and the Gulf Coast in national discourses.

It is also within the framework of cultural trauma that Women of the Storm sought to shed light on the ongoing crisis in New Orleans by keeping the catastrophe in public discourse, collectively endowing the events with heightened meaning and engaging in affective and expressive reactions to fears of being forgotten. The women's participation in the process of constructing cultural trauma through gendered collective actions and appeals to moral responsibility was particularly important when New Orleans seemed to prematurely fade from public memory. In this context of the potential onset of cultural amnesia, whether real or imagined, the women's actions and reactions were a rallying cry for the nation to remember and respond to the material and symbolic needs of New Orleans and the Gulf Coast.

This study suggests that local and regional disaster recovery benefits from cultural interventions at multiple locations of decision making and sites of memory, in this case engaging various disaster memory sites to influence national policy for problems brought on and intensified by catastrophic events. The group resisted the prospect of an organized forgetting of Katrina at different spatial locations and imposed cultural memory through active presence at multiple sites: locally at the sites of the levee breaches, regionally at the stadium in City Park, and nationally at the nation's capitol. In addition to symbolic achievements, two major pieces of legislation speak, to some degree, of the impact of Women of the Storm's collective actions. First, on June 8, 2006, the U.S. Senate reached agreement on a $94.5 billion emergency supplemental spending bill that includes $4.2 billion for housing recovery programs and $3.7 billion for levee upgrades, small amounts in comparison to the money ($66 billion for overseas military operations) provided in the same bill for the wars in Iraq and Afghanistan (Alpert 2006c). Second, on December 20, 2006, President Bush signed legislation giving Louisiana a share of offshore oil and gas royalties, which would be channeled into a "trust fund" for enhanced flood control, hurricane storm protection, and coastal wetlands protection (Deslatte 2006).[8]

At the level of national public policy, remembrance was central to the issue of federal funding for local and regional recovery following the storm and catastrophic flood event. The *New York Times* editorial reminded us that New Orleans, "the city that care forgot," was at risk of death by congressional inaction in the wake of Hurricane Katrina.[9] The scale of the Katrina disaster necessitated responses at all levels of government: local, regional, and national. Yet very few groups were able to successfully organize across these levels to engage in broader public policy deliberations. Women of the Storm constructed arguments that reframed the collective trauma inflicted on local and regional populations in terms of a national disaster. Supported by symbolic, material, and cultural capital, and a love for the city, the group engaged in forms of gendered memory work that were characterized by persistence, repetition, and continuity in the face of change—and that were undeniably integral to disaster recovery efforts. In the context of this unprecedented extreme event, forgetting a whole region and leaving its residents to suffer in limbo would be yet another cruel extension of what has become the cultural trauma of Katrina. To avoid this, Women of the Storm, as caretakers of cultural memory, took on the daunting challenge of helping the nation remember.

By (re)focusing national attention on the ongoing and unfolding crisis in New Orleans through gendered performance activism, I argue that Women of the Storm's collective actions served to maintain the *living cultural memory* of the *dying American city*. By examining Women of the Storm's performances at multiple sites of remembrance and decision making, I situate the group's actions within sociohistorical practices, cultural contexts, and symbol systems unique to (pre- and post-Katrina) New Orleans. In doing so, I demonstrate how the group drew upon and creatively adapted cultural memory through place-based ritual practices and representational systems.[10] This case study shows the importance of the concept of cultural memory for disaster studies. The fate of an American city rested on the ability of Women of the Storm, lawmakers, and the nation as a whole, to resist what Paul Connerton (1989, 14) calls the "method of organised forgetting."

## Acknowledgment

This research was funded, in part, by a Quick Response Grant from the Natural Hazards Center under the Center's National Science Foundation (NSF)–funded Quick Response Program; an Emily Schoenbaum Research and Community Development Grant from the Newcomb College Center for Research on Women at Tulane University; and a Dissertation Expense Award from the Department of Sociology at the University of Colorado at Boulder. I also received support from the Center for Humanities and the Arts (CHA) at the University of Colorado at Boulder, where I participated in a year-long seminar in which I received valuable suggestions for this paper from the other CHA fellows. I would like to thank Jade Aguilar, Elissa Auther, Keri Brandt, Enrico David, Kristine De Welde, Michaele Ferguson, Allison Hicks, Janet Jacobs, Janet Lee, Leith Lombas, Bryce Merrill, Kathleen Tierney, Teresa Toulouse, Sue Zemka, Michael Zimmerman, Naida Zukic, the editors and two anonymous reviewers at *National Women's Studies Association Journal*, and especially Patrick Greaney for their continued support and constructive, insightful, and challenging comments on this manuscript at various stages of its development. Of course, I am responsible for the conclusions and any shortcomings presented in this essay. Finally, my sincere appreciation goes out to all the women who agreed to be interviewed and who allowed me to observe their efforts to help rebuild New Orleans.

## Notes

1. Complete with RSVP card and return envelope, the presentation of the invitation is significant because it reveals how the women drew upon traditionally feminine forms of communication and social practices akin to correspondence that would be sent out for a formal luncheon, tea, or dinner party.

2. These include endorsements by Joe Biden, Sam Brownback, Hillary Clinton, Chris Dodd, John Edwards, John McCain, and Barack Obama.

3. The group included several women from southwestern Louisiana, the area of the state hit by Hurricane Rita. This helped the group frame themselves as Louisiana women rather than just New Orleans women. However, most participants were from the Greater New Orleans metropolitan area.

4. The iconography of the umbrella also resonates in popular images of the Southern Belle. I am grateful to Elissa Auther, who pointed out that the umbrella in these images connects to intersecting discourses of gender, race, and class, since historically many women have tried to shield their skin from the sun so as not to suggest they labored outdoors. This resonates with Joseph Roach's interpretive reading of John Ogilby's folio atlases and his conclusion that the "umbrella seems to represent an icon in the atlas of cultural difference." (2003, 95) and that the parasol is "evocative of prestige, luxury, and pampered excess" (2003, 105), especially when held overhead by others.

5. See for example: Leslie William, 2006, "Storming D.C," *Times-Picayune*, January 26, 2006, A-1, A-8; Mimi Hall, 2006, "'Women of the Storm' Push for More Katrina Funding," *USA Today*, January 30, 2006; Rukimini Callimachi, 2006, "Women's Mission Accomplished as Congressional Leaders Tour City," *Associated Press*, March 4, 2006; "Women of the Storm Working to Rebuild New Orleans," 2006, CNN, February 21, 2006; "First Mardi Gras Celebration after Hurricane Katrina," 2006, CNN American Morning with Miles O'Brien, February 28, 2006.

6. The first Storm Warning event, where America's Wetlands Foundation made the case for coastal restoration as necessary for minimizing disaster impacts, took place *before* Hurricanes Katrina and Rita. On June 1, 2005, America's WETLAND dramatized a flooding in the French Quarter to demonstrate vulnerability to flooding caused by hurricanes, a warning which according to Women of the Storm "proved eerily prophetic three months later when Hurricane Katrina struck, inundating many other parts of the city with water" (2006d). That these warnings went largely unnoticed (among other forewarnings, see especially Laska 2004) and failed to mobilize widespread preparedness measures through environmental protection speaks to a failed intervention in the unfolding, and in many ways foreseeable, catastrophe.

7. Within the context of the privatization of leisure, the choice of this particular football field also points to the lack of public funding for the maintenance of City Park. Although the land occupied by the park is owned by the City of New Orleans, private funds collected through donations and user fees constitute the majority of the park's operating budget. According to the park's Web site, "City Park receives $200,000 (1.8%) of its $10.8 million pre-Katrina annual operating budget from the State of Louisiana and no public support from the City of New Orleans. The remaining $10.6 million needed to operate is self-generated through donations and user fees." Retrieved November 24, 2006, from http://neworleanscitypark.com/index.html.

8. According to Alpert and Walsh (2006), "For Louisiana, the bill is expected to generate $106 million in 2007 and between $11 million and $22 million a year through 2016 before rising to $586 million in 2017, according to Landrieu's office. It is expected to remain well over $500 million a year through 2026, when it is expected to reach an annual total of $721 million. With financing in other existing legislation, the state is expected to take in at least $1.89 billion a year during the next four years for coastal restoration and hurricane protection work. The number drops to less than $300 million a year from 2011 to 2016 before rising again to $888 million in 2017."

9. While completing the final revisions of this manuscript, more than two and a half years after Katrina, remembrance work was made explicitly political through the title of Senator John McCain's weeklong campaign tour of America's "forgotten places," which included a visit to the Lower Ninth Ward of New Orleans (Bumiller 2008).

10. Of course, my examination of Women of the Storm raises important questions about the internal dynamics and politics of power within women's activism, the strengths and limitations of deploying the category "women" for political ends, and how this women-centered group is situated within debates about the future of feminism and contemporary women's movements. These issues will be addressed in my dissertation, *Women of the Storm: Gender, Culture and Social Movements following Hurricane Katrina.*

## References

Alexander, Jeffrey. 2004. "Toward a Theory of Cultural Trauma." In *Cultural Trauma and Collective Identity,* ed. Jeffrey C. Alexander, Ron Eyerman, Bernhard Giesen, Neil J. Smelser, and Piotr Sztompka, 1–30. Berkeley: University of California Press.

Alpert, Bruce. 2006a. "Louisiana Women Storm Washington." *Times-Picayune,* January 31, A-4.

———. 2006b. "Bipartisan tour brings 32 congressmen to N.O.: Leaders to tour devastated areas." *The Times-Picayune,* March 2, National Section, 3.

———. 2006c. "Billions of Relief Dollars Secured for State: Landrieu Helps Seal Deal on Senate Bill." *Times-Picayune,* June 9, 1.

———, and Bill Walsh. 2006. "On the Hill: News from the Louisiana Delegation in the Nation's Capital." *Times-Picayune* 18.

Baumel, Judith Tydor. 1998. *Double Jeopardy: Gender and the Holocaust.* London: Vallentine Mitchell.

———, and Tova Cohen, eds. 2003. *Gender, Place, and Memory in the Modern Jewish Experience: Re-placing Ourselves.* London: Vallentine Mitchell.

Bosco, Fernando. 2004. "Human Rights Politics and Scaled Performances of Memory: Conflicts among the *Madres de Plaza de Mayo* in Argentina." *Social & Cultural Geography* 5(3): 381–402.

Breunlin, Rachel, and Helen A. Regis. 2006. "Putting the Ninth Ward on the Map: Race, Place, and the Transformation of Desire, New Orleans." *American Anthropologist* 108(4): 744–64.

Bumiller, Elisabeth. 2008. "McCain Faults Bush Response to Gulf Storm." *New York Times*, April 25, A1, A23.

Coclanis, Angelo, and Peter Coclanis. 2005. "Jazz Funeral: A Living Tradition." *Southern Cultures* 11(2): 86–92.

Committee on the Future of Coastal Louisiana. 2002. *Saving Coastal Louisiana: Recommendations for Implementing an Expanded Coastal Restoration Program*. Baton Rouge, La.: Governor's Office of Coastal Activities.

Connell, R. W. 1987. *Gender and Power: Society, the Person and Sexual Politics*. Stanford: Stanford University Press.

Connerton, Paul. 1989. *How Societies Remember*. New York: Cambridge University Press.

Crang, Mike, and Penny Travlou. 2001. "The City and Topologies of Memory." *Environment and Planning D: Society and Space* 19:161–77.

DeBerry, Jarvis. 2006. "City of the Dead: We're Still Finding Katrina's Victims, Even as Hurricane Season Looms." *Times-Picayune*, May 28, Metro Section–Editorial, 7.

Deslatte, Melinda. 2006. "Offshore Drilling Royalties Law Will Bring Billions to La." *Associated Press*, December 20.

di Leonardo, Micaela. 1987. "The Female World of Cards and Holidays: Women, Families, and the Work of Kinship." *Signs* 12(3):440–53.

Durkheim, Emile. (1912) 1995. *The Elementary Forms of Religious Life*. Trans. Karen E. Fields. New York: Free Press.

Erikson, Kai. 1976. *Everything in Its Path: Destruction of Community in the Buffalo Creek Flood*. New York: Simon and Schuster.

———. 1995. "Notes on Trauma and Community." In *Trauma: Exploration in Memory*, ed. Cathy Caruth, 183–99. Baltimore: Johns Hopkins University Press.

Fentress, James, and Chris Wickham. 1992. *Social Memory*. London: Blackwell.

Filosa, Gwen. 2006. "Storm Victim's Body Is Found in Mid-City Home: As Death Toll Rises, Search Teams Continue Efforts to Find Missing." *The Times-Picayune*, May 28, Metro Section, 1.

Fine, Gary Alan, and Aaron Beim. 2007. "Introduction: Interactionist Approaches to Collective Memory." *Symbolic Interaction* 30(1): 1–5.

Halbwachs, Maurice. 1992. *On Collective Memory*. Chicago: University of Chicago Press. Trans. from *Les cadres sociaux de la mémoire* by Lewis A. Coser. Paris: Presses Universitaires de France, 1952.

Haskins, K. V., and J. P. DeRose. 2003. "Memory, Visibility, and Public Space: Reflections on Commemoration(s) of 9/11." *Space and Culture* 6(4): 377–93.

Herman, Judith. 1997. *Trauma and Recovery: The Aftermath of Violence—From Domestic Abuse to Political Terror*. New York: Basic Books.

Hirsch, Marianne, and Valerie Smith. 2002. "Feminism and Cultural Memory: An Introduction." *Signs* 28(1): 1–19.

Jacobs, Janet. 2004. "Women, Genocide, and Memory: The Ethics of Feminist Ethnography in Holocaust Research." *Gender and Society* 18(2): 223–38.

———. 2008. "Gender and Collective Memory: Women and Representation at Auschwitz." *Memory Studies* 1(2): 211–25.

Klein, Kerwin Lee. 2000. "On the Emergence of Memory in Historical Discourse." In "Grounds for Remembering," special issue of *Representations* 69: 127–50.

Kousky, Carolyn, and Richard Zeckhauser. 2006. "JARing Actions That Fuel the Floods." In *On Risk and Disaster: Lessons from Hurricane Katrina*, ed. Ronald J. Daniels, Donald F. Kettl, and Howard Kunreuther, 59–73. Philadelphia: University of Pennsylvania Press.

Laska, Shirley. 2004. "What If Hurricane Ivan Had Not Missed New Orleans?" *Natural Hazards Observer* 29(2): 5–6.

Lembcke, Jerry. 1998. *The Spitting Image: Myth, Memory, and the Legacy of Vietnam*. New York: New York University Press.

Lentin, Ronit, ed. 1997. *Gender and Catastrophe*. New York: Zed Books.

Louisiana Coastal Wetlands Conservation and Restoration Task Force and the Wetlands Conservation and Restoration Authority. 1998. *Coast 2050: Toward a Sustainable Coastal Louisiana*. Baton Rouge: Louisiana Department of Natural Resources.

Marcus, George, ed. 1983. *Elites: Ethnographic Issues*. Albuquerque: School of American Research, University of New Mexico Press.

Massey, Doreen. 1994. *Space, Place, and Gender*. Minneapolis: University of Minnesota Press.

Milling, Anne. 2007. "Statement on Presidential Debate Site Selection." Retrieved December 2, from http://womenofthestorm.net.

Nader, Laura. 1972. "Up the Anthropologist: Perspectives Gained from Studying Up." In *Reinventing Anthropology*, ed. Dell Hymes, 284–311. New York: Pantheon Books.

Neal, Arthur. 1998. *National Trauma and Collective Memory: Major Events in the American Century*. Armonk, N.Y.: M. E. Sharpe.

*New York Times*. 2005. "The Death of an American City." December 11.

Nora, Pierre. 1989. "Between Memory and History: Les Lieux de Mémoire." *Representations* 26: 7–24.

Olick, Jeffrey. 1999. "Collective Memory: The Two Cultures." *Sociological Theory* 17(3): 333–48.

Prus, Robert. 2007. "Human Memory, Social Process, and the Pragmatist Metamorphosis: Ethnological Foundations, Ethnographic Contributions, and Conceptual Challenges." *Journal of Contemporary Ethnography* 36(4): 378–437.

Quarantelli, E. L. 2006. "Catastrophes Are Different from Disasters: Some Implications for Crisis Planning and Managing Drawn from Katrina." Retrieved December 2, http://understandingkatrina.ssrc.org/Quarantelli/

Regis, Helen. 1999. "Second Lines, Minstrelsy, and the Contested Landscapes of New Orleans Afro-Creole Festivals." *Cultural Anthropology* 14(4): 472–504.

———. 2001. "Blackness and the Politics of Memory in the New Orleans Second Line." *American Ethnologist* 28(4): 752–77.

Rice, Alan. 2003. *Radical Narratives of the Black Atlantic*. New York: Continuum.

Ringelheim, Joan. 1998. "The Split between Gender and the Holocaust." In *Women and the Holocaust*, ed. D. Ofer and L. Weitzman, 340–9. New Haven: Yale University Press.

Roach, Joseph. 1996. *Cities of the Dead: Circum-Atlantic Performance.* New York: Columbia University Press.

———. 2001. "Cutting Loose: Burying the 'First Man of Jazz.'" In *Joyous Wakes, Dignified Deaths: Issues in Death and Dying*, ed. Robert Harvey, 3–14. Stony Brook, N.Y.: Humanities Institute.

———. 2003. "The Global Parasol: Accessorizing the Four Corners of the World." In *The Global Eighteenth Century*, ed. Felicity A. Nussbaum, 93–106. Baltimore: Johns Hopkins University Press.

Schwartz, Barry. 1982. "The Social Context of Commemoration: A Study in Collective Memory." *Social Forces* 61: 374–402.

Smelser, Neil. 2004. "Epilogue: September 11, 2001, as Cultural Trauma." In *Cultural Trauma and Collective Identity*, ed. Jeffrey C. Alexander, Ron Eyerman, Bernhard Giesen, Neil J. Smelser, and Piotr Sztompka, 264–82. Berkeley: University of California Press.

Sturken, Marita.1997. *Tangled Memories: The Vietnam War, the AIDS Epidemic, and the Politics of Remembering.* Berkeley: University of California Press.

Taylor, Diana. 2003. *The Archive and the Repertoire: Performing Cultural Memory in the Americas.* Durham, N.C.: Duke University Press.

Taylor, Verta. 1994. "An Elite-Sustained Movement: Women's Rights in the Post-World War II Decades." In *Disaster, Collective Behavior, and Social Organization*, ed. Russell R. Dynes and Kathleen J. Tierney, 281–305. Newark: University of Delaware Press.

*Times-Picayune.* 2006. "Another Katrina Victim Found, in Eastern N.O.; Woman Was in House, Buried under Debris." August 1, Metro Section, 3.

———. 2006. "Workers Find Body in Flooded Home." June 18, Metro Section, 1.

Tyler, Pamela. 1996. *Silk Stockings and Ballot Boxes: Women and Politics in New Orleans, 1920–1963.* Athens: University of Georgia Press.

Van Heerden, Ivor. 2007. "The Failure of the New Orleans Levee System Following Hurricane Katrina and the Pathway Forward." *Public Administration Review:* 24–35.

———. 2001. "Commemorating Narratives of Violence: The Yitzhak Rabin Memorial Day in Israeli Schools." *Qualitative Sociology* 24(2), 245–68.

Vinitzky-Seroussi, Vered. 2002. "Commemorating a Difficult Past: Yitzhak Rabin's Memorials." *American Sociological Review* 67(2): 30–51.

Weissman, Terri. 2005. "The Spectacle of Trauma: 9/11 in the Museum." *Visual Resources* 21(2): 155–70.

Williams, Leslie. 2006. "'Women' to Personally Invite Congressmen to Tour the City." *Times-Picayune.* January 25.

Women of the Storm. 2006a. Invitation to Members of U.S. Congress. Unpublished document in author's collection. Acquired February 7.

———. 2006b. "Louisiana Women Storm Capitol Hill, Urge Leaders to Visit New Orleans and America's WETLAND: More than 150 'Women of the Storm' Deliver Personal Invitations on Capitol Hill." Press Release. January 30.

———. 2006c. "National Women's Groups Join Women of the Storm, Urge Congress to Visit New Orleans and South Louisiana." Press Release, March 29.

———. 2006d. "Women of the Storm Raise Hurricane Storm Warnings: First Day of Hurricane Season Used to Illustrate Lack of Congressional Interest in Post-Katrina New Orleans and Increased Threat Caused by Loss of America's Wetland." Press Release. June 1.

CHAPTER TWELVE

# The Representation of the Indigenous Other in *Daughters of the Dust* and *The Piano*

CAROLINE BROWN

> In a world ordered by sexual imbalance, pleasure in looking has been split between active/male and passive/female. The determining male gaze projects its fantasy onto the female figure, which is styled accordingly. In their traditional exhibitionist role women are simultaneously looked at and displayed, with their appearance coded for strong visual and erotic impact so that they can be said to connote *to-be-looked-at-ness*. Woman displayed as sexual object is the *leitmotif* of erotic spectacle: from pin-ups to strip-tease, from Ziegfeld to Busby Berkeley, she holds the look, and plays to and signifies male desire. Mainstream film neatly combines spectacle and narrative.
>
> —Laura Mulvey (2000, 39–40)

## (1)

In the language of traditional feminist film theory the cinematic gaze, conventionally gendered male, consumes the passive female image. As pointed out by Laura Mulvey, this process takes place on two levels: the woman as "erotic object" for both the other characters in the film and the audience itself. The hero pursues and takes possession of the eroticized female, the object of his desire, whether or not the plot is a conventional romance. She is not a presence in and of herself but both an extension and negation of the hero, an idealized figure who signifies his fate. Not only does the very act of looking thus cause the audience to identify with the hero, but the filmmaker is all too often himself a male.

This paradigm is necessarily made problematic when inserting issues related to race into ongoing questions revolving around gender and power. Most often, racial constructions, like those of the sexual, are translated in terms of those who are typically identified as the possessors of *power*: whites and men, usually white men, who invented and are the gatekeepers of what we have come to know as the film industry. Yet, there are presently a greater diversity of filmmakers than ever before, giving voice to new perspectives and tales. This has certainly been the case with the many women directors, who bring their own distinct and often radically unconventional visions and narrative techniques to the cinematic world.

---

Originally published in the Spring 2003 issue of the *NWSA Journal*.

Nevertheless, creating spaces of greater inclusion and sites of resistance can be an extremely complicated and contradictory undertaking. Even as there is a struggle to render new realities on the silver screen, realities diverse, complex, and magical, to challenge the norm and subvert previous representations, there remains the nagging question of how to enact a truly inclusive and egalitarian diversity. Basically, who will speak for whom and how? Or, as posited by Gayatri Spivak: who truly speaks for the subaltern (1988)? What happens when those who have traditionally been marginalized seize the word, when they write the screenplays and direct the films, when they participate in the redistribution of power symbolized by film production? Can they do greater justice to the representation of *themselves* and their own *Others*? In fact, who now becomes the Other? Must there be one? When Spivak puts forth that question, she suggests the many levels of hegemony that intersect to silence the marginalized as well as the mutability of how power is distributed in order to maintain itself. Does that then signify that the process itself is an impossible undertaking and marginalization its inevitable byproduct?

Two films by women that were released within the last decade, *Daughters of the Dust*, directed by Julie Dash (1992), and *The Piano*, directed by Jane Campion (1993), manifest this particular dilemma. While both are subversive tales that rely on unorthodox narrative techniques to examine and challenge female subordination and ethnocentric ideological systems, they are simultaneously foundational epics that mythologize this subordination even as they attempt to resist it, engaging in acts of what I would call *sentimental progressivism*.[1] Referring to a return to the past as a point of narrative reference in contemporary films, sentimental progressivism contains at its core the complementary tension of nostalgia and radical transformation. By presenting the past from the comfort allowed by a late twentieth-century perspective, each film simultaneously sentimentalizes that past while engaging in its critique and revision. What results is an idealized vision of how things could have been based on the peculiar mélange of historical fact, Victorian sentimental conventions, the active revisionism of a politically progressive agenda, and a highly individualized enactment of a feminist sensibility.

In many respects, *Daughters of the Dust* and *The Piano* could not be more disparate films: the former, community focused and womanist, revolves around an ensemble cast of characters who share the dual disenfranchisement of the racial and gender vulnerability experienced by African American women in the land of their birth. The latter is propelled by the image of the independent and rebellious femininity of a lone white woman in a hostile, misogynistic, and alienating foreign culture. Yet, structurally, both films rely on very specific cinematic conventions. Both could easily be labeled women's films. Period dramas, they are set in the past, relying on the twin props of an exotic locale and geographic isolation to establish a romanticized distance. This distance is further enabled by the lush cinematography of soft focus camerawork and a filtered lens; beautifully intricate Victorian/Edwardian wardrobes and elaborate hairstyles; and a charged love story at the center of each. Yet, each is mobilized by a distinctly modern sensibility that destabilizes the carefully scripted codes of Hollywood gender and racial expectations. Both films rotate around a multiethnic cast of characters. Furthermore, women are the agents in each film. They are the protagonists who provide narrative focus, whose conflicts propel the action, and whose strong personalities compel audience attention. However, key to this process is each film's reliance on native Others to both create and sustain a space of individuality and revolt for the female protagonist. Despite significant differences in the structure and perspective of each production, in both, the indigenous characters are silenced in order to permit non-native women the right to speak and affirm themselves and their embattled identities. These *native* characters, American Indian and Polynesian, function in a manner typical of female—often nonwhite—characters in both mainstream Hollywood and independent films.[2] In the process of serving to symbolically liberate the female character from the grip of a type of cultural silence, their own is reiterated. There is a correlation between these cinematic depictions and Aihwa Ong's observation regarding those of the scholarly sort: "For the privilege of making cultural judgements which see their way into print, feminists often speak without reducing the silence of the cultural Other" (1988, 82). What is provocative here is the reliance on specific forms of representation for these culturally liminal characters, representations that twist the balance of racial and gender expectations within the larger film while cleverly borrowing those same expectations in the construction of these cultural Others, regardless of the race of the director. Sites of tension are thus created that reproduce a dynamic similar to what occurs in standard movie fare in relation to the eroticized female. Yet, it is a process more complex than a simple binary opposition. There are truly novel depictions being offered in these films; in addition, many stock representations are being consciously dismantled. What is occurring on one level is the inevitable tension implicit in most transformative processes, as Shari Huhndorf suggests in her own mapping of these cultural struggles:

> While culture never lies outside the realm of social domination and coercion, its function cannot be completely determined by these dynamics. Because culture operates as "a force field of relations shaped, precisely by these contradictory [political] pressures and tendencies," struggles over cultural meanings comprise part of broader struggles for power in society. Popular culture in particular is characterized by a "double movement of containment and resistance." This conception of culture dictates that critics look for multiple

> and contradictory meanings that articulate social struggles. It also compels us to recognize subordinated groups as cultural and political agents rather than simply as victims. (2001, 13)

I believe that the particular tension around the indigenous characters is tied to the struggles taking place in many Western societies as identity is contested and redefined by those who traditionally have not had access to a larger cultural forum, in this case women. An intriguing shift results: in both films the process of looking recorded within the Laura Mulvey excerpt is fundamentally destabilized, becoming a part of the push and pull of containment and resistance (2000). Furthermore, I would argue that while the female becomes the subject and the male the object, it is far from a neat reversal. Rather, the very experience of looking is charged with pressures related to overdetermined gender, sex, and racial expectations, expectations the directors are unable to simply elide and which are thus reincorporated within the cinematic narrative. In intervening in this discourse, I am working to examine the complexity of any process of representational resistance when the very vocabulary of representation often borrows from specific types of images, messages, and conventions that inform larger cultural systems. I will reveal how this process is both specific to race, culture, and gender, and how it transcends it. I will also question whether an artist can work within such conventions without reinscribing them and whether other forms of representation are possible.

## (2)

*Daughters of the Dust*, set in 1902 and released in 1992, unwinds in the rural Gullah communities on the Sea Islands off the coast of South Carolina. It is narrated by the unborn daughter of two of the film's protagonists, Eli and Eula, a young married couple. Traumatized by the rape of the now pregnant wife by a man, presumably white, she refuses to identify, the newlyweds argue over whether to leave the islands with the exodus of a handful of fellow community members for the promise of the urban North. What results is an exploration of the tensions in an African American community experiencing the dramatic change of migration even as they deal with racism, class tensions, gender conflicts, and the legacy of slavery. Toni Cade Bambara calls *Daughters of the Dust* oppositional cinema that challenges the normative forms and values of contemporary filmmaking (Dash with Bambara and hooks 1992). Joel Brouwer writes that the film "has claimed a new center, historically, artistically, and economically" (1995, 15). He argues that

> historically, [Dash] has reconfigured the history of a marginalized people . . . by foregrounding the experiences of the Gullah, a group marginalized within

> the African American community. Artistically, she has employed an African narrative technique to break down the expectation that a story must be told with a single voice. . . . In the production and distribution of the film, she has confounded the normal expectations of the hegemonic Hollywood system and forced the system to recognize (albeit grudgingly and temporarily) the legitimacy of her subject and her artistic method, and the existence of her audience. (15)

This takes on new meaning in examining the strategies that Dash used to get the film made, including contracting with public television and working with a small distribution company that marketed *Daughtersof the Dust* as a foreign film.[3] In her essay "The Black South in Contemporary Film," Jacquie Jones explores some of the cinematic strategies that Dash relies on to mobilize her work:

> Finally, on the screen, African American life is freed from the urban, from the cotton picking, from the tragic integrationist ladder-climbing. Here, in the unlikely arena of American film, the complexity and shaded histories of Black women's lives take center stage. There are no whores or maids in this film. No acquiescent slaves. No white people. Instead, *Daughters of the Dust* offers an historical moment in African American culture, plain and imperfect, blended with such subtle charm, such careful technique that the preparation of food and a stroll along the beach become overwhelming in their beauty. And Dash has conceded that the film does have a certain preoccupation with beauty. Cinematographer Arthur Jafa holds close-ups far longer than is customary, not only allowing the audience to contemplate the specific grace of his subjects but also forcing viewers into intimate proximity with each one. The entire film . . . allows very little space for those who are not Black and not women. (1993, 19)

As all three argue, Dash's approach is an unusual one. The political is cloaked within the lyricism of cinematography that celebrates the beauty of the land and its haunting relationship to the sea, the sustenance offered by prosaic rituals, and the elegance of the black body. The black body, and the black female body in particular, so commonly maligned in mainstream cinematic encounters, portrayed as ugly and undesirable, viewed as asexual or hypersexual, mutilated, satirized, sensationalized or simply ignored, becomes an object of an awed and adoring gaze. While the viewer is necessarily external to the unwinding narrative, there is an intimacy established, as Jones points out, and he or she is allowed to be privy to the secrets of the African Americans, male but particularly female, who interact within this familiar yet exotic community. In accomplishing this, Dash explains that

> it's not just how the scenes are set up. We could get more specific and say it's the way the cameras are placed . . . , the closeness. Being inside the group rather than outside, as a spectator, outside looking in. We're inside; we're

> right in there. We're listening to intimate conversation between the women, while usually it's the men we hear talking and the women kind of walk by in the background. This time we overhear the women. So it's all from the point of view of a woman—about the women—and the men are kind of just on the periphery. (Dash with Bambara and hooks 1992, 33)

As mentioned by both Dash and Jones, there is truly little space reserved in the narrative for those who are not black and/or female. Dash herself has stated that she wanted to privilege "black women first, the black community second, and white women third. . . . And everyone else after that" (40). Subsequently, the gaze is a black female gaze. This is particularly resonant in light of the marginalization experienced by blacks on all levels in the American film industry. It is here, however, that I would like to examine the contradiction that is represented by positioning the indigenous Other within the film and this co-optation in ways that I perceive as both conventional and innovative.

Located on the periphery of the ensemble cast and community drama, Saint Julian Last Child, "Son of the Cherokee Nation," is objectified on several levels: as a male character by a female filmmaker; as a nonblack by an African American; as an indigenous American by a culture asserting its own reconstituted yet distinctively foreign slave heritage. Within this process, what is perhaps most disarming and later disconcerting about Saint Julian is how profoundly yet conventionally seductive he is. Through the camera's lens, he becomes the feminized male, enacting a symbolic cross-dressing that relies on reified images similar to those of the traditional African American female lead: his hair is long and silken; his skin a caramel; his features are filtered to a blur of perfection; most suspiciously, like the ordinarily female object of desire, he himself never talks. Rather he is spoken for. On the one occasion when we have access to his thoughts, it is through Iona, the young Geechee woman he loves, who reads his letter aloud to her female relatives:

> With the greatest respect for yourself and the Peazant family I beg that you stay by my side here on this island. Please do not leave me on this flood of migration. I feel that if I lose you I will lose myself. Consider the stories we share of growing up together. We are the young, the eager up from slavery. Eager to learn a trade, eager to live a better life for ourselves and our children who will follow. Our love is a very precious, very fragile flowering of our most innocent childhood association. . . . We must call out to higher forces that they may guide us. Iona, as I walk toward the future with your hand embracing mine everything seems new and . . . possible. (Dash 1992)

Captured from a distance, he becomes a romanticized ideal: Saint Julian sitting in a tree gazing at the sky; Saint Julian working with the other men in the fields; Saint Julian riding off into the distance with Iona on horseback as Iona's protesting mother and relatives sail toward the supposed progress of the North. It is impossible either to disregard Saint Julian's overwhelming silence in so oral a film, or his lack of place in this close-knit family drama. Saint Julian wordlessly floats. The details of his family and early life, his own ancestry and specific connection to Iona remain unknown. He comes to symbolize the rustic past, unchanging and bucolic, although ironically associated with African American slavery and Native American dispossession. What thus occurs is that he and Iona are able to flee the pressures of migration and urbanization. Yet the film, while powerful and moving, becomes trapped in an agrarian landscape, at once hopelessly beautiful and static, that signals this past but refuses to more deeply engage it.

*Daughters of the Dust* is an important intervention in this past in that it acknowledges the complexity of African American culture and identity in a medium which is often loathe to do so. A significant aspect of this history is the ongoing and complex interactions among the indigenous peoples of the Americas and the Africans in their midst. A multiplicity of cultural exchanges has occurred, influencing food, music, and social organization and affiliation. In the continental United States, *maroons*—runaway slaves—were often assisted by various Native American communities, most notably the Seminoles of Florida. Many African Americans and Native Americans share bloodlines and intersecting histories of triumph and oppression, from the eastern seaboard to the founding of California itself.[4] Yet, there is a more troubling side to this history. Blacks and American Indians have often been played off each other. Buffalo soldiers were used to suppress Indian political uprising and rebellion and Native Americans worked as slave trackers. In fact, members of the Cherokee nation, before their expulsion from the verdant lands of the Southeast, were often slave owners themselves; African Americans were excluded from participation in tribal politics; and there were violent divisions within the larger community related to power struggles and divided loyalties about the Civil War.[5]

Saint Julian's silence is indicative of the role played by Native American culture in the minds of many Americans—and it is a perspective that transcends race—as individuals not readily identified as Native American proudly proclaim: "My great-grandmother was a Cherokee" or, "We have some Indian blood." This often-unnamed ancestor becomes a site of cultural reclamation, the process through which *American* authenticity is appropriated and justified. As Shari Huhndorf writes in *Going Native*: "Indians, . . . safely 'vanishing,' began to provide the symbols and myths upon which white Americans created a sense of historical authenticity, a 'real' national identity which had been lacking in the adolescent colonial culture" (2001, 22). Thus, one is allowed access to the exotic while never having to experience the complexities of claiming and working through that identity. However, it is not a process limited to white Americans. Saint Julian becomes the ultimate manifestation of this co-optation.

I do not want to equate white co-optation, which suggests institutional power, with Dash's work of political and artistic resistance. But I do think it important to show how ideologies and approaches overlap without the necessary contextualization. Saint Julian's words are profoundly moving, particularly in that they suggest a more varied trajectory than was seemingly the case following Andrew Jackson's enforced Trail of Tears. They are the words of a thoughtful, sensitive, and, perhaps educated man. They also point to this alliance between the two communities that could otherwise be easily overlooked in which a respect for, and bond with, the land is shared. In fact, it is Nana Peazant, the grandmother and matriarch, who becomes its ultimate embodiment, who urges her lost kin to remain, poignantly waging an intergenerational battle to keep her family together. Saint Julian reiterates her strength and respect for culture and tradition, pointing to a past of shared oppression and hope for the future of their union and that of their possible progeny. Unlike Nana, however, he is not allowed to express himself—his hopes and dreams and deepest convictions—in his own words and voice. Rather than an agent, he is a passive recipient and helpmate who portends Iona's fate and helps to uncover her emotions, much as the eroticized white woman and Native American so often function in mainstream films. The gender roles and races are switched but the process itself remains the same. Here, Iona struggles with her domineering and shamelessly striving mother who arrogantly dismisses the worth of their collective heritage for the newfangled, the shiny, the modern. Saint Julian is both the knight on a white horse who literally carries her into the sunset and the feminized object of desire.

There is a fascinating story beneath the romantic conventions, including the effects of Christianity on these embattled cultures, as indicated by Saint Julian's name, the fact that both characters appear to have been educated, the nature of their personal and cultural connection, and the intersection of these communities. Does Saint Julian have a family, if so who and where are they? Is he of mixed heritage? Was he raised as a part of the Gullah community or did he migrate somewhat later? Even a short reference could have supplied more depth for the character.

Here I think it is necessary to examine Dash's own perspective on her project. In an interview with bell hooks, Dash explains her desire to subvert Hollywood stereotypes related to both Native Americans and African Americans. "The Cherokees," Dash states, "were some of the original inhabitants of the Sea Islands. So I thought it was important to have one remaining Native American there. . . . I see his family as having held back [after the Trail of Tears] and him the lone survivor. Because the whole film . . . is about retention, the saving of tradition, persistence of vision"

(Dash with Bambara and hooks 1992, 46). Later, she emphasizes, "Where have you ever seen a Native American win in the end and ride off in glory? When have you ever seen an African American woman riding off into the sunset for love, only, and not escaping?" (49). Interestingly, however, Dash fails to interrogate her particular use of images related to Saint Julian, including his positioning within (the maternal crotch) of a tree and his speechlessness.[6] (It is hooks who offers specific prompts, more thoroughly contextualizing the contradictions of some of these images, reiterating: "I think *Daughters* tries to show that something which, however flawed, we have no other cinematic example of" [hooks 1992, 49]). Hearing Saint Julian interact with the members of his community, whether Gullah, Cherokee, or another, or knowing he no longer belongs to a conventional community, could have established his presence as a dynamic character, allowing the viewer to appreciate his individuality and, for lack of a better word, authenticity. It also could have traced the intersections between Native American and African American communities in a more resonant manner. Saint Julian is not allowed the gift of unpredictability and an intimacy with the viewer that Dash generally grants the other characters. It can be argued that Dash is implicitly indicating her inability and/or unwillingness to speak *for* Saint Julian. Yet, both his very presence and his letter—his mediated words and formal tone that simultaneously establish a class-bound propriety and distance him as an individual—convey his imprint on the film.

## (3)

Of Jane Campion's film, Carolyn Gage writes:

> *The Piano* is a gorgeously shot, utterly repellent film about a woman trapped between two rapists: a sleazy, blackmailing rapist and a violent possessive rapist. The woman "chooses" the sleazy, blackmailing rapist, falling deeply in love with him apparently because her experience of coerced sex was so hot, and ends up blissfully married to him in a cozy English cottage. And in case the misogyny of this scenario isn't enough to turn you off there is an extra fillip of ableism at the end: the woman, who is mute and communicates very effectively through sign language, is taught to speak by the sleazy rapist—thereby consolidating the film's claim to a happy ending. (1994, 12)

While I share many of Gage's reservations on the gender politics of *The Piano*, which I believe fetishizes female powerlessness through the seduction allowed by a seemingly subversive masculine sexual economy, I would also stress that Campion's general cinematic sensibility, from *Sweetie* (1989) and *AnAngel at My Table* (1990) to *The Portrait of a Lady* (1996), embraces the odd, the unconventional, the eccentric. She does so in a manner that causes discomfort, eroding the security permitted by a more convenient and tasteful distance. Campion, like Dash, is always visually engaging. Rather than the seeming intimacy of Dash's work that is based on the warmth of shared humanity, Campion offers the disconcerting intrusion of the bizarre, of becoming unwillingly yet fantastically consigned to the position of the voyeur. Still, what I find both disturbing and instructive in this scenario are the uses to which the native Other is put. As in *Daughters of the Dust*, the native presence becomes eroticized, gripping a cinematic gaze that simultaneously records and erases it. Once again, it reverses Mulvey's gendered paradigm through the substitution of a masculine body racialized as nonwhite. However, even as it performs this transference, *The Piano* manifests a tension particular to the manner in which it makes use of Ada, its female protagonist. In Ada's development, Campion falls into a form of viewing that both deconstructs and reinscribes Mulvey's example of the passive female. She teases the spectator by mixing narrative forms that veer from the assertively feminist to a Victorian pastoral with undertones of the true woman. In doing so, however, Campion reveals the fault lines around race, sex, the consumption of the female body, and the tensions around the creation of new discourses in film.

*The Piano*, released in 1993, takes place in mid-nineteenth-century New Zealand. Newly colonized and experiencing the onslaught of Victorian ideals and technologies, the Maoris, the region's indigenous population of Polynesian origin, are being increasingly marginalized within their native land. Under assault to sell that land and assimilate to the dominant British cultural norms, their adversary is embodied in Alisdair Stewart, Ada's husband. An entrepreneurial bachelor who orders the mute Ada, the unmarried Scottish mother of a young child, as a mail order bride, he is afflicted with the many curses of the imperialist: pride, prudishness, distrust, greed, sanctimoniousness, and the capacity for an explosive and self-righteous violence. Standing in stark contrast is George Baines, the tribalized European who lives in harmony with the native population and who longs for Ada's love.

Unlike the lone survivor of the Cherokee in *Daughters of the Dust*, Campion's Maoris are allowed to speak. And speak they do. They willingly and not so willingly oblige the demands of the European settlers. Even as they do, they are practiced in the art of dissimulation, insulting the rude and grasping Stewart, calling him "dry balls" in their native language even as they labor for him. They also challenge him outright when their way of life and heritage are threatened. With Baines as translator, they refuse the former's offer of guns for land: "The rivers and burial caves of our ancestors lie within these lands. Are you saying we should sell the bones of our ancestors? Never! There is no price you can pay." With Baines himself, the Maoris are mischievous and jovial. As he broods over Ada, he is playfully informed: "You need a wife. It's no good having it sulk between your legs for the rest of your life."

There is a significant role reversal that takes place between the whites and the Maoris. It is Ada who is mute, though she narrates the film in voiceover. The white husband, shunned by her, is portrayed as emotionally rigid and emasculated, so repressed as to lack an appealing sexuality. Baines, acting as intermediary between the colonial whites and the Maori, with whom he lives but does not cohabit, is hypermasculine. His body, tattooed and darkened by exposure to the elements, is firm and muscled like those of his Maori counterparts, unlike the pale, soft, cosseted body of the rejected Stewart. He becomes the symbolic native whom Ada comes to desire. Yet the Maoris inhabit an interstitial sexuality, childlike and androgynous. Their sexuality is omnipresent but unthreatening. As mentioned previously, the women tease Baines with sly sexual innuendo. He is then propositioned by a young man, homosexual or transgendered, who offers: "I save you Baines." While Baines responds with silence, the young man, walking a thin line between male and female, is insulted by his fellow Maoris. Yet other Maoris, and Hira, the older woman who serves as Baines's maternal surrogate, are oddly androgynous; she sports tails and a top hat that mock European pretensions. It is with difficulty that the viewer identifies her as male or female, lover or friend. Later, as their mothers watch, indifferent, Maori children lead Ada's daughter in a sexualized game in which trees are embraced and humped. While the white child is punished by her stepfather, who forces her to wash the trees with soap and water, for the Maori, sexuality appears a natural occurrence about which no shame is felt. Though an empowering construction, the portrayal of Maori sexuality in the film is problematic. Leonie Pihama in "Are Films Dangerous? A Maori Woman's Perspective on *The Piano*" argues that "the imagery of Maori people is located firmly in colonial constructions" (1994, 241). Maori women, she adds,

> were the "sexual servants." It is the Maori women who cook for Baines in line with a colonial agenda that focused on Maori girls as house servants. Maori men are irrational, naïve, simpleminded and warlike. It is Maori men with whom Baines attempts to do his suspect land deals, which again fits neatly in line with colonial expectations that men are the owners of property and therefore the decision makers in regard to its usage or sale. (241)

I would add that Maori sexuality enables Ada and Baines to manifest sexual agency in the unhealthy Victorian world of the parochial, racially stratified colonies. Ada and Baines play a taboo, dangerous, and addictive game of sexual barter. Ada provides favors, from a view of her corseted cleavage to a touch of her flesh through a torn undergarment, which will eventually permit her to buy her piano back from the sexually starved

Baines, who cleverly bought the piano from the mercenary Stewart. Ada, the bartered object becomes an agent, lowering her defenses as she is increasingly attracted to Baines. As he touches the curves of her naked flesh, the viewer is transported to the land itself. Luxuriant with flora, dripping with moisture, opulent yet rough and largely uncharted, it is the paradise envisioned by Europeans in their imaginings of unclaimed foreign territories. Though initially presented to the viewer by the scornful Stewart as runtish and unattractive, Ada, with loosened hair and nude body, embodies that unclaimed territory. Baines becomes the working-class cultural mongrel who *honestly* earns access after refusing to participate in their risky exchange because it makes Ada a *whore* and he has had a crisis of conscience. Their relationship is consummated which eventually leads to their discovery by Stewart who severs Ada's finger, the phallic symbol through which she asserts her individuality. Ada and Baines then leave for a new life together with Ada's child. Baines, increasingly Europeanized himself, builds Ada a mechanical finger and teaches her vocalized speech. She gives piano lessons and the two become a part of their new European community though she is admittedly a *freak*. By this point, as the film nears its conclusion, no mention is made of the Maori and their plight.

Though an intriguing narrative, *The Piano* is also perplexing on several levels. Yet I am as concerned with the unintentional racial dynamic as the more consciously wrought gender one, not because one is more insidious than the other, but because each so smoothly reinforces the other. Behind the radical chic of Campion's iconoclastic work lies the conservatism of an old-fashioned true romance. Or as Gage angrily declares:

> What she started to say was something about a woman in patriarchy who decides to stop speaking and who channels all of her passion and all of her love into her piano and her daughter. Jane Campion, the filmmaker and screenwriter, started to say something about male trivialization and appropriation of women's art. She started to say something very important about men as enemies, men as colonizers. (1994, 12)

A strong argument in support of this can be found in the narrative and its perspective on the independence Ada claims through her artistry. Still, I do not think it is necessarily this simple. I am not so certain Campion views men as enemies or colonizers or that she particularly needs to in order to make her point. But, what I do find especially striking is the manner through which the film becomes the ultimate colonizing project, appropriating Maori culture as a site of radical and quirky difference. Despite the cleverness of their presence in the film—their humor, the fact that they speak their own language, their boldness—the Maori, though symbolically juxtaposed against the stodgy avariciousness of the European colonizers, do not in any way exist as individuals. Furthermore, their responses, while a space of radical opposition, are also perhaps too easily reincorporated into a host of earlier cultural stereotypes.

Here it is necessary to examine some other critical evaluations of Campion's cinematic text that refuse to acknowledge the use of cultural distortions and thus succeed in reinscribing them. For example, Peter Chumo, in examining the inability of cultures to more effectively communicate, writes:

> The play within the film also shows the limitations of art bounded by social conventions. When Bluebeard is attacking his wife, the Maori natives, thinking a woman is really being attacked, storm the stage to save her. They have an honest, untutored reaction to the play—the art affects them on a gut level the way Ada's piano playing originally affected Baines. (1997, 175–6)

Jeanne Dapkus asserts:

> *Piano* makes fun of Victorian restrictions and contrasts them with earthy, erotic images. Ada is an "alien" to the New Zealand coast. At the beginning of the film she is someone arriving from a far-away, civilized land. She and her piano are distinctly out of place on the savage shore. However, her character progressively changes to accommodate the natural surroundings along with her awakening sexual desires. The film makes fun of the prudish Victorian limitations on humanity, and it highlights the freeing aspects of the passionate, sexual sides of humanity. This is most apparent in the many scenes which involve native New Zealanders, the Maoris, as they contrast the Victorians and, often, mock them. . . . This taunting undercurrent by the Maoris continues throughout the film, and Ada's eventual migration to Baines's hut shows that she will eventually align herself with the more natural, sexually open natives. (1997, 180–1)

Both writers, in validating Maori culture as a legitimate site of cultural contestation, also flatten it through this process of naturalization. Despite novel representations, the mode of seeing reinforces a Eurocentric perspective. In the end, Baines compels viewers as the white native. Though the Maori talk, they are even less individualized than Saint Julian. It is harder to truly see them. They remain largely nameless and what happens to them, their land, their culture and traditions, is airbrushed in favor of Ada's tempestuous affair with and satisfaction in the now re-Europeanized Baines (which also averts the threat of miscegenation). Their difference, at once carnal and devoid of sexuality, enables Ada's ultimate sexual liberation. And it seems limited to that. As the androgynous native woman sleeps outside of Baines's cottage and the symbolic hermaphrodite flirts with him, he cannot respond to them. (Though I must admit that for me it was a relief to see the native Other portrayed as anything other than sexually available for the white hero.[7]) Rather, Baines, like Campion, is blinded and enraptured by Ada's whiteness, a rare commodity, in a land where whiteness comes to represent an object of startling uniqueness and value. Simultaneously, Baines, as exoticized white, becomes an object of erotic fascination, particularly in the tight focus of the camera on his naked and vulnerable body. His is the Other body the audience actually perceives. While we stare in erotic fascination, his sexuality, which nurtures Ada's into existence, intensifies the ascendance of European culture. Campion relies on the Maoris to provide the spaces of ambiguity that will propel her tale of the reconstitution of the white family according to a more liberated gender and sexual ideal. However, once the film has ended, there is little to be said about the Maori characters because the audience does not have to see or engage with them as individual subjects. This includes the fact that during the era that *The Piano* takes place there were escalating tensions between the Maoris and Europeans over land and political power. Campion's film hints at this. In fact, the original screenplay provides an indication of this, citing the 1840 Treaty of Waitangi that was not honored by European colonizers and subsequently led to a series of wars from 1860 to 1872.[8] Instead, in the final adaptation the Maoris are members of the crowd, the idiosyncratic objects of Campion's anthropological gaze, her cryptic and charming artistic creation.

## (4)

It is telling that in attempting to articulate her own cinematic sensibility in very different and difficult ways, both Dash and Campion return to the source of the nation-state itself, revisiting, re-envisioning, and representing the foundation of the nation. Each director performs a cultural archeology of sorts, acknowledging and incorporating the presence, perspective, and struggles of the region's original inhabitants. Dash appears to desire to depict an underrepresented minority with justice and thus relies on the rejection of stereotypes of Native American savagery and primitivism, accentuating instead the dignity and polish of an industrious respectability tied to both Edwardian and modern American civic ideals. Conversely, Campion emphasizes Maori humanity by undermining the proper and expected; while risking offense, Campion's portrayal is steeped in the earthy humor of the ribald and idiosyncratic, destabilizing the contemporary middle-class preoccupation with conformity and achievement. Nonetheless, the process is replete with the dynamic of containment and resistance referred to by Huhndorf and which I am mapping in my own examination (2001). As indigenous culture is reclaimed in a dual show of cooperation and co-optation, the viewer is able to see not only how women from quite distinct subject positions operate against but within the traditions of which they are a part.

The structure of these films underscores the fluidity of the colonizing process as well as the fact that the traditionally invisible and powerless are still capable of co-opting others, often with the best of intentions. Applying the format of progressive sentimentalism to validate a feminized gaze, each film lays claim to the quotidian events of the past that have all too often been effaced in favor of the masculinist metanarrative. Here, men's stories become secondary to women's stories, concerns, forms of labor, modes of conduct, and communication. Nonetheless, in each film, the indigenous Other, though distinctively drawn, serves a similar function. They are the repositories of truth and purity bound to the land, untouched by the contradictions and complexity of progress. Eroticized objects of a feminine gaze, they do not stand on their own as fully formed characters. Rather they present a backdrop to further dramatize the dilemma of its nonindigenous heroines.

As I asserted earlier, however, this is far from an orderly process. Even as stereotypical images are deployed in a move of cinematic Orientalism, it can be argued that subversive representations are built into these portraits. Despite reinscribing many conventions around the native, these stereotypes are also scrambled and diffuse. It is difficult to attach a single meaning to many of these images. By packaging this history in the trappings of nostalgia, both directors make their films more palatable and compelling to their audiences. Simultaneously, new forms of reading the text are also validated, forcing the viewer both to respect a female-oriented perspective and to revisit this past from a very different point of view. As Dash insists, how many sensitive, eloquent Native American characters ride off into the sunset with the women of their choice, particularly when she is African American and not fleeing slavery or a lynch mob? Furthermore, how many representations are there of African American and Native American coexistence in the American vernacular? Indeed, Saint Julian's humanity, though silenced and perceived from afar, is palpable. The reciprocity of the care and respect between Saint Julian and the larger community is poignant, particularly in that its representation does not rely on words, but rather images which demand a more visceral response. On the other hand, how many representations are there of natives signifying on the colonizers? How many images are there of an oppositional sexual identity of natives, an identity with which they—if not their communities—seem completely comfortable? How often do viewers see indigenous people who feel justified in actively resisting colonial incursions onto their land and into their cosmology? Far from a static process, the novelty and complexity of the images force the viewer to expand his or her definitions of both the native characters and the non-natives as well as how we determine meaning. The small, insignificant, and "quirky" become worthy of attention and exploration. Such images compel us to ponder the nature of history as we know it, based as it is on hierarchies of interest and action. Finally, however, these images press the issue of whether a character has to be central to the narrative, an individualized speaking subject, to effectively challenge established patterns of cinematic representation.

Reversing subject positions can create powerful representations that challenge the insidious silencing that nonwhite and women characters have all too often experienced. In pointing this out, I believe it especially important to acknowledge recent films made from the perspective of American Indians (*Smoke Signals* [Eyre 1999] and *Naturally Native* [Red-Horse and Farmer 1998]) and Maoris (*Once Were Warriors* [Tamahori 1994] and *Broken English* [Nicholas 1996]).[9] While their reception has been mixed and examining them is outside the parameters of this paper, these films represent significant inroads into filming the experiences of indigenous peoples from the point of view of modern-day urban dwellers who navigate a complex and contradictory sense of subjectivity. Even though these are very different projects and positing such radically disparate alternatives is not entirely fair, the image of an individualized speaking subject, who even briefly returns the gaze of the filmmaker/spectator and speaks as an independent individual, can be empowering. It reverses Mulvey's paradigm and permits the spectator to perceive and/or identify with previously nonexistent images (2000). But simultaneously, dominant forms of representation are not necessarily transformed by doing so. Highly individualized, vocal Maoris and Native Americans would not necessarily change the texture of being a character of significance within each film or the reality of what it means to be an actual person living with this identity. In fact, doing so could easily extend this form of entitlement to remake the Other in the semblance of the dominant group, thus enabling a type of symbolic progress that becomes a form of artistic tokenism, obscuring the systemic inequalities that exist outside of the celluloid world. What it does, however, particularly in our media-obsessed culture, is make accessible a broader range of images and experiences.

In the end, these films are already made and distributed; they will not change. Nor should they have to. Yet, as viewers, it is important that we read them with critical and informed perspectives. An important aspect of that is acknowledging the complexity of any process of representation and the cultural forces at work in its enactment. Only then can we honestly take part in the production of radically new discourses of being and representation.

## Notes

1. I would like to thank my colleague Linda Dittmar of the University of Massachusetts Boston for familiarizing me with this term.

2. Two examples of this can be seen in vehicles starring Brad Pitt. In both, he is the troubled brother, the prodigal son. In *A River Runs Through It*, he is a gambler, a drunk ne'er-do-well whose outlaw status is embodied in the brazen Indian woman with whom he consorts, clad in red, face painted not as the warrior but as the harlot, barred from respectable European-American society and thrown in jail (Redford 1992). Her ostracism signals Pitt's own, his own doomed fate. Once again in *Legends of the Fall*, Pitt's chosen mate is a Native American woman (Zwick 1994). Rather than the scarlet woman, it is the beautiful, chaste Karina Lombard who serves to redeem the previously corrupted Pitt. The daughter of a family servant, Lombard's regal yet simple presence ties her to the pristine land over which the white brothers feud. Her reward for sticking by the reformed Pitt and bearing his children is an accidental bullet and premature death. Though a forceful signifier, she is incidental. In both films, the native woman serves to point to the white man's status and fate. Although she serves to critique the corrupt, the wasteful, the discriminatory and hypocritical in white society, she herself is an oppositional force, idealized and abstracted, who never really crystallizes into an individual presence. Hers is the walk-on; Pitt's humanity is purchased at her expense.

3. See Dash's *Daughters of the Dust: The Making of an African American Woman's Film* for an in-depth description of her experiences in getting the film made (Dash with Bambara and hooks 1992).

4. *Africans and Native Americans: The Language of Race and the Evolution of Red-Black Peoples* by Jack D. Forbes contextualizes this larger process throughout the Atlantic region (1993). His painstaking analysis of color perception and racial categories within ideological, linguistic, and legal systems reflect the evolution and intersections of these shifting communities of people.

5. *Slavery and the Evolution of Cherokee Society 1540–1866* by Theda Perdue (1987).

6. Dash reveals that the person in the tree could have been Nana but for the logistics of placing an elderly woman so high above the ground.

7. Cyndy Hendershot offers an intriguing reading of this process in a footnote of her article, "(Re)Visioning the Gothic": "extensive scenes involving Baines and the Maoris have been cut from the final version of the film. The screenplay, however, makes it clear that Baines is not sexually involved with the Maoris. Possibly one explanation for this is that he does not want

to replicate the European man's use of the 'native' woman which was so common in colonial/imperial situations. More strongly, I would suggest, is the possibility that he wants to remain European but wants a different European subjectivity to be possible." (1998, 196, n. 8).

8. See Hendershot (1998) and Thornley (2000).

9. In addition, *Naturally Native*, the first crossover film starring, written, directed, and produced by (female) Native Americans, deals specifically with three sisters from a woman-oriented perspective (Red-Horse and Farmer 1998).

## References

Brouwer, Joel. 1995. "Repositioning: Center and Margin in Julie Dash's *Daughters of the Dust*." *African American Review* 29(1):5–16.

Campion, Jane, dir. (1989). *Sweetie*. Australia: Electric/Arena Film. Motion picture.

———. (1990). *AnAngel at My Table*. Australia: Hibiscus Films. Motion picture.

———. 1993. *The Piano*. West Hollywood, Calif.: Miramax Films. Motion picture.

———. (1996). *The Portrait of a Lady*. Los Angeles: Gramercy Pictures/Propaganda Films. Motion picture.

Chumo, Peter N. 1997. "Keys to the Imagination: Jane Campion's *The Piano*." *Literature/Film Quarterly* 25(3):173–6.

Dapkus, Jeanne R. 1997. "Sloughing Off the Burdens: Parallel/Antithetical Quests for Self-Actualization in Jane Campion's *The Piano* and Henry James's *The Portrait of a Lady*." *Literature/Film Quarterly* 25(3):177–87.

Dash, Julie, dir. 1992. *Daughters of the Dust*. New York: Kino International. Motion picture.

———. with Toni Cade Bambara and bell hooks. 1992. *Daughters of the Dust: The Making of an African American Woman's Film*. New York: New Press.

Eyre, Chris, dir. 1999. *Smoke Signals*. West Hollywood, Calif.: Miramax. Motion picture.

Forbes, Jack D. 1993. *Africans and Native Americans: The Language of Race and the Evolution of Red-Black Peoples*. Urbana: University of Illinois Press.

Gage, Carolyn. 1994. "*The Piano*: Dangerous Music." *Feminist Voices* (February):12–3.

hooks, bell. 1992. *Black Looks: Race and Representation*. Boston: South End Press.

Hendershot, Cyndy. 1998. "(Re)Visioning the Gothic: Jane Campion's *The Piano*." *Literature/Film Quarterly* 26(2):97–108.

Huhndorf, Shari M. 2001. *Going Native: Indians in the American Cultural Imagination*. Ithaca, N.Y.: Cornell University Press.

Jones, Jacquie. 1993. "The Black South in Contemporary Film." *African American Review* 27(1):19–24.

Mulvey, Laura. 2000. "Visual Pleasure and Narrative Cinema." In *Feminism and Film*, ed. E. Ann Kaplan, 34–47. New York: Oxford University Press.

Nicholas, Gregor. 1996. *Broken English.* Culver City, Calif.: Sony. Motion picture.

Ong, Aihwa. 1988. "Colonialism and Modernity: Feminist Re-Presentations of Women in Non-Western Societies." *Inscriptions* 3–4:79–93.

Perdue,Theda. 1987. *Slavery and the Evolution of Cherokee Society 1540–1866.* Knoxville: University of Tennessee Press.

Pihama, Leonie. 1994. "Are Films Dangerous: A Maori Woman's Perspective on *The Piano.*" *Hecate* 20(2):239.

Redford, Robert, dir. 1992. *A River Runs Through It.* Culver City, Calif.: Columbia. Motion picture.

Red-Horse, Valerie, and Jennifer Wynne Farmer, dirs. 1998. *Naturally Native.* Los Angeles: Red-Horse Native Productions. Motion picture.

Spivak, Gayatri Chakravorty. 1988. "Can the Subaltern Speak?" In *Marxism and the Interpretation of Culture*, ed. Cary Nelson and Lawrence Grossberg, 217–313. Urbana: University of Illinois Press.

Tamahori, Lee, dir. 1994. *Once Were Warriors.* Los Angeles, Fine Line. Motion picture.

Thornley, Davinia. 2000. "Duel or Duet? Gendered Nationalism in *The Piano.*" *Film Criticism* 24(3):61–76.

Zwick, Edward. 1994. *Legends of the Fall.* Los Angeles: Tristar Pictures. Motion picture.

# Contributors

VIVYAN C. ADAIR is the Elihu Root Peace Fund associate professor of women's studies and the founder and director of the ACCESS Project at Hamilton College. She is the author of *From Good Ma to Welfare Queen: A Genealogy of the Poor Woman in American Literature, Photography, and Culture* (Routledge, 2000). Her research focus is studying representations of women on welfare and analyzing the impact of welfare reform, education, and public policy.

DENISE BAUER, PH.D., is currently the associate dean of liberal arts at the Culinary Institute of America. She has been researching and writing about Alice Neel since 1992. Her current research interests include gender and leadership. Denise is the mother of two children, Marygrace and Thomas Bauer-Gluckmann. They live together in New Paltz, New York.

CAROLINE BROWN is an assistant professor in the English department at the University of Montreal. She specializes in twentieth-century U.S. literature, women's studies, and the literature of the African Diaspora. Her articles have appeared in diverse publications, including *African-American Review, Obsidian, NWSA Journal*, and *Comparative Studies of South Asia, Africa, and the Middle East.* She is currently at work on her book-length project, *Black Women's Artistry, American Identity: Performing the Postmodern Body,* which examines intersections between African American women writers and visual artists.

JILL R. CHANCEY, a New Orleans native, has been curator of the Lauren Rogers Museum of Art in Laurel, Mississippi, since 2001. Chancey was educated at Trinity University of Texas and Tulane University in New Orleans. She received her doctorate in American art history from the University of Kansas, Lawrence, with the dissertation "Elaine de Kooning: Negotiating the Masculinity of Abstract Expressionism." She recently edited *The Floating World: Ukiyo-e Prints from the Wallace B. Rogers Collection* (Lauren Rogers Museum of Art, 2008) and has contributed to the forthcoming *Mississippi Encyclopedia.* She has organized exhibitions by Mississippi natives Sam Gilliam, William Dunlap, and Ethel Wright Mohamed.

EMMANUEL DAVID is a doctoral candidate in the department of sociology at the University of Colorado at Boulder, where he also teaches in the women and gender studies program. He has published on art and social movements in New Orleans and on collective behavior following disasters. He also co-edited two special issues of *Social Justice: A Journal of Crime, Conflict, and World Order* on the role of art in social justice struggles. His current research focuses on social movements that emerged in response to Hurricane Katrina, with particular attention to women's participation in efforts to rebuild New Orleans and the Gulf Coast.

MARY K. DESHAZER is a professor of English and women's and gender studies at Wake Forest University, where she teaches transnational feminisms and women's literature. She is the author of *Fractured Borders: Reading Women's Cancer Literature* (University of Michigan Press, 2005), *A Poetics of Resistance: Women Writing in El Salvador, South Africa, and the United States* (University of Michigan Press, 1994), and *Inspiring Women: Re-imagining the Muse* (Pergamon Press, 1987) and the editor of *The Longman Anthology of Women's Literature* (2001). Her current research addresses contemporary autobiographical and photographic representations of breast cancer.

MILA GANEYA is an associate professor of German at Miami University of Ohio and author of the book *Women in Weimar Fashion: Discourses and Displays in German Culture, 1918–1933* (Camden House, 2008). Her research interests include mass media, film history, and contemporary German film. She has published numerous articles on fashion journalism, fashion photography, and mannequins in the Weimar Republic; early German film comedies; and Berlin in film.

LORI LANDAY is an associate professor of cultural studies in the liberal arts department at Berklee College of Music, where she teaches interdisciplinary courses in visual culture, film studies, and American culture. She is the author of *Madcaps, Screwballs, and Con Women: The Female Trickster in American Culture* (University of Pennsylvania Press, 1998); articles on topics including silent film, digital narrative, virtual worlds, and *I Love Lucy*; and *Lucy TV*, forthcoming from Wayne State University Press. She is also a new media artist.

ANNE MCLEER is currently the director of research and strategic planning at the Service Employees International Union, Local 500. She holds a Ph.D. in the human sciences from George Washington University, where she led the successful effort to form a part-time faculty union. She works on part-time faculty unionization and collective bargaining in the metropolitan Washington area and occasionally teaches graduate courses in women's studies. She is raising two feminist, socialist children with her husband, Travis Keller, in Washington, D.C.

OLGA M. MESROPOVA is an associate professor of Russian at Iowa State University. Her area of research is contemporary Russian cultural discourse focusing on post-Soviet film, television, gender studies, and performance. She has published extensively on such subjects as Russian women stand-up comedians, popular Russian women-writers, and representation of women in post-Soviet film and television. She is the author of *Kinotalk: Russian Cinema for Conversation* (Slavica Publishers, Indiana University, 2006) and the co-editor of *Uncensored? Re-Inventing Humor and Satire in Post-Soviet Russia* (Slavica Publishers, Indiana University, 2009). She is currently working on a new manuscript that examines the representation of women in Russian popular literature, film, and television of the past decade.

KIM MILLER is an assistant professor of art history and women's studies at Wheaton College in Norton, Massachusetts, where she is also the coordinator of the women's studies program.

DIANE SHOOS is an associate professor of visual studies and French in the humanities department at Michigan Technological University. She teaches and publishes on cinema, feminist film theory, and gender and visual representation. Shoos recently completed a book manuscript on Hollywood films about domestic violence and is currently working on a project on adoption in the media.

MARGARET D. STETZ is the Mae and Robert Carter professor of women's studies and professor of humanities at the University of Delaware. She has been the curator or co-curator of exhibitions at venues such as the National Gallery of Art Library, Harvard University's Houghton Library, the Bryn Mawr College Library, the University Gallery at the University of Delaware, and the Grolier Club of New York City. Her exhibition titled *Facing the Late Victorians* was on view at the Henry B. Plant Museum in Tampa, Florida, in Spring 2010. She is also the author of a number of books, including *British Women's Comic Fiction, 1890–1990* (Ashgate Publishing, 2001); *Gender and the London Theatre, 1880–1920* (Bryn Mawr College Library, 2004); and the forthcoming *Oscar Wilde, New Women, the Bodley Head and Beyond*; and she has co-edited volumes such as *Legacies of the Comfort Women of World War II* (East Gate Books, 2001) and *Michael Field and Their World* (Rivendale Press, 2007).

STACEY WEBER-FÈVE, PH.D., is an assistant professor of French at Iowa State University (Ames). She is a specialist of French and Francophone cinemas, concentrating on the constructions and performances of gender and identity on screen and in print. She has published numerous articles on North African filmmakers/writers Assia Djebar and Raja Amari and has a forthcoming book (Lexington Books, 2010) on "transvergent" women's filmmaking and lifewriting of France, Algeria, and Tunisia.

# Index

Other Books Available in the Series

*Diversity and Women's Health,*
edited by Sue V. Rosser

*Feminist Pedagogy: Looking Back to Move Forward,*
edited by Robbin D. Crabtree, David Allan Sapp,
and Adela C. Licona